THE NEW HAMBURGER & HOT DOG COOKBOOK

THE NEW HAMBURGER & HOT DOG COOKBOOK

METTJA C. ROATE

WEATHERVANE BOOKS • NEW YORK

CONTENTS

PART I

INTRODUCTION

TO MANY PEOPLE the word "hamburger" conjures up a picture of a limp, slightly browned piece of ground meat between two soft roll halves, oozing with onions, catsup, mustard and pickle slices. But to a cook who enjoys experimenting with this inexpensive but nutritious menu staple, hamburger is much more than that.

In the raw stage, hamburger has many different versions. The meat departments of supermarkets, good butchers, and reputable freezing concerns usually do not put more than 25% fat or suet in their hamburger. If you buy packaged meats at a supermarket, you can usually tell how much fat filler has been ground with the hamburger by the appearance. If the meat is a light pink, with lots of white flecks showing, beware! The fat content is probably high. If you buy it you will end up with 50% grease and only 50% meat protein.

To taste good, hamburger should contain no more than 12% to 25% fat. The presence of this moderate amount of fat adds to the meat's juiciness and flavor. Without any fat content, hamburger is dry and flavorless.

The color of good hamburger is like that of the loin in a T-bone steak—red and rich, slightly flecked with white. Good hamburger is ground from flank, brisket, portions of the shanks, neck meat, etc. Most hamburger is of a medium-coarse grind. If it is ground too fine, the structure of the meat is completely broken down and the result is a dry, flavorless dish.

The freshness of the meat is another prime factor to bear in mind in hamburger cookery. A reputable butcher never grinds the meat too long before he sells it. Good hamburger can keep its flavor and freshness for at least two or three days after you buy it. Always store it in a tightly covered glass, porcelain or plastic dish in the coldest spot in the refrigerator.

Hamburger can be frozen with great success. It is one of the few meats you can remove from the freezer stone hard and immediately start sautéing without making it lose its flavor. When freezing hamburger, remove it from the paper store bag and put it into an airtight plastic container. If you are going to freeze casserole dishes for future meals, always encase them in airtight plastic bags. Keeping air away from frozen foods is of the utmost importance.

If you make hamburger patties for freezing, be sure to layer each one in aluminum foil. When you have to rush, this eliminates waiting for thawing. You can separate the patties easily and start cooking them immediately. I also find those little plastic bags that come on a roll are wonderful for storing hamburger patties. With each patty encased in its own plastic bag, storage is simple after they are frozen. The little bags also permit you to take out one or two separate patties for a latecomer to dinner, or six or eight from your frozen cache without having to thaw the whole lot.

All of the recipes in this book are designed to serve four people with good healthy appetites. If you get into a spot where you find you have only one package of hamburger, and ten people to feed—remember hamburger is elastic in flavor; it can be stretched and stretched!

Many spices and flavorings are used in this book. Substitution of a spice can prove the downfall of an otherwise good dish. If you do not have the spice called for in your cabinet, it's better to skip the recipe than have to toss good food away uneaten. If you are not familiar with a spice or herb, put a little on the tip of your tongue to see if you find its flavor agreeable. If you don't care for it, that recipe is probably not for you.

In this day of high-protein diets, hamburger can be your nutritious, economical stand-by. After all, good hamburger is protein laden.

In fact, any way you look at it, hamburger is America's all-purpose meat!

Chapter I
LOAVES FOR LOAFERS

MEAT LOAVES are excellent one-dish meals. And they need not be only for pot-luck occasions; they can come to the table with the elegance of a seven-rib crown roast. Meat loaves are easy to make, easy to serve, and easy to digest. They slice well, both hot and cold; if you have lunch carriers in your clan, they will enjoy meat loaf more than Bologna sandwiches.

Meat loaves are wonderful for people who like to loaf and take a day off from cooking. All you have to do is double the recipe, bake two loaves, freeze one and serve the other. Then when that day of freedom comes along, take out the frozen loaf early enough to let it thaw. You can serve it cold, if you can't get up enough strength to turn on the oven!

MEAT LOAF WITH CHEESE

2 pounds hamburger
¼ chopped onion, or ¼ cup dehydrated onion flakes, soaked in ¼ cup milk
2 eggs, slightly beaten
1 teaspoon salt
¼ teaspoon pepper
1 teaspoon celery seed
1½ cups whole milk
1 cup dry bread crumbs
¾ cup diced American cheese (reserve 10 pieces for the top)
¾ cup diced Swiss cheese (reserve 10 pieces for the top)
¼ teaspoon paprika

Mix all of the ingredients except the cheese and the paprika; stir well so that all are thoroughly mixed. Add the cheese (except for the reserved pieces) with a light hand so that you do not break up the pieces. Press the mixture into a well-greased baking tin. Slightly indent the center, and decorate with the pieces of cheese you have reserved; sprinkle with paprika. Put into a 350° F. preheated oven and bake for 1 hour. When removing from the loaf tin, be sure to loosen all four sides with a spatula before lifting out so the loaf will not crumble.

This loaf is excellent with mashed potatoes and frozen fresh peas arranged around the edge of the platter.

11

MILK-RICH MEAT LOAF

If some members of your family refuse to drink their quota of milk, this is a marvelous way to slip in an extra pint.

¼ teaspoon paprika
1 egg
1½ pounds ground veal, pork and beef (most supermarkets
    sell it packaged in equal portions of these three kinds of
    meat)
¼ cup flour
2 cups scalded milk
1 small onion, grated, or ¼ cup dehydrated onion, soaked in
    ¼ cup milk
2 cups soft bread crumbs
½ teaspoon salt
¼ teaspoon pepper
½ teaspoon Accent
⅛ teaspoon nutmeg
⅛ teaspoon cinnamon

A fluted type of mold is wonderful for this meat loaf; if you do not own one, a regular loaf tin will do. Butter all sides of the mold and sprinkle lightly with paprika. (Paprika gives a rich brown color to meat.) Beat the egg slightly and add to the meat mixture. Alternately add the flour and the scalded milk to the meat mixture. Add the onion, and work in the bread crumbs. Add the salt, pepper, Accent, nutmeg and cinnamon. Stir all well to mix the flavors thoroughly. Turn into greased mold form or baking tin.

Place mold in a pan of hot water in a preheated 350° F. oven. Bake for 1 hour, or until the center of the loaf is firm to the touch. Turn out on a warmed platter. Garnish with parsley and rings of boiled carrots, if desired.

WHEATIES MEAT LOAF WITH VEGETABLE SOUP

1½ pounds hamburger
¼ cup chopped onion
½ teaspoon salt
¼ teaspoon ground pepper
½ teaspoon Accent
2 cups Wheaties cereal
1 egg, beaten with 1 tablespoon water
1 can beef-vegetable soup

Mix all of the ingredients with the exception of the soup. Stir until all are well blended. Finally, fold in the soup, taking care that you do not mash the vegetables beyond identification.

Put into a greased loaf pan and bake in a preheated 350° F. oven for 1 hour, or until center of loaf is firm to the touch. Baste from time to time with the liquid which gathers around the loaf.

This loaf is very colorful when sliced. It is excellent served cold.

Variations:

Substitute 1 can cream of mushroom soup for the beef-vegetable soup.
Substitute 1 can cream of chicken soup for the beef vegetable soup.
Substitute 1 can cream of celery for beef vegetable soup.
For a wonderful flavor, add 3 tablespoons wheat germ.
Substitute corn flakes for Wheaties.
Substitute Cheerios for Wheaties.
Substitute 4 shredded wheat biscuits for Wheaties.
Substitute Rice Chex for Wheaties.

HAM-HAMBURGER MEAT LOAF

This is one of my favorite meat loaf recipes because it tastes so good in sandwiches. It blends well with either whole wheat or rye bread.

1½ pounds hamburger
1 pound ground ham (we usually ask the butcher to save boiled ham ends to grind for this)
2 eggs, beaten until lemon yellow
½ cup condensed milk
1 cup soft bread crumbs
¼ teaspoon pepper
¼ teaspoon dry mustard
1 teaspoon Accent
⅛ teaspoon ground cloves
4 slices pineapple
1 tablespoon brown sugar

Mix very thoroughly all of the ingredients except the pineapple and brown sugar. Form into a loaf and place in a buttered loaf tin. If your family likes a crisp outside on a loaf, this one can be made in an oblong shape and baked on a flat coffee-cake tin.

Place the pineapple slices on the top and hold them in place with toothpicks. Sprinkle the brown sugar over each slice. Place loaf in a preheated 350° F. oven and bake for 1 hour, or until firm to the touch.

Left-over ham can be frozen successfully. The next time you bake a big ham, freeze the scraps to use in this recipe.

RUSSIAN MEAT LOAF

1 cup rice
2 cups water
3 hard-boiled eggs
1 medium-sized onion, chopped fine
1 tablespoon butter
3 slices white bread, broken into coarse crumbs and moistened in ¼ cup water
1 pound hamburger
½ teaspoon monosodium glutamate
½ teaspoon salt
¼ teaspoon pepper

Boil the rice in the water for 15 minutes in a covered pan. At the end of this time the grains should be fluffy and tender. Rinse in warm water and drain thoroughly. Chop the hard-boiled eggs into coarse pieces so that they keep their yellow and white identity. Fold the eggs into the boiled rice. In a small pan, sauté the onion in the butter until it is transparent but not brown.

Mix the sautéed onion and the moistened bread crumbs with the hamburger. Add the monosodium glutamate, salt and pepper. Flatten the meat mixture on a piece of aluminum foil, making a circle about the size of a pie plate.

Place the rice and egg mixture in the middle of the meat circle. Using the foil for support, bring up the sides of the meat until the rice and egg mixture is completely hidden. Leave a small opening in the top of the foil for the steam to escape.

Place in a flat pan and bake in a preheated 350° F. oven for 45 minutes. Garnish with chopped parsley if you want additional color.

FRENCH MEAT LOAF WITH LEEK

Leek is an unusual vegetable which few but the French know how to use. If you want a meat loaf that is both different and delightful in flavor, try this one.

2 eggs, beaten to a lemon-yellow color
½ cup water
4 slices white bread with the crusts removed
½ cup chopped onion
1 can tomato soup
1 pound hamburger
½ teaspoon salt
¼ teaspoon pepper
⅛ teaspoon nutmeg
2 good-sized leeks

Beat the eggs, then add the water. Break up the bread and add to the egg-and-water mixture. Add the onion and ¼ of the can of tomato soup. Reserve the remainder of the soup until later. Add the meat to the softened bread mixture, along with the salt, pepper and nutmeg. Mix all very thoroughly and set aside.

Thoroughly butter the sides and bottom of a loaf tin. Wash the leeks and remove the harsh outer leaves. Cut into ⅛" slices. Line the bottom of the buttered loaf tin with slices of leek, reserving the rest of the slices until later.

Gently spoon the meat mixture into the loaf pan over the leek. Pour over the meat mixture the remainder of the tomato soup. Arrange the rest of the leek over the top. Place in a preheated 350° F. oven and bake for 1 hour.

This loaf is excellent served with plain boiled potatoes.

FESTIVE MEAT LOAF

Here is a meat loaf made with, of all things, fruit. There is a festive air about it, and an outstandingly different flavor.

1½ pounds hamburger
1 pound lean ground pork
1 teaspoon salt
¼ teaspoon pepper
2 eggs
1 teaspoon monosodium glutamate
4 cups soft bread crumbs

Filling

¾ cup seedless raisins
¼ cup dried apricots, cut into ⅛" slices
½ cup chopped onion
¼ cup chopped parsley
¼ teaspoon sage
¼ teaspoon thyme
½ cup water or bouillon

Mix the meat, salt, pepper, eggs, monosodium glutamate and bread crumbs thoroughly. Spread on a sheet of aluminum foil, forming a rectangle about ½" thick.

Mix the ingredients of the filling and spread evenly over the meat mixture. Now, carefully roll up the meat as you would a jelly roll. Bring up the top and bottom edges of the foil and fold them together tightly; the sides of the foil should be folded over to keep in the juices and the flavor.

Place the foil-wrapped roll on a flat tin in a 350° F. preheated oven for 1½ hours. At the end of the first hour, open the foil and spread away from the sides of the loaf to allow browning.

SIMPLE MEAT LOAF

1½ pounds hamburger
½ pound lean ground pork
¼ cup chopped onion
⅛ teaspoon pepper
1 medium carrot, grated*
1 medium raw potato, grated
2 eggs, beaten until lemon yellow
¾ cup condensed milk or rich milk from the top of the bottle
2 cups bread crumbs

Mix all of the ingredients in the order in which they are listed. Stir thoroughly. Press into a greased loaf tin and bake in a preheated 350° F. oven for 1 hour.

When serving, garnish with chopped parsley.

*If you have left-over cooked carrots or potatoes, these may be used instead of the raw ones.

MEAT LOAF WITH MUSHROOM SOUP

4 slices white bread with crusts removed
2 eggs, beaten to a lemon yellow
1½ pounds hamburger
¼ teaspoon salt
¼ teaspoon pepper
1 can condensed cream of mushroom soup
½ cup dried mushrooms (optional, but very nice to add)

Crumble the bread into the beaten eggs, then mix in all the rest of the ingredients in the order listed above. Spoon gently into a greased loaf tin. Place in a preheated 350° F. oven for 1 hour.

Fresh mushrooms, quartered, may be used in this recipe instead of the dried ones. If you are using the fresh ones, sauté a few to be used for a garnish around the edges of the plate when serving.

18

CHINESE CHOW MEIN LOAF

2 pounds hamburger
1 cup celery, cut into ¼" pieces
1 cup onion, cut into ¼" pieces
1 cup rice
1 can cream of mushroom soup
1 can cream of celery soup
¼ cup milk
½ teaspoon salt
¼ teaspoon pepper
1 #2 can chow mein noodles

Brown the hamburger in a deep skillet until it is all separated. Add the celery and onion. Cook over low heat until the onion is transparent and glazed. Meanwhile, place the rice in two cups of water and cook for 15 minutes, or until fluffy and tender. Rinse the rice in warm water, drain and add to the hamburger mixture.

Stir in the mushroom soup and celery soup. Add the milk, salt and pepper. Mix all very thoroughly. Put into a greased 1½ quart casserole; sprinkle the chow mein noodles over the top. Place in a 350° F. oven for 30 minutes. Serve with soy sauce if desired.

VEAL LOAF

2½ cups moist bread crumbs
3 eggs, beaten until lemon yellow
2 tablespoons grated onion
Juice of 1 lemon
2 teaspoons salt
½ teaspoon pepper
2 pounds ground veal
¼ pound salt pork, ground with the veal
½ cup cracker crumbs
4 strips salt pork

Add the bread crumbs to the beaten eggs; stir in the grated onion and the lemon juice. Add the salt and pepper. Mix in the ground veal and pork. Stir all very well.

Shape into an oblong loaf and place on a sheet of heavy aluminum foil. Press the cracker crumbs into the sides and over the top. Place the strips of salt pork diagonally across the loaf. Fold up the sides of the aluminum foil to retain the juices. Bake in a preheated 425° F. oven for 30 minutes. Then reduce heat to 300° F. and bake for an additional 1 hour and 30 minutes.

SELF-GLAZING MEAT LOAF

1 cup V-8 vegetable juice cocktail
3 slices bread, fresh and soft
3 eggs
1 teaspoon salt
¼ teaspoon pepper
1 tablespoon minced onion
1 pound ground chuck
½ pound ground ham
½ pound ground veal
4 tablespoons dark brown sugar
4 tablespoons cider vinegar
¼ teaspoon dry mustard
Dash of cayenne
2 tablespoons Worcestershire sauce
1 tablespoon water

Put the V-8 juice into a small saucepan and heat thoroughly. Place the bread, well broken up, into a medium-sized mixing bowl. Pour the vegetable cocktail over it. With the beaters of your mixer at low speed, beat until the bread and juice are thoroughly mixed and cooled. Then turn your mixer to its highest speed and add the eggs, one at a time. Add the salt, pepper and onion.

Now stir in the ground meat by hand. Be sure that all is thoroughly mixed. Mix the sugar, vinegar, dry mustard, cayenne, Worcestershire sauce and water together. Pour this into the bottom of a loaf tin. Form the meat mixture into a loaf and place in the tin. Bake in a 375° F. oven for 1 hour. At the end of this time, invert the loaf on an ovenproof platter and continue to bake for 30 minutes longer. The glaze which was at the bottom of the loaf will now glaze the top. If you wish, spoon the glaze over the top and sides from time to time.

MEAT LOAF WITH APPLE SAUCE

1 pound lean ground beef
¾ pound pork sausages (remove casings)
½ teaspoon sage
1 tablespoon Worcestershire sauce
½ teaspoon salt
2 cups canned apple sauce
1½ cups very dry bread crumbs
4 twists of pepper mill

Mix all of the ingredients together in the order in which they are given. Butter a loaf tin and pack them into it. Bake in a 350° F. oven for 45 minutes. This delicious meat loaf is excellent served cold in sandwiches.

LIMA BEAN, RICE AND HAMBURGER LOAF
(a good stretcher recipe)

1 pound hamburger
½ teaspoon paprika
½ cup chopped onion
½ teaspoon salt
¼ teaspoon pepper
1 tablespoon parsley flakes
1 cup rice
2 #2 cans lima beans, drained
1 cup stock, or 2 bouillon cubes dissolved in 1 cup water
1 can condensed tomato soup

Sauté the hamburger in a skillet until it loses its reddish color. Add the paprika and the chopped onion and continue to cook over low heat for 5 minutes longer. Then remove from heat.

Add the salt, pepper and parsley flakes; stir in the rice just as it comes from the package. Last, stir in the lima beans, stock and tomato soup. Take care not to break up the lima beans.

Place the mixture in a well-greased loaf tin and bake at 350° F. for 45 minutes, or until the center of the loaf is firm.

MEAT LOAF RING WITH CREAMED BEANS

½ pound ground veal
½ pound ground pork
½ pound ground ham
½ teaspoon salt
4 twists of pepper mill
2 eggs
4 tablespoons instant flour
2 tablespoons instant onion
1 can cream of mushroom soup
½ cup dry bread crumbs
1 package frozen green beans in cream sauce

Mix the ground veal, pork and ham together very well. Add the salt, pepper and eggs. Mix until all are thoroughly blended. Add the flour and the onion and stir again. Stir in the cream of mushroom soup. Grease a ring mold with butter and coat the inside with the bread crumbs. Carefully pour in the meat mixture; spread evenly with a rubber spatula.

Place in a 375° F. oven in a pan of water. Bake in the pan for 1 hour. Remove from oven and let cool for 5 minutes. Cook the green beans in a double boiler until they are thoroughly thawed and tender.

Invert the meat mold on a platter and pour the green beans into the center. Serve piping hot.

Variations:

Substitute 1 can cream of mushroom soup and 1 cup mushroom stems and pieces for the green beans.
Substitute 1 package frozen creamed peas for the green beans.
Substitute 1 package frozen cream-style corn for the green beans.
Substitute 1 can cream of celery soup plus 1 cup cooked celery for the green beans.
Substitute 1 package frozen peas and 1 can cream of celery soup for the green beans.

MEAT LOAF WITH YOGHURT

1 cup yoghurt
1 package onion soup mix
3 eggs, well beaten
¼ teaspoon pepper
1 teaspoon salt
1 tablespoon butter or margarine
1 cup soft bread crumbs (do not use crusts)
1½ pounds chopped beef

Mix the yoghurt, onion soup mix and eggs very well. Add the pepper and salt and set aside to allow the flavors to blend. Melt the butter or margarine in a large skillet. Add the chopped beef and brown evenly until all of the meat is well separated. Mix the bread crumbs with the eggs, yoghurt and onion soup.

Strain the browned meat through a sieve so that there is no fat left in it. Reserve the drippings. Add the browned meat to the other ingredients and mix very well. Use a small portion of the drippings to grease a loaf tin. Place the meat mixture in the tin and bake at 375° F. for 30 minutes, or until the center of the loaf is firm.

Invert the loaf on a hot platter and place under the broiler for 5 minutes to brown the bottom; then remove from oven.

FESTIVE MEAT LOAF #2

1 pound ground beef
1 pound ground veal
3 eggs, beaten to a lemon yellow
½ cup catsup
1 teaspoon salt
¼ teaspoon pepper
½ cup onion, chopped very fine
½ cup green pepper, chopped very fine
1 cup cracker crumbs
1 can tomato soup
¼ cup water

Mix the ground meat with the eggs, catsup, salt, pepper, onion and green pepper. Add the cracker crumbs and mix all very thoroughly. Place in a suitable loaf pan, cover tightly with aluminum foil and bake at 400° F. for 45 minutes. Then remove foil and pour the tomato soup, mixed with the water, over the loaf. Continue to bake for 15 minutes.

Invert on a heated platter and garnish with parsley sprigs. This will serve about 8.

CAULIFLOWER MEAT LOAF

1 large head cauliflower (approximately 8" in diameter) or
two small heads
4 strips bacon, diced into ¼" pieces
1 pound ground chuck
½ teaspoon salt
4 twists of pepper mill
2 tablespoons dehydrated onion
1 cup moist bread crumbs
¾ cup milk
4 eggs, beaten until lemon yellow
Dash of paprika

Wash the cauliflower well and break it into pieces. If there
is a large core, cut it into slices. Place in cold water and bring
to a boil. When the larger stems can be pierced with a fork,
remove from heat and drain. Set aside to cool. Brown the
diced bacon in a frying pan. Remove bacon and set aside;
then brown the ground chuck in the bacon drippings. Add
the salt, pepper and dehydrated onion.

Cover the bottom of a greased loaf pan with pieces of cauliflower. Sprinkle with some of the bread crumbs. Follow this
with a layer of the ground meat. Repeat until all of the cauliflower, bread crumbs and meat are used up. Add the milk
to the eggs and mix very well. Pour this over the ingredients
in the loaf tin. Sprinkle bacon over the top.

Place in a 300° F. oven for 45 minutes, or until the egg
mixture has set like a custard. Invert on a hot platter and
garnish with paprika.

HAMBURGER PANCAKE LOAF

This is a recipe from the Ukraine region of Russia. When I first heard of it, it seemed impossible that you could make meat loaf with pancakes; but you can, and it is delicious.

1 cup flour
½ teaspoon salt
½ teaspoon baking powder
2 raw eggs
1 cup milk
1 tablespoon butter or margarine
1 pound ground chuck
1 small onion, minced
¼ teaspoon salt
½ teaspoon pepper
½ teaspoon Accent
2 hard-boiled eggs, chopped
¼ cup stock, or ¼ cup water with 1 bouillon cube dissolved in it
¼ cup buttered browned bread crumbs

Place the flour in a bowl and mix in the ½ teaspoon salt and the baking powder. Beat the raw eggs in the milk. Slowly stir the egg and milk mixture into the flour. Stir very well, then set aside for 25 minutes.

Meanwhile, melt the butter in a skillet, then place the ground meat in the skillet and fry until golden brown. Add the onion, ¼ teaspoon salt, pepper and Accent. Remove from heat and add the chopped hard-boiled eggs, then the stock. Stir, mixing all well.

Heat a griddle and place 1 tablespoon of batter for each of the pancakes on it. Brown on both sides; set the finished pancakes aside until all the batter is used up.

Place pancakes to cover the bottom of a greased loaf tin. Follow with about a half-inch layer of the meat mixture. Continue alternate layers of pancakes and meat until all is used up. You should end with pancakes on the last layer. Sprinkle the bread crumbs over all. Bake in a 350° F. oven for 20 minutes.

CHICK PEA-HAMBURGER LOAF

1 cup dried chick peas*
5 strips bacon, cut into ¼" cubes
2 medium onions, diced
1 pound ground beef
¼ teaspoon grated nutmeg
½ teaspoon Accent
¼ teaspoon grated lemon rind
½ teaspoon salt
¼ teaspoon pepper
Juice of 1 lemon
½ cup catsup
¾ cup precooked rice
½ cup stock, or 2 bouillon cubes dissolved in ½ cup water

After having soaked the chick peas for at least 6 hours, drain them and cover with cold water. Bring them to a boil, then lower the heat and cook for at least 30 minutes, or until they can be pierced with a sharp fork. Drain and set aside to cool.

Fry the cubed bacon until it is brown and crisp. Remove bacon with a slotted spoon and set aside until later; reserve half of the bacon drippings in the skillet. Fry the onions in the bacon fat until they are glazed and transparent. Now fry the ground beef until it loses its red color. Add the grated nutmeg, Accent, lemon rind, salt and pepper. Continue to cook for 5 minutes longer and then add the lemon juice and catsup. Stir in the rice just as it comes from the package, and then add the stock.

Arrange half of the chick peas on the bottom of a greased loaf pan. Over this place the hamburger mixture. Arrange the remainder of the chick peas on top. Pour the stock over it, and place in a 350° F. oven for 35 minutes. Turn loaf onto a heated platter and sprinkle bacon cubes over the top.

* If your local grocer does not have them, they can be purchased in an international food store or one specializing in Greek, Armenian or Turkish food.

Chapter II
CASE THAT CASSEROLE

IT TOOK YEARS for me to get my husband within ten feet of a casserole. To him a casserole meant something gooey, soupy, and totally without distinctive flavor. Even macaroni and cheese had to have the tar baked out of it before he would condescend to try a forkful of it. Hamburger Hot Pot, the first dish listed in this chapter, is the first casserole he liked enough to ask for a second helping.

Men seem to love casseroles that have some "chew" to them. Here are recipes for casseroles that have been tested by the severest critic I know—my husband.

HAMBURGER HOT POT

1 pound hamburger
1 can Spam or similar canned meat, cut into 1" x ½" pieces
1 8-ounce package medium-wide egg noodles
1 #2 can red kidney beans, drained
1 clove garlic, minced
1 cup sliced whole mushrooms or 1 cup pieces and stems
¼ cup chopped green pepper
½ teaspoon salt
5 twists of pepper mill, or ¼ teaspoon ground pepper
1 teaspoon Accent
1 cup tomato sauce
2 cups water
2 tablespoons butter

Sauté the hamburger until it is separated into pieces about the size of pecans, and slightly browned. Then combine it and all the other ingredients in a 2½-quart casserole. The noodles are put into this mixture just as they come from the package—no precooking.

Toss the ingredients to mix them thoroughly. Cover the casserole and bake in a 375° F. oven for 30 minutes. At the end of this time, remove cover from casserole, With a broad spoon or spatula, turn over the top ingredients so that they will get the benefit of the juice which has accumulated.

Bake 30 minutes longer without a cover. Stir occasionally to insure even cooking of the noodles. This is a wonderful and very nutritious one-dish meal.

CHUCK WAGON WESTERN BEAN CASSEROLE

1 pound hamburger
1 #4 can pork and beans
1 teaspoon prepared mustard
¼ teaspoon salt
¼ teaspoon pepper
1 large onion
½ cup catsup
1 tablespoon Worcestershire sauce

Sauté the hamburger until quite brown and separated. Drain off any excess fat. Add the beans and the other ingredients. Stir well, taking care not to mash up the beans in the process. Place in a 1½-quart covered casserole dish in a preheated 350° F. oven for 40 minutes.

This is an excellent picnic dish because it can be prepared ahead of time and warmed right in the casserole on the grill outdoors.

Variations:

Substitute 1 #2 can butter beans and 1 #2 can pork and beans for the #4 can of pork and beans.

Substitute 1 #2 can black-eyed peas and 1 #2 can pork and beans for the #4 can of pork and beans.

Substitute 1 #2 can chick peas and 1 #2 can pork and beans for the #4 can of pork and beans.

Substitute 1 #2 can lima beans and 1 #2 can pork and beans for the #4 can of pork and beans.

Substitute 1 #2 can pork and beans and 1 #2 can macaroni and cheese for the #4 can of pork and beans.

Substitute 1 #2 can pork and beans and 1 #2 can spaghetti for the #4 can of pork and beans.

MADRID RICE CASSEROLE

3 slices bacon, cut into ¼" pieces
½ cup onion, chopped fine
1½ pounds hamburger
¼ teaspoon thyme
¼ teaspoon sweet basil
1 #2 can tomato juice
1½ cups precooked rice
1 green pepper, cut into ¼" pieces
½ teaspoon paprika

Sauté the bacon in a skillet until slightly browned. Pour away most of the fat; add the onion and continue to sauté until the onion is slightly transparent. Add the hamburger to the onion and bacon, along with the thyme and basil. Cook for a few minutes longer, until the meat loses its reddish color. Remove from heat, and add the tomato juice. Stir in the rice just as it comes from the package. Add most of the green pepper, reserving a few pieces for later. Place the entire mixture in a 1½ quart casserole and sprinkle the paprika over the top.

Place the casserole in a 350° F. oven and bake for 35 minutes, uncovered. Five minutes before removing from the oven, sprinkle the remaining green pepper over the top for color. Serve right from the casserole used to bake in.

I usually bake a double quantity of this casserole, one for serving and one for freezing. This is a satisfying main dish for a hurry-up meal.

Variations:

Add 1 package frozen okra.
Add 1 package frozen zucchini squash.
Add 1 package frozen French-style green beans.
Omit the green pepper and use 1 8-ounce can of mushrooms.
Add 1 package frozen niblet-style corn.

EAT-MORE CASSEROLE

1 pound hamburger
½ pound elbow macaroni
1 cup chopped onion or ½ cup dehydrated onion soaked
   in ½ cup water
1 #2 can tomatoes
1 cup tomato sauce
¼ teaspoon salt
¼ teaspoon pepper
¼ teaspoon garlic powder
1 teaspoon Accent
1 can niblet-style corn with pimento, drained

Sauté the hamburger until a golden brown. Meanwhile, boil the macaroni in slightly salted water until tender. Drain the macaroni and combine it with the hamburger; add the onion, tomatoes, tomato sauce, salt, pepper, garlic powder and Accent to the meat. Last, fold in the corn.

Place this mixture in a 1½-quart buttered casserole and put into a preheated 350° F. oven; bake for 45 minutes.

If you are entertaining teen-agers with ravenous appetites, this is a good mixture to serve on hamburger buns as "sloppy joes." However, if you want the real "sloppy joe" recipe, it is included in the chapter called "Shades of Lord Sandwich."

WALNUT-MEAT BALL CASSEROLE

2 pounds hamburger
1 cup chopped walnuts
1 cup bread crumbs
3 eggs, beaten to a lemon yellow
¾ cup milk
1 package dehydrated French onion soup
½ cup boiling water

Mix the hamburger, walnuts, bread crumbs, eggs and milk thoroughly. Form into 1" diameter meat balls and brown them a few at a time. Shaking the skillet back and forth slowly over the flame will assure even browning.

Mix the dehydrated onion soup with the boiling water and pour over the meat balls. Place in a preheated 350° F. oven for a half hour. Add more water if necessary. Should you desire additional gravy, remove meat balls, add ¾ cup of water with tablespoon cornstarch mixed in it. Simmer for 5 minutes longer, and return meat balls to the gravy.

Variations:

Substitute 1 cup blanched Virginia peanuts for the walnuts.
Substitute 1 cup cashew nuts for the walnuts.
Substitute 1 cup pecans for the walnuts.
Substitute 1 cup pine nuts for the walnuts.

RED LETTER DAY CASSEROLE

This casserole combines meat, potatoes and other vegetables all in one dish, and is both colorful and flavorful. If your family doesn't like vegetables, it's a painless way to get them to eat them.

1 pound hamburger
8 cooked beets, peeled and coarsely chopped
8 medium-sized cooked potatoes, coarsely chopped (left-over potatoes, even hashed brown ones, are all right in this recipe)
8 cooked carrots, coarsely chopped
1 teaspoon salt
¼ teaspoon pepper
1 teaspoon Accent
2 tablespoons butter
¼ cup soup stock, or 1 bouillon cube dissolved in ¼ cup water

Sauté the ground beef until it is in pieces about the size of pecans, and slightly brown. Drain off any excess fat. To the browned meat add the chopped beets, potatoes and carrots. Add the salt, pepper and Accent. Place in a well-greased casserole. Dot the top with pieces of butter. Add the stock or bouillon. Place in a preheated 350° F. oven and bake for 35 minutes.

MEAT BALL-BEER CASSEROLE

The first time I was served this casserole, I thought the cook had flipped her lid. Beer and meat? Well, it turned out to be delicious. Try it; you too are in for a pleasant surprise. Some strange alchemy of flavors takes place that's hard to beat.

10 onions, approximately 2" in diameter
1 pound hamburger
1 egg, whipped to a lemon yellow
½ teaspoon salt
1 teaspoon monosodium glutamate
¼ teaspoon pepper
1 tablespoon olive oil, or any good cooking oil
1 tablespoon flour
1 teaspoon dry mustard
1 teaspoon sugar
1 small bay leaf
¼ teaspoon thyme
1 12-ounce bottle beer
1 pound fresh mushrooms, or 1 #2 can mushrooms
Water cress, parsley or spinach for garnish

Peel the onions and put a toothpick through the middle of each one to prevent them from coming apart. Cover with warm water and boil until the outer shell begins to get transparent. Do not cook them completely—the final cooking takes place in the casserole. Drain and set aside to cool. Do not remove toothpicks until the onions are cool.

Mix the hamburger with the egg, salt, monosodium glutamate and pepper. In this instance, because you want a tightly held-together meat ball, knead the mixture for several minutes by hand. Form into very small meat balls, about 1" in diameter. I use the large end of my melon-ball maker to keep the meat balls uniform in size.

Heat the oil in your largest skillet; brown the meat balls by gently rolling them around in the pan. Try not to crowd them, or they will lose their shape. When all the meat balls are evenly browned, sprinkle the flour, mustard and sugar over their surface. By shaking the pan, roll the meat balls so that the flour mixture is evenly distributed.

Remove from the heat, add the bay leaf and thyme. Now pour over them the bottle of beer. Cover and set aside for approximately a half hour for all of the flavors to get acquainted. This wait is not a must, but it does improve the flavor.

32

In a 1½ quart casserole arrange the meat balls, mushrooms and onions (with toothpicks now removed) and pour over all the beer you have left in the skillet. Place in a 300° F. oven and bake for 35 minutes. Garnish with shredded water cress, parsley, or a few leaves of spinach, chopped fine.

RIPE OLIVE HAMBURGER CASSEROLE

1 tablespoon butter or margarine
1 pound ground chuck
2 cups dry fine egg noodles
3 quarts slightly salted water
1 cup sour cream
1 cup large-curd creamed cottage cheese
1 tablespoon dehydrated onion
1 clove garlic, chopped fine
1 teaspoon Accent
1 teaspoon Worcestershire sauce
1 drop Tabasco
1 #2 can pitted ripe olives
1 teaspoon paprika

Melt the butter or margarine in a deep skillet. Add the ground meat and cook until the reddish color disappears. Set aside. Boil the egg noodles in the water. Drain and add to the meat.

Stir in the sour cream, cottage cheese, onion, garlic, Accent, Worcestershire sauce and Tabasco. Chop the ripe olives rather coarsely and add to the meat mixture.

Put into a greased 1½-quart casserole. Bake at 350° F. for 30 minutes. Sprinkle with the paprika just before serving.

YAMBURGERS

¾ pound ground chuck
¾ pound lean ground pork
½ teaspoon salt
4 twists of pepper mill
6 rings pineapple
2 tablespoons butter
2 #2 cans yams or sweet potatoes, drained
¼ cup muscat raisins
¼ cup dried currants

Mix the ground beef and pork, salt and pepper together thoroughly. Form into six meat patties about the same size as the pineapple rings. Melt the butter in a skillet and brown the meat patties on each side. Mash the yams with a potato masher until they are quite fluffy. Add the raisins and currants and stir very well.

Butter the bottom and sides of a deep baking dish, and place the mashed yam mixture on the bottom. Cover the top with the pineapple rings, pushing each down into the mixture about a half inch. Place one hamburger patty on each of the pineapple rings. Bake in a preheated 350° F. oven for 30 minutes.

BUTTER BEAN-HAMBURGER CASSEROLE

1 #2 can butter beans or 1 cup uncooked lima beans
1 pound hamburger
¼ teaspoon pepper
½ teaspoon salt
Dash of nutmeg
1 egg, slightly beaten
2 tablespoons margarine or cooking oil
1 small can tomato paste
¼ teaspoon paprika
1 cup sour cream

If you are using uncooked lima beans, cover with water and boil until tender. Drain and set aside.

Thoroughly mix the hamburger, pepper, salt, nutmeg and egg. Form into meat balls about the size of apricots. Brown the meat balls in a skillet in the margarine or cooking oil. Add the tomato paste to the butter beans or lima beans, then stir in the paprika and sour cream. Last, add the browned meat balls, discarding any fat left in the skillet. Pour into a greased casserole and bake for 25 minutes at 350° F.

This casserole is equally good served either hot or cold.

DEER HUNTER'S PIE

1 pound hamburger
4 large boiled potatoes, peeled and sliced ⅛″ thick
2 large onions, peeled and sliced ⅛″ thick
3 large apples, preferably tart baking variety, sliced ⅛″ thick
1 cup beef stock, or 1 cup water with 3 bouillon cubes dissolved in it
¼ teaspoon grated nutmeg
¼ teaspoon pepper
½ teaspoon salt
½ cup bread crumbs

Sauté the hamburger in a skillet until it is lightly browned and completely separated.

Arrange a layer of potatoes over the bottom of a 1½ quart greased casserole, follow with a layer of meat, a layer of onions and a layer of apples. Repeat until you have used up all of the ingredients.

Heat the beef stock, add the nutmeg, pepper and salt. Stir well so that all of the salt is dissolved. Pour this over the casserole. Sprinkle the bread crumbs over the top, and add little dabs of butter if you like. Bake in a 350° F. oven for 50 minutes.

HAMBURGER OYSTER CASSEROLE

2½ pounds hamburger
1 pint oysters (save the liquor)
1 cup dry bread crumbs
4 sprigs parsley, chopped fine
1 small onion, chopped very fine
1 teaspoon salt
¼ teaspoon ground pepper

Fry the hamburger loosely until it is all browned, turning with a spatula during frying so that it is not broken up too much. Then add the drained oysters, and continue frying until the oyster edges curl—about 5 minutes. Set aside, and mix the liquor from the oysters with the bread crumbs, parsley and onion. Season with the salt and pepper. Add to the browned meat and oysters, tossing lightly to mix. Put into a well-greased casserole and bake at 350° F. for 45 minutes. Before removing from oven, slip under the broiler for a few seconds so the top can brown.

MEXICAN CASSEROLE

¾ pound ground chuck
¾ pound lean ground pork
2 cups cooked broad noodles
1 8-ounce can tomato sauce
2 cups American process cheese, diced into ¼" pieces
¼ cup minced parsley
3 preserved pimentos, sliced into long strips ¼" wide
1 green pepper, diced into ¼" pieces
2 cups onion, diced into ¼" pieces
½ teaspoon paprika
1 teaspoon salt
4 twists of pepper mill
4 strips bacon, diced into ¼" pieces

Mix together all of the ingredients except the diced bacon. Sprinkle the bacon over the bottom of a 1½-quart buttered casserole. Top the bacon with the meat and vegetable mixture. Bake in a 350° F. oven for 1 hour.

HAMBURGER-CABBAGE CASSEROLE

1 pound hamburger
1 tablespoon dehydrated onion
4 eggs
1 cup of milk
1 teaspoon sugar
½ teaspoon salt
¼ teaspoon pepper
1 2-pound cabbage
½ cup bread crumbs

Brown the hamburger and cook until it is all separated. Add the onion and cook for a few minutes longer. Remove from the heat. Beat the eggs until they are lemon yellow, add the milk gradually and continue beating. Add the sugar to the milk and eggs. Stir in the hamburger. Add the salt and pepper. Mix well.

Slice the cabbage very fine. Cover with water and cook for 7 minutes; drain, discarding the water. Place the boiled cabbage in a deep, greased casserole. Pour the hamburger mixture over the cabbage. Sprinkle the top with bread crumbs. Bake in a 350° F. oven for 50 minutes.

The bread crumbs should become golden brown during this cooking time. If they are not, place the casserole under the broiler for a few minutes before serving.

RAW POTATO CASSEROLE

½ pound ground chuck
½ pound lean ground pork
1 can condensed tomato soup
½ teaspoon salt
4 twists of pepper mill
1 tablespoon flour
2 tablespoons butter or margarine
1 8-ounce can mushroom stems and pieces (do not drain)
1 large onion, diced
3 cups raw potatoes, diced in ½" pieces

Mix the ground meat with the tomato soup, salt and pepper. Work in the flour. Form into meat balls about the size of golf balls. Melt the butter in a skillet and brown the meat balls on all sides.

Place the meat balls on the bottom of a well-greased 1½-quart casserole. Mix the mushrooms, onion and raw potatoes very well, and pour over the meat balls. Cover with aluminum foil and bake at 350° F. for 45 minutes. Then remove the foil and continue to bake for 15 minutes longer. Serve piping hot.

HEARTY CASSEROLE

1 tablespoon butter or margarine
½ cup chopped onion
1 pound ground chuck
½ pound American process cheese, cut into ¼" cubes
1 8-ounce package elbow macaroni, cooked in 3 quarts salted, boiling water
1 tablespoon mustard
1 package frozen corn
½ teaspoon salt
¼ teaspoon pepper
1 can condensed tomato soup

Melt the butter in a skillet, add the onion and cook until transparent. Then add the meat and continue to cook until it loses its reddish color. Set aside to cool.

Mix the cheese, macaroni, mustard, corn, salt, pepper and tomato soup. Stir in the mixture of meat and onion. Place in a 1½-quart buttered casserole and bake at 350° F. for 1 hour. Serve piping hot.

WILD RICE AND HAMBURGER CASSEROLE

¾ cup wild rice
2 cups slightly salted water
1 pound combined beef, veal and pork ground together
½ cup chopped onion
½ cup celery, chopped fine
½ teaspoon salt
½ teaspoon Accent
½ teaspoon Worcestershire sauce
1 can condensed cream of mushroom soup
¼ cup sherry wine
¼ cup grated Parmesan cheese
1 cup quartered canned or fresh mushrooms, if desired

Cook the wild rice in the water until each grain is doubled in size. Drain rice, rinse in warm tap water, and set aside in strainer to drain thoroughly dry.

Sauté the ground meat till brown, add the onion, celery, salt, Accent and Worcestershire sauce. Stir in the wild rice and mushroom soup. Add the wine. Place in a well-greased casserole; sprinkle the cheese over the top. Bake in a 350° F. oven for 1 hour.

Since wild rice and mushrooms complement each other, you may also use a cup of canned or fresh mushrooms in this recipe.

Variations:

Substitute ¼ cup grated American cheese for the Parmesan cheese.
Substitute ¼ cup feta (Greek) cheese for the Parmesan cheese.
Substitute 1 can cream of celery soup for the mushroom soup.
Substitute 1 can cream of asparagus soup for the mushroom soup.
Substitute 1 can cream of chicken soup for the mushroom soup.

38

EGGPLANT, LAMB AND CRACKED WHEAT
CASSEROLE

3 tablespoons olive oil
1 pound ground lamb
½ cup chopped onion
½ cup chopped green pepper
1 #2 can tomatoes
1 medium-sized eggplant, peeled and cut into 1″ pieces
2 cloves garlic
1 teaspoon salt
4 twists of pepper mill
1 tablespoon lemon juice
1 teaspoon lemon rind
¾ cup cracked wheat
1 cup water
½ cup Parmesan-Romano cheese

Place 1 tablespoon of the olive oil in a skillet and brown the ground lamb. Add the onion and green pepper and cook until they are glazed and soft. Stir in the tomatoes and set aside.

Meanwhile, in another skillet, heat the remaining 2 tablespoons of olive oil and sauté the eggplant cubes until they are almost tender. Add the garlic, salt, pepper, lemon juice and rind. Cook the cracked wheat in the water until all the kernels are separated, doubled in size and tender. All of the water should be absorbed in the cooking.

Place half of the cracked wheat in the bottom of a well-buttered 2-quart casserole. Put half the lamb mixture over this, then half the eggplant, and repeat the layers with the other half of each. Sprinkle the cheese over the top and place in a 350° F. oven for 30 minutes. Serve piping hot.

You can make variations on this delicious casserole by substituting ground beef, ground ham, or a mixture of ground beef, veal and pork for the lamb.

HAMBURGER AND RICE CASSEROLE

1 pound hamburger
1 teaspoon onion juice or 1 tablespoon onion, chopped very fine
½ cup celery, chopped fine
¼ teaspoon ground black pepper
1 teaspoon salt
Dash of nutmeg
1 8-ounce can tomato sauce
1 egg
2 cups cooked regular rice
½ cup dry bread crumbs
1 tablespoon butter or margarine

Put the hamburger into a good-sized mixing bowl; add the onion, celery, black pepper, salt and nutmeg. Mix all very thoroughly; then stir in the tomato sauce.

In another mixing bowl, beat the egg with a rotary beater until light and lemon colored. Add the rice and mix thoroughly. Press half the rice-egg mixture around the sides and over the bottom of a well-greased casserole. Reserve the other half of the rice to go over the top.

Place this casserole under the broiler for 5 minutes, or until the rice begins to brown and is set firmly around the sides. Remove from the oven, and put in the meat mixture carefully, using a rubber spatula to spread it evenly. Cover with the remainder of the rice-egg mixture, and sprinkle the bread crumbs over the top. Dot with the butter or margarine.

Bake at 350° F. for 45 minutes. Just before serving, place under the broiler for a few seconds to brown the crumbs on top.

Chapter III

SERVE IT IN ONE DISH

IF I CAN MAKE ONE-DISH MEALS, I generally do. To the busy housewife there is nothing more discouraging than a sinkful of cooking pots in addition to the piles of plates, knives and forks. Even if you are fortunate enough to own an automatic dishwater, washing pots is still a chore. So here are one-dish recipes I love because they save so much washing-up.

ONION HAMBURGER STEW

2 pounds hamburger
2 eggs, beaten until lemon yellow
½ cup olive oil
10 medium-sized red Italian onions (if not available, use white or yellow)
1 #2 can tomatoes
½ cup white vinegar
1 teaspoon pickling spices, tied in a little cloth sack so they can be removed
2 cloves of garlic, minced (optional)
½ teaspoon salt
¼ teaspoon pepper
½ teaspoon monosodium glutamate

Thoroughly mix the ground hamburger with the two beaten eggs. Knead by hand so that the meat balls will be very firm. With the large end of your melon-ball scoop, form 1″ diameter meat balls. Heat the olive oil in a large skillet and slowly brown the meat balls. Shake the pan in a back and forth motion to keep them round and to insure even browning.

Peel the onions and add them; continue to cook until the outer skins begin to glaze. Add the tomatoes, vinegar, spice bag, garlic, salt, pepper and monosodium glutamate. Cover and simmer for 2 hours.

If desired, you can add about 8 medium-sized potatoes 45 minutes before the dish is done. If additional water is needed, add enough to keep the stew from scorching. Remove the bag of spices before serving the stew.

STUFFED TOMATOES, ITALIAN STYLE

1 pound hamburger
4 large ripe tomatoes
½ cup precooked rice
¼ cup grated Parmesan-Romano cheese
2 tablespoons chopped parsley
2 4-inch square slices of Swiss cheese, cut into ¼″ cubes
1 teaspoon monosodium glutamate
¼ teaspoon salt
¼ teaspoon pepper
¼ teaspoon sweet basil

Brown the hamburger in a skillet until it is completely separated; turn off the heat and let cool until you have the tomatoes ready. Boil the rice in 1½ cups of water until double in size; rinse and drain. Set aside to cool.

Cut off ¼″ of the top of each tomato. With a teaspoon, very carefully scoop out the center pulp, leaving about a ½″ wall. Add the pulp you have removed to the hamburger, and turn the heat low. Cook for 5 minutes longer, or until the tomato pulp is broken up; now add the Parmesan-Romano cheese, parsley, Swiss cheese, monosodium glutamate, salt, pepper and basil. Lastly, fold in the cooked rice.

Fill each tomato cavity with the mixture; use a teaspoon to pack it in. Place the stuffed tomatoes in a greased shallow baking dish and bake in a 350° F. oven for 35 minutes.

Care must be taken not to overcook this dish; you want the tomatoes to retain their shape, not become a mushy mess.

Variations:

Substitute grated American cheese for the Parmesan-Romano.
Substitute feta (Greek) cheese for the Parmesan-Romano.
Substitute ½″ cup crushed fine egg noodles for the rice.
Add ½ cup green pepper, diced very fine.
Add ½ cup niblet-style corn.
Wrap each tomato with a slice of bacon fastened with a toothpick before putting it in the oven.

HAMBURGER CHOW MEIN

1 pound of pork, veal and beef, ground together
6 medium-sized onions cut in ¼″ slices
2 cups celery, cut in ¼″ slices
1 #2 can of tomatoes
1 #2 can of bean sprouts
1 #2 can of mushroom stems and pieces
1 7-ounce can water chestnuts (optional)
1 tablespoon soy sauce
1 teaspoon bead molasses
1 teaspoon monosodium glutamate
1 #2 can chow mein noodles

Slowly sauté the meat until it is in lumps about the size of hickory nuts, and light brown in color. The pork in the mixture should supply enough fat for sautéing.

Add the onions, celery and tomatoes and simmer slowly for 35 minutes. Do not cover, or celery will lose its green color. Add the bean sprouts, mushrooms, water chestnuts, soy sauce, molasses and monosodium glutamate. Simmer for 10 minutes longer. Heat the noodles in the oven at 250° F. for 10 minutes. Serve the chow mein over the heated noodles.

If you really want to show off, add about 10 sliced almonds and a few cubes of pimento to the recipe and sprinkle a little of each over the top of each serving.

Variations:

Substitute 1 10½-ounce can cream chicken soup and 1 can of water for the tomatoes.
Substitute 1 10½-ounce can cream of mushroom soup and 1 can of water for the tomatoes.
Substitute 1 10½-ounce can cream of celery soup and 1 can of water for the tomatoes.
Substitute 1 8-ounce package medium-sized egg noodles, boiled until tender, for the chow mein noodles.
Substitute 3 cups cooked rice for the chow mein noodles.
Substitute 2 packages frozen French-fried onion rings for the chow mein noodles.

ONIONS AND HAMBURGER, MILAN STYLE

4 large Bermuda onions, or 8 medium-sized onions
1 pound hamburger
8 soda crackers, soaked in enough milk to soften
¼ cup Parmesan cheese
2 3" diameter ginger snaps, broken into small pieces
¼ teaspoon salt
¼ teaspoon pepper, or 4 twists of pepper mill
½ teaspoon monosodium glutamate
2 tablespoons chopped parsley
2 eggs, beaten until lemon yellow
½ teaspoon paprika

Very carefully peel the onions, removing only the first layer of the peeling. Cut a ½" slice from the top of the onion —enough so that all the inner rings are exposed. Stick a toothpick into the side of the onion straight through the center. If the onions are very large, insert toothpicks from each side. This is to keep the onions from losing their shape during cooking. Place the onions in a saucepan, cover with water and boil very slowly for 20 minutes. Set them aside in their own liquid to cool so that you can handle them with ease.

Brown the hamburger in a skillet until it is all separated and in small pieces. Now remove the toothpicks from the onions and, using a teaspoon, carefully scoop out the centers. Leave about a ½" wall. Add to the hamburger the onion centers you scooped out.

Cook the hamburger and onion centers until the onion breaks apart and is glazed. Remove from the heat and stir in the drained soda crackers. Stir in the Parmesan cheese. Next add the pieces of ginger snaps and stir until they are completely dissolved. Add the salt, pepper, monosodium glutamate and parsley. When the mixture has cooled, add half of the beaten eggs. Reserve the other half until later.

Using a teaspoon, pack the filling into each onion shell, taking care not to break through the outer walls. Place the onions in a buttered baking dish. Pour the remainder of the beaten eggs, by tablespoonfuls, over the onions. Sprinkle a little of the paprika over them. Place in a preheated 350° F. oven and bake for 35 minutes.

Variations:

Substitute ground lean pork for the hamburger.

Substitute a mixture of pork and veal for the hamburger.

Substitute a mixture of ham and hamburger for the straight hamburger.

Add ¼ teaspoon cloves and ¼ teaspoon allspice, if you like food to be spicy.

ONE-DISH MEAL

1 pound hamburger
2 onions, peeled and cut in ⅛" slices
1 teaspoon salt
¼ teaspoon pepper
3 large raw potatoes, peeled and diced into ½" pieces
3 large carrots, peeled and diced into ½" pieces
1 cup precooked rice
Water to cover

Brown the hamburger in a skillet until it loses its reddish color. Add the onions and continue to cook until they are glazed and transparent. Add the salt and pepper.

In a greased 1½ quart casserole, place the potatoes first; follow with a layer of carrots, then a layer of rice. Last, add the sautéed meat and onion mixture. Pour on enough water to cover. Leave the casserole uncovered and place in a 350° F. oven for 1 hour.

Serve hot, right from the casserole.

Variations:

Substitute 1 #2 can of peas and carrots for the raw potatoes.

Substitute 1 #2 can boiled onions for the fresh onions; leave them whole.

Substitute 1 #2 can of boiled potatoes for the fresh ones; leave them whole.

Substitute 1 #2 can corn, cream or niblet style, for the carrots.

Substitute 1 8-ounce package fine egg noodles (uncooked) for the rice.

KIDNEY BEAN SPECIAL

4 large potatoes, scrubbed, unpeeled, cut in ¼" slices
4 onions, cut in ¼" slices
1 cup precooked rice
1 pound hamburger
1 #2 can peas, drained
1 #2 can red kidney beans, not drained
1 8-ounce can tomato sauce
1 cup warm water
1 cup crushed potato chips

Butter a 1½-quart casserole and place the slices of potato in the bottom. Add a dash of salt and pepper, then a layer of onions. Next add a layer of precooked rice, as it comes from the package. Then place the raw hamburger, broken into pieces, over the rice. Salt and pepper again.

Next add the peas, then the kidney beans. Mix the tomato sauce with the water and pour over the top of the casserole. Sprinkle with the potato chips. Place in a 375° F. oven for 1½ hours. Serve piping hot.

Variations:

Substitute 1 cup dry fine noodles for the rice.
Substitute 1 cup brown rice for the white rice.
Use ½ cup wheat germ and ½ cup rice instead of all rice.
Substitute 1 #2 can pork and beans for the kidney beans.
Substitute 1 #2 can butter beans for the kidney beans.
Substitute 1 #2 can chick peas for the kidney beans.
Substitute 1 #2 can black-eyed peas for the kidney beans.
Substitute 1 #2 can niblet-style corn for the kidney beans.

HAMBURGER-FILLED ACORN SQUASH

6 tablespoons butter
2 cloves garlic, cut into very thin slices
1 pound hamburger
4 slices white bread with crusts removed
1 cup milk
1 egg, beaten to a lemon yellow
½ cup chopped parsley
½ cup chopped celery
¼ teaspoon salt
¼ teaspoon pepper
1 teaspoon monosodium glutamate
4 acorn squash, sliced lengthwise, with the seeds and pulp
  removed
⅓ cup water

Melt the butter in a skillet, being careful not to burn it. Add the cut-up garlic and sauté for 5 minutes. Now remove the garlic and discard it. Here garlic is used as a very subtle flavoring agent, if left in it would overwhelm the squash flavor.

Brown the meat in the garlic-flavored butter; break up the slices of bread and soak in the milk; to the bread mixture add the egg, parsley, celery, salt, pepper and monosodium glutamate. Stir in the meat mixture, and continue to mix and stir until all is very smooth.

Fill each squash half with a portion of the mixture, then place the filled squash in a shallow baking pan. Pour the water into the bottom of the pan. Do not cover. Place in a preheated 350° F. oven and bake for 1 hour, or until the sides of the squash can be pierced with a fork.

Variations:

Substitute lean ground pork for the hamburger.
Substitute lean ground ham for the hamburger.
Substitute a mixture of half pork sausage with casings removed and half hamburger for all hamburger.
Substitute a mixture of half ham and half hamburger for all hamburger.
Use 1 cup cooked rice in place of the bread; diminish the milk by half.

HAMBURGER ENCHILADAS

Meat Filling

1 pound ground chuck
1 tablespoon olive oil
½ teaspoon salt
4 twists of pepper mill
1 clove minced garlic

Sauce

1 can condensed tomato soup
¼ teaspoon garlic salt
Dash of cayenne pepper
½ cup water
Pinch oregano

Tortillas

1 cup instant flour
1 cup yellow corn meal
½ teaspoon salt
¼ cup shortening
½ cup warm milk

Vegetable Filling

½ cup chopped onion
1 cup shredded chopped lettuce
½ cup sharp American cheese

Brown the meat in olive oil. Add the salt, pepper and garlic. Set aside while you make the sauce.

Put the tomato soup, garlic salt, pepper, water and oregano in a saucepan and bring to the simmering point. It can continue simmering while you prepare the tortillas.

Mix the flour, corn meal and salt together. Cut in the shortening until it is very crumbly. Slowly add the warm milk. Mix until you have a soft dough. Knead on a lightly floured board 60 times. Divide into 10 balls and set them aside for 15 minutes, covered with a cloth. Then roll the dough into 8″ rounds. Fry on a hot ungreased griddle until they start to turn brown in spots.

Dip each tortilla into the sauce until it is soft. Put a heaping tablespoonful of the meat mixture in the middle of each one. Add a little of the chopped onion, some of the lettuce and a teaspoonful of the cheese. Roll each tortilla and place it seam side down in a buttered baking dish. Pour the remainder of the sauce over the tortillas and bake in a 350° F. oven for 20 minutes.

Serve piping hot. This will serve 5 people, allowing two enchiladas for each.

MEXICAN HAMBURGER AND RICE

1 tablespoon olive oil
1 cup rice
1 pound ground chuck
1 medium onion, chopped fine
2 cloves garlic, minced
1 #2 can tomatoes
2 bouillon cubes dissolved in 1 cup warm water
1 tablespoon chili powder
1 teaspoon salt
Dash of cayenne

Heat the olive oil in a deep skillet with a tight-fitting cover. Add the rice and cook until it turns white. Add the ground meat and cook until it is golden brown. Add the onion and garlic, and cook until the onion is transparent. Add the tomatoes, bouillon, chili powder, salt and cayenne. Mix all very well.

Cover and simmer for 35 minutes, stirring from time to time. During this process all of the liquid should be absorbed by the rice. If it is not, cook for 5 minutes longer with a double thickness of dish towel between the lid and the top of the pan. The towel will absorb any additional moisture.

QUICK HAMBURGER GOULASH

2 pounds hamburger
1 cup onions, sliced
2 cups wide noodles, previously cooked
1 tablespoon dehydrated parsley
1 #2 can tomatoes
1 #2 can corn
1 teaspoon salt
4 twists of pepper mill
½ teaspoon paprika

Place the hamburger in a large skillet with a tight-fitting cover and brown the meat until it loses its reddish color. Add the onions and cook until they are transparent. Stir in the remainder of the ingredients and let simmer for about 40 minutes. Keep tightly covered all the while it is cooking.

HAMBURGER AND ZUCCHINI

2 pounds zucchini squash, unpeeled
4 slices ham, diced in ¼" pieces
3 slices bacon, diced in ¼" strips
½ cup onion, chopped
1 pound hamburger
1 tablespoon parsley flakes
½ teaspoon salt
4 twists of pepper mill
¼ cup chopped pimento, fresh or preserved

Wash the zucchini in cold water. Put in a pot with enough cold water to cover, and bring to a boil. Drain and set aside to cool. Do not cover pan while boiling zucchini, as that would make it lose its beautiful green color.

Place the ham and bacon in a skillet and fry until the bacon is a golden color. Now add the onion and fry until it is clear and glazed. Add the hamburger and fry until its red color has disappeared. Remove from heat and stir in the salt, pepper, pimento and parsley.

Cut the cooled zucchini in half and arrange in the bottom of a greased baking dish. Place the hamburger mixture over the zucchini. Bake in a 350° F. oven for 45 minutes.

HAMBURGER BAKE

2 pounds ground chuck
2 tablespoons butter or margarine
4 medium onions, sliced ¼" thick
½ cup catsup
1 tablespoon dehydrated parsley
1 tablespoon Worcestershire sauce
1 teaspoon salt
4 twists of pepper mill
1 lemon, cut into ⅛" slices

Form the meat into a huge patty about 2" thick. Place it on a piece of aluminum foil large enough to wrap the patty tightly. Melt the butter in a skillet and brown the onions in it. Place the buttered onions on top of the ground meat.

Mix the catsup, parsley, Worcestershire sauce, salt and pepper. Bring up the sides of the foil to form a border around the meat, and pour the catsup mixture over the meat and onions. Place the lemon slices on top.

Tightly seal the foil, and place meat in a 350° F. oven

for 40 minutes. Just before removing from oven, roll back the foil to form a dishlike arrangement, move the onions and lemon off to the sides and put the dish under the broiler for 5 minutes.

HAMBURGER WITH CORN MEAL BISCUITS

1 tablespoon olive oil
1 pound hamburger
1 #2 can tomatoes
4 onions, chopped very fine
1 4-ounce can mushroom stems and pieces
½ cup catsup
½ cup water
½ teaspoon salt
¼ teaspoon sweet basil
3 green peppers, chopped

Biscuits

1 cup yellow corn meal
1 cup instant or all-purpose flour
1 teaspoon salt
1 tablespoon baking powder
¼ cup shortening
¾ cup milk

Heat the olive oil in a skillet, add the hamburger and cook until all the reddish color disappears. Add the tomatoes, onions and mushrooms. Mix the catsup with the water and add to the meat mixture. Add the salt, basil and green peppers. Place the mixture in a well-greased 1½-quart casserole.

Mix the corn meal, flour, baking powder and salt together. Cut in the shortening. Blend until the mixture is crumbly. Slowly add the milk. Mix until a soft dough is formed. Turn out on a lightly floured board and knead 20 times. Roll out the dough until it is ½″ thick. Cut into 3″ circles. Arrange the circles on top of the meat mixture.

Place the casserole in a 400° F. oven for 15 minutes, or until the biscuits are golden brown. Serve hot. This dish will serve 6.

MEAT BALLS, MACARONI AND BROCCOLI

1 pound hamburger
¼ teaspoon oregano
½ teaspoon salt
4 twists of pepper mill
Pinch of thyme
¼ cup olive oil
1 pound elbow macaroni
1 pound broccoli
½ cup Parmesan cheese

Mix the hamburger meat with the oregano, salt, pepper and thyme. Form into meat balls about the size of golf balls. Sauté until golden brown in 2 tablespoons of the olive oil.

Boil the elbow macaroni until it is tender. Rinse in tepid water and set aside. Clean the broccoli under running water. Break apart the blossoms, and cut the stalks into ¼" slices. Boil for 8 minutes in salted water. Drain.

Put the remainder of the olive oil into a large baking dish. Swirl it around so that the bottom and sides are completely covered. Place the macaroni in the bottom of the baking dish. Add the meat balls, and sprinkle with half of the cheese. Put the broccoli over this and sprinkle the remainder of the cheese over the top.

Bake in a 350° F. oven for 20 minutes. Serve piping hot.

HAMBURGER, HERBS AND RICE

1 pound hamburger
2 tablespoons butter
2 tablespoons dehydrated onion
½ cup chopped celery
¼ cup chopped parsley
¼ teaspoon salt
¼ teaspoon pepper
1 #2 can chicken broth
2 cups precooked rice
⅛ teaspoon oregano
Pinch of thyme
Pinch of rosemary
Pinch of marjoram

Sauté the hamburger in the butter until well separated and slightly browned. Add the onion, celery and parsley, and cook for 5 minutes longer. Add the salt, pepper and chicken broth. Stir in the rice and herbs. Cook over very low heat,

covered, for 15 minutes, or until the rice is tender.
Serve garnished with a little additional parsley.

CABBAGE LEAVES STUFFED WITH HAMBURGER

1 medium-sized white cabbage
1 pound hamburger
2 tablespoons butter or margarine for browning meat
1 large onion, chopped very fine
1 cup precooked rice
2 tablespoons butter or margarine for browning cabbage rolls
1 tablespoon flour
1 10-ounce can beef consommé or 1½ cups of beef stock
1 cup sour cream
½ teaspoon salt
¼ teaspoon pepper
Juice of lemon
1 cup canned tomatoes or 1 cup chopped fresh tomatoes

Clean the cabbage by removing the tough outer leaves and rinsing under cold running water. Place the whole cabbage in a large kettle of slightly salted water. Bring to a boil, then reduce heat to a simmer until the outer leaves of the cabbage begin to pull away easily. Remove it from the water, let drain and cool. Discard the water it was boiled in.

Brown the hamburger in the butter or margarine. Add the onion to the meat and continue to cook until the onion is transparent. Remove from the heat and stir in the rice just as it comes from the package.

Carefully remove the cabbage leaves from the head, using a sharp knife to cut them off from the core or heart. In the center of each leaf place a tablespoonful of the meat and rice mixture. Fold the leaf around very tightly and fasten with a toothpick. Melt the butter or margarine and brown the cabbage rolls on all sides. When browned, place in a casserole in layers.

To the butter you have left after browning the cabbage rolls, add the flour. Brown the flour and then add the consommé or stock; cook until slightly thickened. Remove from the heat; stir in the sour cream, add the salt and pepper; add the lemon juice and tomatoes. Blend all well and pour over the cabbage rolls. Bake in a 350° F. oven for 45 minutes.

HAMBURGER PATTIES IN HORSE-RADISH AND SOUR CREAM SAUCE

1 pound ground beef
½ pound ground pork
1 large onion, grated or minced
1 clove garlic, chopped very fine
2 tablespoons dehydrated parsley flakes
2 shredded wheat biscuits, rolled very fine
1 egg
1 teaspoon salt
4 twists of pepper mill
¼ cup Parmesan-Romano cheese

Sauce

2 tablespoons butter
2 tablespoons horse-radish, thoroughly drained
2 beef bouillon cubes
1 cup warm water
1 tablespoon cornstarch
2 tablespoons cider vinegar
1 cup sour cream

Mix the beef, pork, onion, garlic, parsley flakes and shredded wheat biscuits together. Add the egg, salt, pepper and cheese. Again mix very thoroughly. Form into 3″ round patties and brown on both sides in the butter. Remove the patties from the skillet and set aside.

In the butter which remains in the skillet, brown the horse-radish for a few seconds. Dissolve the bouillon cubes in the warm water and then stir in the cornstarch. Add this bouillon-cornstarch mixture to the horse-radish. Cook for 5 minutes, or until slightly thickened, and then add the vinegar. Remove from the heat and slowly stir in the sour cream. Put the hamburger patties in the sour cream-bouillon mixture, and cook very slowly for an additional 15 minutes.

This is a good dish to prepare ahead of time, as it can be rewarmed without losing its flavor.

CURLY KALE AND HAMBURGER

2 pounds curly kale
6 medium-sized potatoes, peeled and quartered
4 tablespoons dry quick-cooking oatmeal
1 can bouillon or 1½ cups soup stock
½ teaspoon salt
¼ teaspoon pepper
1 pound hamburger
2 tablespoons butter or margarine

Place the kale, potatoes, oatmeal and bouillon in a sauce-pan and cook for approximately 15 minutes. Turn frequently so that all of the kale is thoroughly cooked. Mix the salt and pepper with the hamburger and form into little meat balls; brown in the butter or margarine.

Mash the kale-potato mixture thoroughly, place on a platter and garnish with the browned meat balls.

HAMBURGER-HAM AND ORANGES

1 pound hamburger
½ pound ground lean ham
½ teaspoon salt
¼ teaspoon pepper, or 4 twists of pepper mill
1 egg
1 cup soft bread crumbs
1 teaspoon prepared yellow mustard
½ cup milk
4 large oranges, peeled
½ cup catsup
¼ cup brown sugar

Mix the hamburger with the lean ham. Add the salt, pepper, egg, bread crumbs, mustard and milk. Mix all very well. Form into eight patties about ¾" thick and 3" in diameter.

Cut the round ends off each orange. Slice each orange in half so that you end up with 8 generous slices. Place the orange halves in a flat baking dish. Mix the catsup and brown sugar together and put a generous tablespoonful of the mixture on top of each orange. Place the meat patties on top of this.

Bake in a 350° F. oven for 1 hour. Ten minutes before serving, carefully turn over each patty and orange half so that the meat can absorb the juice in the bottom of the pan. Serve with the orange slice up. Garnish with parsley, if desired, for additional color.

ONIONS STUFFED WITH HAMBURGER

10 yellow onions approximately 2-3" in diameter
1 cup cooked regular rice
½ cup condensed milk
1 pound hamburger
1 egg, slightly beaten
1 teaspoon salt
¼ teaspoon pepper
1 tablespoon butter or margarine
2 tablespoons lemon juice

Cut off the stem ends of the onions to a depth of ½"; pare the root end just enough to remove the roots. Then peel each onion carefully, making sure that the outside first layer is completely intact. Put the onions in a kettle and cover with salted water; boil for 10 minutes, or until the outer three layers of each onion can be pricked easily with a toothpick.

Meanwhile, simmer the cooked rice in the condensed milk until it is thick and the consistency of rice pudding. Set aside to cool. When cool, mix with the meat and egg. Add the salt and pepper.

Drain the cooked onions, reserving ½ cup of the liquid. With a teaspoon, scoop out the centers of the onions and re-place with the meat mixture, packing as firmly as possible. Place the stuffed onions in a casserole dish, using the center portions to fill in between the stuffed onions. Heat the half cup of onion liquid in a saucepan, add the butter and the lemon juice. When hot, pour over the onions. Then place the casserole in a 350° F. oven for 30 minutes.

LITTLE MEAT LOAVES

¾ pound ground chuck
¾ pound ground ham
1 cup left-over or instant mashed potatoes
3 eggs, beaten to a golden yellow
½ cup condensed milk
1 cup dry bread crumbs or 1 cup crushed Wheaties
1 teaspoon salt
4 twists of pepper mill
1 cup water with 2 bouillon cubes dissolved in it

Mix the chuck, ham and mashed potatoes. Add the eggs and milk. Work in the bread crumbs or Wheaties. Add the salt and pepper.

Form into little loaves about 3″ long and 2″ wide. Place them in rows in a buttered coffee-cake tin. Add the water with the bouillon cubes in it. Cover the tin with aluminum foil.

Place in a 375° F. oven for 1 hour. Just before serving, remove the foil and brown the tops of the loaves under the broiler.

STEAK AND POTATOES

2 pounds ground beef (preferably chuck)
½ cup powdered dry milk
1 teaspoon salt
¼ teaspoon pepper
1 egg
¾ cup soft bread crumbs
4 or 5 potatoes, baked or boiled
1 large onion
1 large green pepper
1 teaspoon prepared mustard
1 tablespoon Worcestershire sauce
2 cups tomato juice
6 tablespoons grated Parmesan cheese

Thoroughly mix hamburger, milk, salt, pepper, egg and bread crumbs. Form into six large patties approximately 4″ in diameter. Brown the patties in a skillet and then pour away any excess grease. Place patties in a large rectangular baking dish. Cut the potatoes in half and arrange around the patties. On the top of each patty place several rings of onion and several rings of green pepper.

Mix the mustard and Worcestershire sauce with the tomato juice. Pour around the meat patties and the potatoes. Cover with aluminum foil and place in a 350° F. oven for 30 minutes. Then remove the foil and place a tablespoonful of cheese on top of each patty. Place under broiler for 5 minutes longer before serving.

Chapter IV
SHADES OF LORD SANDWICH!

BACK IN THE 17TH CENTURY, the fourth Earl of Sandwich was so involved in a hot card game that he did not want to stop to eat. So he demanded his roast beef between two slices of bread—and this, according to history, is the way the sandwich was born.

How the American hamburger evolved from that, we'll never know. However, here is a chapter loaded with variations on Lord Sandwich's idea. Hamburgers between buns have found an honored place in America. This chapter is going to be longer than the rest, for we have what is probably the largest collection of hamburger sandwich recipes in captivity!

A GOOD BASIC HAMBURGER

(to pan fry, foil wrap, or grill outdoors)

1 pound hamburger
1 teaspoon salt
4 twists of pepper mill
1 tablespoon grated onion
1 tablespoon minced parsley
½ teaspoon sugar
1 tablespoon salad oil, if hamburger is very lean
4 or 6 hamburger buns
4 to 6 tablespoons soft butter for buns

Mix together, in the order in which they are listed, all of the ingredients for the hamburger mixture. Form into 4 generous or 6 smaller patties, and brown in a skillet. Serve on the buns, after spreading them with the soft butter.

TEN VARIATIONS FOR THE BASIC HAMBURGER

Cashew Burgers
   Add ¾ cup chopped salted cashew nuts to the hamburger mixture.

Pecan Burgers
   Add ¾ cup chopped pecans to the hamburger mixture.

Walnut Burgers
   Add ¾ cup chopped walnuts to the hamburger mixture.

Zippy Burgers
   Add ½ cup chili sauce and ½ teaspoon cinnamon to the hamburger mixture.

Stretch-that-Meat Burgers
   Add ¾ cup mashed potatoes and 1 well-beaten egg to the hamburger mixture.

Cheesits
   Add 8 slices American process cheese, diced into ¼" cubes, to the hamburger mixture.

Italian Burgers
   Add 2 cloves minced garlic or 1 tablespoon garlic juice, and ½ cup Parmesan cheese, to hamburger mixture.

Hungarian Burgers
   Add 1 large grated carrot to the hamburger mixture, and sprinkle generously with paprika before browning.

Herb Burgers
   Add ¼ teaspoon thyme, ¼ teaspoon rosemary and ¼ teaspoon oregano to the hamburger mixture.

Indian Burgers
   Add ⅛ teaspoon curry powder and ⅛ teaspoon corriander to the hamburger mixture.

TWENTY-FIVE GARNISHES FOR THE
BASIC HAMBURGER

After you have made the hamburgers according to the basic recipe, and put them on the buttered buns, prepare any of the following garnishes and spread them on the hamburgers while the meat is still hot:

1. Soften 4 tablespoons of butter and mix with 4 tablespoons of Heinz 57 Sauce or A-1 Steak Sauce.

2. Chop 4 sweet-sour pickles very fine. Add 4 tablespoons mayonnaise and beat together.

3. Mix together very thoroughly: 2 tomatoes, chopped very fine; ½ teaspoon sweet basil and 3 tablespoons soft butter.

4. Mix to spreading consistency: 1 4-ounce package cream cheese, softened; ¼ teaspoon thyme; ¼ teaspoon oregano and ¼ teaspoon sage.

5. Mix together 4 tablespoons softened butter, 2 tablespoons grated onion and 1 tablespoon mayonnaise.

6. Mix to spreading consistency: 4 tablespoons softened butter and 4 tablespoons pine nuts, chopped very fine.

7. Mix to spreading consistency: 4 tablespoons softened butter and 4 ounces feta (Greek) cheese.

8. Mix together ½ cup catsup; ¼ cup green pepper, chopped very fine and 1 pimento, chopped fine.

9. Mix to spreading consistency: 1 4-ounce package cream cheese, 4 tablespoons Bleu cheese and 1 tablespoon mayonnaise.

10. Mash 1 medium-sized avocado, then add to it 1 tablespoon lemon juice and a dash of Tabasco.

11. Mash 1 medium-sized avocado, then add to it 2 tablespoons lime juice, ½ teaspoon grated lime rind and a dash of cayenne.

12. Whip to spreading consistency: ¾ cup Cheese Whiz, 1 tablespoon onion juice and 1 tablespoon lemon juice.

13. Whip together to spreading consistency: ¾ cup Cheese Whiz and ¾ cup French-fried onions, crumbled.

14. Mix together ¾ cup Cheese Whiz and 5 strips of bacon, fried crisp, broken into small pieces.

15. Beat together: 4 tablespoons softened butter, 1 tablespoon bead molasses and 1 tablespoon soy sauce.

16. Place ¼"-thick slices of onions on burgers when nearly done, and brush three or four times with the following, all mixed together: 1 tablespoon sugar, 1 teaspoon salt, 1 teaspoon mustard, ½ teaspoon celery seed, ½ cup olive oil and juice of 1 large lemon.

17. Put in a saucepan and let simmer for 15 minutes: 1 cup pitted tart pie cherries, juice of 1 lemon, 1 tablespoon sugar, ½ teaspoon cinnamon and ¼ teaspoon ground cloves.

18. Put in a jar: 1 cup evaporated milk, ½ cup sugar, 2 tablespoons dry mustard, 2 tablespoons cornstarch, 1 teaspoon Accent, ½ teaspoon salt and ¼ teaspoon pepper. Shake all the ingredients together in the jar; then put them in a saucepan and cook over low heat until thick.

19. Blend together: ½ cup horse-radish, grated; 1 cup thick sour cream; 1 teaspoon sugar; ½ teaspoon salt and ¼ teaspoon pepper.

20. Melt ¾ cup Cheese Whiz in a double boiler. Add 1 small can mushroom stems and pieces, drained and chopped fine. Stir mushrooms and cheese together well.

21. Whip together until of spreading consistency: 4 tablespoons soft butter, ½ teaspoon dill seed and ½ teaspoon celery seed.

22. Put in a fruit jar: 2 tablespoons fresh dill, chopped very fine; 1 cup water; 2 beef bouillon cubes; 1 tablespoon flour; ½ teaspoon cider vinegar and 1 egg yolk. Shake all the ingredients together in the jar, then put in a saucepan and cook over low heat until thickened. Add 1 tablespoon butter. Spread over burgers and serve immediately.

23. Whip together: ½ cup mayonnaise, 1 tablespoon lemon juice and 1 tablespoon capers, crushed.

24. Mix together: 1 cup mushrooms (fresh ones, preferably), chopped very fine; ¼ cup Heinz 57 Sauce and ¼ cup mayonnaise.

25. Mix well 1 small can deviled ham; ¾ cup Virginia peanuts, chopped fine; ¼ cup sweet pickle relish and ¾ cup mayonnaise.

SESAME BURGERS

1 pound hamburger
¼ cup onion, chopped fine
1 egg, slightly beaten
¼ teaspoon nutmeg
½ teaspoon salt
4 twists of pepper mill
½ cup sesame seeds
2 tablespoons butter or margarine
4 hamburger buns

Mix the hamburger with the onion, egg, nutmeg, salt and pepper. Dipping your hands into cold water, form the mixture into 4 generous patties. Press a teaspoon of sesame seeds into each side of the raw hamburgers.

Melt the butter or margarine in a skillet and brown the hamburgers on each side. Place the hamburgers in the buns and put into the oven at 350° F. for 5 minutes.

LAMBURGERS

Ground lamb is a wonderful source of protein. When you buy it, look for lamb which is a rich reddish color; the lighter it is in color, the more fatty it is—and, naturally, the less nutritional value it contains.

1 pound ground lamb
2 cloves garlic, minced very fine, or 1 tablespoon garlic juice
1 teaspoon salt
¼ teaspoon pepper
1 tablespoon dehydrated parsley
4 tablespoons grated Parmesan cheese
4 hamburger buns

Mix the lamb with the garlic, salt, pepper and parsley. Form into 4 generous patties and place in a skillet over low heat. Fry the patties until they are golden brown. Place each patty on the bottom half of a hamburger bun; top the lamb with a tablespoonful of the cheese. Put under the broiler for 5 minutes, or until the cheese starts to bubble. Put the tops of the buns in place and serve piping hot.

Lamb is one meat which should be served hot, especially if it is ground; otherwise it loses a lot of its wonderful flavor.

GLAZED BURGERS

1 pound hamburger
1 tablespoon minced onion
1 tablespoon minced parsley
1 can dehydrated mushroom soup
1 egg, beaten until lemon yellow
2 tablespoons butter or margarine

Glaze

1 cup apple butter
1 tablespoon grated orange rind

Mix the hamburger with the onion, parsley, mushroom soup and egg. Form into 8 patties. Melt the butter or margarine in a skillet and brown the patties well on each side.

To make the glaze, put the apple butter and orange rind in the skillet. Simmer for 15 minutes, turning each patty several times so it will be well covered with the glaze.

Serve on hot hamburger buns.

BURGERS IN FOIL

1 pound hamburger
½ teaspoon salt
4 twists of pepper mill
1 tablespoon Worcestershire sauce
1 tablespoon catsup
¼ pound butter or margarine
⅛ teaspoon thyme
10-15 dill seeds
1 teaspoon soy sauce
8 hamburger buns

Mix the hamburger, salt, pepper, Worcestershire sauce and catsup very well. Form into 8 patties. Broil on each side enough to brown. Melt the butter or margarine, add the thyme, dill seeds and soy sauce. Brush the bottoms and tops of the hamburger buns generously with the flavored butter. Place a meat patty in each bun. Wrap tightly in squares of aluminum foil. Place in a 350° F. oven for 30 minutes. If onions on hamburgers are a favorite, put a large onion slice on each burger before placing in the bun.

These burgers are equally good served on an outdoor grill. All ingredients can be prepared ahead of time, and then heated around the edge of the grill while corn or potatoes are roasting.

UPSIDE-DOWN SANDWICHES

½ cup bread crumbs
1 tablespoon dehydrated onion
½ cup milk
1 pound ground beef
1 egg, beaten to a lemon yellow
2 tablespoons capers, chopped very fine
4 tablespoons butter or margarine
6 slices white bread

Place the bread crumbs and onion in the milk and let the crumbs swell and absorb all of the milk. Place the meat in a bowl and mix with the bread crumbs and milk. Add the egg and the chopped capers. Mix all very well.

Melt the butter in a skillet and place each slice of bread in it until it is golden brown on one side. Spread a generous portion of the meat mixture on the unbrowned side of the bread. Place the bread, meat side down, in the skillet and cook until the meat is browned. Serve piping hot.

BLEU CHEESE BURGERS

1 pound ground chuck
1 medium onion, chopped very fine
1 tablespoon Worcestershire sauce
1 teaspoon sugar
½ teaspoon Accent
1 teaspoon prepared mustard
¼ cup tomato sauce or ¼ cup chili sauce
6 hamburger buns
6 tablespoons soft butter or margarine
½ cup Bleu cheese mixed in ½ cup mayonnaise

Mix the ground meat, onion, Worcestershire sauce, sugar, Accent, mustard and tomato sauce very thoroughly. Set aside to allow the flavors to blend. This meat mixture can be made several hours before serving, or even the day before.

Butter the hamburger bun halves and place under the broiler until they are toasted a golden brown.

Place 1 heaping tablespoonful of the cheese and mayonnaise mixture in the center of each bun half. Form the meat into ½" thick patties the size of the buns; place the meat patty over the Bleu cheese mixture. Press the edges of each patty so that the cheese mixture is completely sealed inside. Put under the broiler for 15 minutes, or until the meat is completely browned. Serve piping hot.

This will yield 12 half buns, or 2 portions per person.

TEEN-AGERS' SPECIAL SANDWICHES

1 tablespoon dehydrated onion
2 tablespoons water
¼ teaspoon nutmeg
½ teaspoon salt
¼ teaspoon pepper
¼ teaspoon cardamon
1 pound ground round steak or very lean ground chuck
10 slices white bread
4 tablespoons butter or margarine
2 eggs
¼ cup milk

Place the dehydrated onion in the water for 10 minutes. Then mix it very thoroughly with the nutmeg, salt, pepper, cardamon and meat. Spread the meat mixture on one side of each of 5 slices of bread. Press the remaining 5 slices of bread tightly over the meat mixture.

Melt the butter or margarine in a large skillet. Meanwhile, beat the egg in the milk. Dip the sandwiches in the beaten egg mixture and then put the sandwiches in the skillet and fry slowly until each side is browned. Serve with pickle slices.

TEENS' RIB LINERS

1 pound hamburger
1 tablespoon butter or margarine
1 teaspoon salt
½ teaspoon pepper
¼ cup chopped onion
2 cloves of garlic, minced
1 #2 can red kidney beans, drained and chopped very fine
½ teaspoon oregano
½ teaspoon chili powder
8 hamburger buns

Brown the hamburger in the butter or margarine, add the salt, pepper, onion and garlic. Stir in the kidney beans. Add the oregano and the chili powder and simmer for 10 minutes longer. Put a generous spoonful of this mixture on each bun and serve with potato chips and pickles.

This is an ideal teen-age treat because it can be kept warm in the top of a double boiler and served whenever needed. This is also a good item to freeze. You can double or even triple the recipe and freeze the extra portions against that day when you are suddenly invaded by a tribe of hungry youngsters.

SLOPPY JOE

There are many versions of "Sloppy Joe" sandwiches, but the following three recipes are our favorites. Once you get the knack of making this teen-agers' delight, you will think of many variations. Sloppy Joes take only a short time to prepare, and being a mother who knows what to serve while the Beatles are bleating will mark you as "cool" forever.

2 pounds hamburger
1 large onion, diced
½ cup catsup
1 cup water
1 7-ounce can mushroom stems and pieces, drained
½ teaspoon salt
¼ teaspoon pepper
1 10½-ounce can minestrone soup
8 hamburger buns

Brown the hamburger and break it apart until it is quite fine. Add the onion and continue to cook until the onion is transparent and glazed. Add the catsup, water, mushrooms, salt, pepper and soup. Cook over low heat for 25 minutes. Stir from time to time to prevent scorching.

Place heaping spoonfuls in the middle of each hamburger bun and serve.

SLOPPIER JOES

2 pounds hamburger
1 large onion, diced
1 #2 can tomatoes
8 hamburger buns
6 slices bacon, diced and fried crisp
½ cup grated American cheese

Brown the hamburger until it is all broken apart; add the diced onion and cook until it is glazed. Add the tomatoes and simmer for 25 minutes without a cover. Stir from time to time to prevent scorching.

Remove from heat and place a heaping spoonful of the meat mixture on the bottom of each hamburger bun. (Set aside the tops temporarily.) Sprinkle with the crisp bacon, then top with the grated cheese. Place under the broiler until the cheese is melted. Cover with bun tops, and serve.

SLOPPIEST JOES

2 pounds hamburger
Dash of nutmeg
½ teaspoon salt
¼ teaspoon pepper
1 cup fresh mushrooms, cut into quarters
1 can cream of mushroom soup
1 package frozen French-fried onion rings
8 hamburger buns

Brown the hamburger until it is all broken apart. Add the nutmeg, salt and pepper. Add the mushrooms and cook for 8 minutes longer. Toss frequently during this time so that the mushrooms are warmed through. Add the soup and continue to cook for 10 minutes longer.

Place the onion rings in a 350° F. oven for 10 minutes, or until warmed through. Then place 3 or 4 onion rings on each bun bottom; top this with a heaping spoonful of the hamburger mixture. Place an additional 3 or 4 rings on top of the hamburger mixture. Put under the broiler for 5 minutes, then cover with tops of buns and serve.

SCHNITZEL BURGERS

6 tablespoons butter
2 tablespoons instant flour
1 tablespoon parsley flakes
½ teaspoon salt
4 twists of pepper mill
Pinch of mace
3 tablespoons water
1 pound ground veal
6 eggs

Melt half the butter in a saucepan over low heat. Stir in flour, parsley flakes, salt, pepper and mace. When the flour begins to brown, add the water. Cook until thickened, and then set aside to cool.

When the above mixture is cool, add the ground veal and mix very thoroughly. Form into 6 patties about 3″ in diameter. Melt the rest of the butter in a skillet and brown the patties on one side. Turn them carefully and make an indentation in each one large enough to hold an egg. Carefully break the eggs and place one in each of the indentations you have made. Cover pan tightly and cook for 20 minutes.

Serve on hot hamburger buns.

SPANISH SLOPPY JOES

1 tablespoon butter or margarine
1 pound ground chuck
1 tablespoon vinegar
1 tablespoon lemon juice
1 tablespoon Worcestershire sauce
1 cup celery, chopped very fine
1 cup onion, chopped fine
1 cup tomato catsup
1 can condensed tomato soup
1 tablespoon sugar
1 teaspoon garlic juice
1 teaspoon salt
½ cup water
4 hamburger buns

Place the butter or margarine in a deep skillet with a tight-fitting cover. Add the meat and sauté until the reddish color disappears. Stir in the vinegar and the lemon juice. Add the Worcestershire sauce, celery, onion and catsup. Bring to a simmer, and add the tomato soup. Add the sugar, garlic juice, salt and water. Cover and simmer for 1 hour.

At the end of this time the meat mixture should be thick enough to spoon onto the buns. If it is not, continue to simmer for a few minutes longer without the cover.

SPANISH HAMBURGERS

¾ pound ground beef
½ pound ground ham
½ teaspoon monosodium glutamate
2 tablespoons butter
3 tablespoons flour
3 tablespoons grated onion
1 tablespoon dehydrated parsley
1 sweet pepper (red or yellow)
1 small bay leaf, broken into tiny pieces
¼ teaspoon grated nutmeg
¼ teaspoon ground cloves
1 10½-ounce consommé, or 1¼ cups rich stock
1 cup canned tomatoes
½ cup light sherry wine

Mix the beef and the ham with the monosodium glutamate; set aside while you make the sauce, as follows:

Melt the butter in a skillet and stir in the flour. Let the mixture get slightly browned. Add the onion, parsley, sweet pepper, bay leaf, nutmeg, cloves and consommé or stock. Cook for 5 minutes or until the sauce is slightly thickened. Add the beef-ham mixture and continue to cook over low heat for 1 hour. Stir from time to time during this period to break up the ham and beef.

Then stir in the tomatoes and wine. Simmer for 5 minutes longer. Serve like Sloppy Joes on hamburger buns, or pour over boiled rice, spaghetti or macaroni.

HAMBURGERS MADE WITH WINE

1 pound ground chuck
1 pound lean ground pork
2 eggs, beaten to a lemon yellow
3 tablespoons melted butter (reserve one tablespoonful for browning patties)
½ teaspoon salt
¼ teaspoon pepper
Juice of 1 lemon
1 tablespoon grated lemon rind
3 tablespoons dehydrated onion
3 tablespoons dehydrated parsley
1 cup soft bread crumbs
½ cup light sherry wine
8 hamburger buns

Thoroughly mix the ground chuck and the ground pork; add the eggs, 2 tablespoons of melted butter, salt and pepper. Mix again, and then add the lemon juice and rind. Add the onion, parsley and bread crumbs. Mix all very thoroughly. Form into 8 patties about 1″ thick.

In the remaining tablespoonful of butter, brown the patties on both sides. Lower the heat to simmer and then add the wine. Cook over very low heat for 30 minutes. Turn the patties frequently during the cooking time so that the wine flavor penetrates the entire patty. Serve on warmed hamburger buns.

SORBONNE SANDWICHES

¾ pound ground round steak
2 egg yolks, beaten until lemon yellow
1 small onion, chopped very fine
1 medium boiled potato, chopped very fine
3 pickled beets, chopped rather coarsely
10 capers, chopped fine
½ teaspoon salt
4 tablespoons soft butter for spreading
6-8 slices bread
4 tablespoons butter or margarine for frying

Mix the meat, egg yolks, onion, potato, pickled beets, capers and salt very thoroughly. Set aside for 20 minutes to let the flavors blend.

Butter 6 to 8 slices of bread (depending on how thick your family likes the meat spread). Heat some of the butter in a skillet, and fry one side of the bread until golden brown. Spread the unbrowned side with the meat mixture and fry until brown. Serve piping hot.

If you want these sandwiches to be especially festive use circles cut out of the center of very fresh bread slices. Save the crusts for crumbs or croutons.

QUICK-AND-EASY PIZZA SANDWICHES

1 pound ground chuck
½ teaspoon salt
½ cup chili sauce
Pinch of oregano
4 English muffins
1 medium onion, sliced very thin
8 slices sharp process American cheese

Mix the ground chuck, salt, chili sauce and oregano together lightly. Split the English muffins in half. On each half, spread the meat mixture about ½" thick. Place several slices of onion on top of meat. Cut the pieces of cheese in half and crisscross them on top of the meat and onion mixture.

Place in a 400° F. oven for 8 to 10 minutes, or until the cheese is melted and bubbling. Serve immediately.

Chapter V

YOU'RE IN THE DOUGH

FOR CENTURIES, in those countries where fresh meat was scarce or there wasn't enough refrigeration to keep a supply on hand, homemakers have been dreaming up ways to make a little ground meat go a long way.

Since then we have learned that a protein-rich diet is good for us. However, many of these "stretch the meat" recipes are too delicious to pass up. Besides, in this day of high prices, high taxes, high everything, one is sometimes forced to stretch the meat.

Try these recipes at times when there is too much month left at the end of the money.

HAMBURGER PASTIES

The origin of pasties is variously attributed to the Cornish, Welsh, French, Irish, Swedes. In fact, so many people got into the act of taking credit for them, it's hard to tell exactly where they did start. But whatever their origin, the important thing is that pasties are a wonderful food, both filling and nourishing.

¾ pound hamburger
3 medium-sized cooked potatoes, diced in ½" cubes
1 onion, chopped finely, or ¼ cup dehydrated onion flakes
2 coarsely chopped cooked carrots
1 teaspoon salt
1 teaspoon pepper

Dough

1¾ cups sifted all-purpose flour
1 teaspoon baking powder
¼ teaspoon salt
6 tablespoons shortening
6 tablespoons cold water

Lightly sauté the ground meat until it is browned and about the size of hickory nuts. Add the diced potatoes, onion and carrots. (If you have bits of left-over peas, lima beans or other vegetables in the refrigerator, add them too. Anything goes in a pastie.) Add the salt and pepper and set aside to cool slightly.

71

Mix the flour, baking powder and salt together. Cut in the shortening with two knives or a pastry blender until it is the consistency of pie dough. Add the cold water, 1 tablespoonful at a time, and knead into a dough.

Place the dough on a floured board and roll out until it is about ¼" thick. Cut into squares or circles about 3" in diameter. On half of each square or circle, place 1 heaping tablespoonful of the meat mixture. Wet one edge of the square or circle, and bring the other half down over the meat mixture. Press the edges together. You wet the edge of the dough to insure its staying together.

Place the filled circles or squares on a greased and floured cookie sheet and bake in a 325° F. oven for 1 hour, or until the tops are golden brown.

Variations (if you have not already included left-over vegetables)

Add ¾ cup canned peas.
Add ¾ cup butter beans.
Add ¾ cup lima beans.
Add 1 coarsely chopped tomato.
Add ¾ cup cooked navy beans.
Add ¾ cup niblet-style corn.

BRITISH TOADS

½ pound ground beef
½ pound ground pork
¼ teaspoon pepper
½ teaspoon salt
¼ teaspoon nutmeg
1 tablespoon cooking oil
¾ cup flour
1 egg
½ cup milk
¼ teaspoon salt

Mix the beef, pork, pepper, salt and nutmeg together. Form into small patties about 1½" in diameter. Place the oil in a long coffee-cake tin and heat. Put the patties into the tin and brown on both sides. Remove from heat.

Make a batter of the flour, egg, milk and salt. Set aside for about 30 minutes, or until the browned patties are thoroughly cool. Pour the batter over the meat patties, place in a 350° F. oven, and bake for about 30 minutes, or until outer edges of the batter are well browned.

BURGER SAUSAGE ROLLS

½ pound ground chuck
½ pound ground pork
½ teaspoon salt
¼ teaspoon pepper
¼ teaspoon ground cloves
¼ teaspoon garlic powder
1 teaspoon monosodium glutamate
1 egg, separated

Pastry

½ cup vegetable shortening
1 cup all-purpose flour
½ teaspoon salt
3 brimming tablespoons water

Mix the chuck, pork, salt, pepper, cloves, garlic powder and monosodium glutamate. Add only the egg yolk to the meat; reserve the white to brush top of pastry. Mix very well and set aside.

Cut the shortening into the flour with two knives or a pastry blender. Add the salt and continue to cut until the mixture is the consistency of bread crumbs. Add the water and knead the mixture into a dough. Place on a floured board or pastry cloth and roll into an oval until the dough is about ¼" thick. Cut into eight pieces about 3" x 3".

Form the meat mixture into eight finger-shaped sausages and sprinkle them lightly with flour on all sides. Place the sausages in the center of each square of pastry. Fold over the two sides, but leave the ends open. Pinch the pastry tightly so that the bottoms are well sealed. Make three gashes on the top of each roll with a sharp knife. Brush the top of each roll with the egg white, slightly beaten.

Place the rolls on a cookie sheet, leaving about 1" space between them. Place in a 400° F. oven for 20 minutes. As soon as the edges get brown, reduce the heat to 300° F. and bake for 20 minutes longer. Serve piping hot.

DUTCH SAUSEASONS

The story behind sauseasons (pronounced saw-seasons) is that the Dutch housewives used to make these in the month of November, after the fall butchering. They would bake them and then store them in some safe place outdoors so they could freeze solid. The fishermen would then thaw them as needed, and take them along on the fishing boats to use as a quick snack when the fish were running and the men didn't have time to stop to cook meals.

Filling

1 pound ground lean pork (or half pork and half beef)
1 teaspoon salt
½ teaspoon monosodium glutamate
½ teaspoon ground pepper

Dough

4 cups sifted enriched flour
1 cup lukewarm milk
1½ teaspoons salt
4 tablespoons melted butter or margarine
1 package powdered dry yeast dissolved in ½ cup lukewarm water

Mix the meat, salt, monosodium glutamate and pepper very thoroughly. Set aside in refrigerator while you make the dough.

Place the flour in a large mixing bowl; make a dent in the center and add the milk, salt and melted butter; add the yeast and then stir with a slotted spoon until almost all of the liquid is absorbed. Knead with your hands until the whole ball of dough is shiny and smooth. Form into a large ball and place in a greased mixing bowl to rise. Cover with a cloth and place in the warmest spot in your kitchen. The dough should rise to double its bulk in about 2 hours.

When it has risen, place on a floured board or pastry cloth and knead again for about two minutes. Cut off pieces about the size of an egg, flatten out and place about two tablespoonfuls of the meat mixture, shaped like a little sausage, in the middle. Fold the dough over and around and shape it to look like a miniature loaf of bread about 3″ long. Be sure the dough is sealed all around the meat.

Place the loaves in two rows in a 7″ x 11″ greased coffee-cake tin. When you have used all of the dough, place the pan in a warm place to rise again. When almost doubled in size, place in a 350° F. preheated oven and bake for 1 hour or until the tops are golden brown. During the baking process the little loaves will swell up and fill the whole pan, much in the manner of Parker House rolls. The bottom crust becomes a crisp golden brown, too, as a result of the fat content in the pork.

Sauseasons are equally delicious hot or cold; they make excellent party fare because they can be prepared ahead of time.

BACON BURGER SURPRISE

Batter

2 eggs
¾ cup milk
¾ cup all-purpose flour
1 tablespoon dry yeast, dissolved in ¼ cup lukewarm water
¼ teaspoon salt
1 tablespoon brandy (optional)

Filling

1 pound hamburger
1 egg
¼ cup soft bread crumbs
1 teaspoon minced onion
⅛ teaspoon thyme
⅛ teaspoon nutmeg
½ teaspoon salt
¼ teaspoon pepper
8 to 10 slices bacon
Enough cooking oil for French frying

Beat the eggs until golden yellow. Alternately add the milk and flour and continue beating. Add the dissolved yeast, salt and brandy. Continue to beat for 3 minutes longer. Set aside.

Thoroughly mix the hamburger and the remaining ingredients, with the exception of the bacon and the cooking oil. Place mixture in the refrigerator for 15 minutes, then take out and form into finger-shaped sausages. Wrap each sausage in a slice of bacon, starting at the top and winding barberpole fashion. Place on a piece of waxed paper and return to the refrigerator for 30 minutes.

Dip each chilled sausage wrapped in bacon in the batter and then drop into hot cooking fat until golden brown. Serve piping hot.

HAMBURGER-MACARONI PIE

Pastry

½ cup vegetable shortening
1 cup instant flour
1 teaspoon salt
3 brimming tablespoons water

Filling

1 12-ounce package elbow macaroni
1 pound hamburger
1 small can tomato paste
4 tablespoons Parmesan-Romano cheese
½ teaspoon salt
¼ teaspoon pepper
2 eggs

Cut the shortening into the flour and salt mixture until it is the consistency of bread crumbs. Add the water and continue to cut and blend until you have a stiff dough. Divide into two portions and roll out until you have circles large enough to fill the bottom and top of your favorite pie dish.

Cook the elbow macaroni until tender. Rinse in cold water, drain and set aside. Brown the hamburger until it has separated into lumps about the size of large peas, add the tomato paste, cook for a few seconds longer, then remove from heat. Add the cheese, and stir in the macaroni. Add the salt and pepper and stir again.

Line your pie tin with the pastry. Be sure the outer edges are firmly in place. Pour into the pastry-lined tin the macaroni and meat mixture. Beat the two eggs until they are golden yellow. Pour the eggs over the macaroni-meat mixture. Cover with the remaining pastry, making sure that the edges are well sealed. Pierce with a sharp knife in several places. Place in a preheated 350° F. oven and bake for 35 minutes, or until crust is golden brown. Serve piping hot.

Variations:

Substitute grated American cheese for the Parmesan-Romano.
Substitute grated Swiss cheese for the Parmesan-Romano.
Substitute feta (Greek) cheese for the Parmesan-Romano.
Use half a package of macaroni and add 1 #2 can of niblet-style corn.
Substitute broad noodles for the macaroni.
Substitute rice for the macaroni.
Substitute thin spaghetti for the macaroni

PELMENY, OR MEAT DUMPLINGS

Filling

½ pound lean ground beef
½ pound lean ground pork
½ pound ground veal
1 tablespoon minced onion
½ teaspoon salt
¼ teaspoon pepper
¼ teaspoon nutmeg
⅛ teaspoon marjoram

Dumpling mix

1 cup flour
½ teaspoon salt
½ teaspoon baking powder
1 egg
3 brimming tablespoons cold water

Mix the beef, pork and veal very thoroughly. If you are fortunate enough to have an accommodating butcher, ask him to double grind all of the meat. Add the onion, salt, pepper, nutmeg and marjoram. Mix until the onion and seasonings are thoroughly blended throughout the meat. Set aside while you make the dumplings.

Place the flour in a mixing bowl, stir in the salt and baking powder. Break the egg into the center, add the water and mix thoroughly. Knead into a stiff dough. Now roll the dough out on a floured board until it is about as thin as pie crust. Using a 2″ round cookie cutter, cut circles. Place a teaspoonful of the meat mixture in the center of each circle. Fold up the sides and press the edges together, carefully sealing in all of the meat mixture. You may reroll the portions of the dough left around the circles without fear of its getting tough.

Drop the dumplings into a kettleful of rapidly boiling salted water. When the dumpling rises to the top, remove from the water with a slotted spoon.

Place the cooked dumplings on a heated platter. These dumplings are delicious just as they are; however, if you want to be festive, pour about ¼ cup melted butter or ½ cup sour cream over them. Garnish with parsley if you want to add color.

HAMBURGER PIE CRUST

1 pound ground chuck
½ pound ground pork
1 cup whole wheat flakes, rolled fine
2 eggs, beaten until lemon yellow
1 6-ounce can condensed milk
1 tablespoon grated onion
½ teaspoon garlic juice
1 teaspoon salt
½ teaspoon monosodium glutamate
¼ teaspoon pepper
¼ teaspoon grated nutmeg
1 teaspoon granulated sugar
1 #2 can niblet-style corn, drained
2 canned pimento, cut into ¼" pieces
1 8-ounce can tomato sauce

Mix the chuck and pork together; add the whole wheat flakes, eggs and milk alternately. Stir well; add the onion, garlic juice, salt, monosodium glutamate, pepper, nutmeg and sugar. Mix all very thoroughly. Press the meat mixture over the bottom and sides of a greased pie tin. Mix the corn, pimento and tomato sauce together and pour into the meat-lined tin. Bake in a 350° F. oven, uncovered, for 1 hour. Garnish with chopped parsley if you desire additional color.

Ten other fillings for Hamburger Pie Crust:

1. Substitute 1 #2 can of drained pork and beans for corn and omit the tomato sauce.
2. Substitute 1 8-ounce package of broad egg noodles, boiled until tender, for the corn.
3. Substitute 1 cup of fresh mushrooms and 1 10½-ounce can of cream of mushroom soup for the corn, pimento and tomato sauce.
4. Substitute 1 package frozen lima beans and ½ cup cubed onion for the corn.
5. Substitute 2 cups cooked rice plus 1 10½-ounce can cream of mushroom soup for corn, pimento and tomato sauce.
6. Substitute 1 package frozen green peas and 1 10½-ounce can cream of celery soup for corn, pimento and tomato sauce.
7. Substitute 1 package frozen succotash for the corn.

8. Substitute 1 #2 can beef chow mein for the corn, pimento and tomato sauce. Top with chow mein fried noodles if you like.
9. Substitute 1 #2 can spaghetti in meat sauce for corn, pimento and tomato sauce.
10. Substitute 2 cups boiled macaroni for the corn and sprinkle ¼ cup Parmesan cheese over the top.

TINY HAMBURGERS

1 pound ground round steak
2 tablespoons grated onion
2 egg yolks, beaten until lemon yellow
½ teaspoon salt
3 tablespoons olive oil
⅛ teaspoon salt
2 cups biscuit mix
¾ cup milk
1 tablespoon water
2 egg whites
¼ cup minced parsley

Mix the ground meat, onion, egg yolks and ½ teaspoon salt together. Using a tablespoon, form little patties about the size of silver dollars. Heat the olive oil and fry the patties until they are well browned. Set aside while you make the biscuits.

Mix the ⅛ teaspoon salt into the biscuit mix, add the milk. Stir until the dough forms into a large ball. Place on a lightly floured board and pat flat until it is about ½" thick. With a small cookie cutter about the size of the meat patties, cut enough biscuits to equal the number of patties. Add the water to the egg whites and beat with a fork. Brush the top of each biscuit with the egg white mixture. Place on a lightly greased cookie tin and bake at 375° F. for 15 minutes, or until they are golden brown.

Sprinkle the minced parsley on top of the meat patties. Cut the biscuits in half and put the meat patties inside. Place in a 350° F. oven for 10 minutes. You can prepare these hamburgers ahead of time and keep them refrigerated until you need them. This is excellent fare for a buffet-style meal.

HAMBURGER MINCEMEAT

2 pounds ground chuck
½ pound suet ground with the chuck
5 tart baking apples, peeled, cored and chopped very fine
1½ cups dark brown sugar
2 cups apple butter
1 tablespoon cider vinegar
¾ cup raisins, chopped fine
¾ cup currants
2 tablespoons bead molasses
1½ teaspoons cinnamon
¼ teaspoon nutmeg
¼ teaspoon cloves
¼ teaspoon allspice
Pinch of mace
1 teaspoon lemon extract
Juice and grated rind of 1 lemon
1 cup water

Cook the meat in a deep saucepan until it loses all of its reddish color and is well done and separated into small pieces. Stir in all of the other ingredients in the order which they are given. Simmer for 1 hour. This mincemeat can be kept for several days in the refrigerator. If you want to use it for holiday cooking, you can preserve it by placing it in a sterilized canning jar with a rubber top closure. This mincemeat can be used in any recipe calling for mincemeat—pie, cookies, scones, cup cakes, etc.

HAMBURGER STUFFED LOAF

1 pound ground chuck
½ pound ground ham
1 cup apple butter
10 slices American cheese, cut into ¼" cubes
1 small onion, chopped very fine
2 eggs, beaten lemon yellow
1 teaspoon salt
¼ teaspoon pepper
1 loaf white bread, unsliced, Vienna style
3 tablespoons butter

Mix the ground meat with the apple butter, cheese, onion, eggs, salt and pepper. Cut the loaf of bread through the middle, crosswise. Scoop out the soft bread from each half. Shred up the soft bread and add to the meat mixture. Brush the bottom crust of the loaf with the butter and place on a piece of foil large enough to wrap the entire loaf.

Place the meat mixture in the bottom half of the loaf, heaping up a mound to fit the hollow in the top half. Put top half in place and wrap the loaf securely in the foil. Pierce foil in a few places so it can emit the steam.

Place on a baking tin in a 350° F. oven for 1 hour. Fifteen minutes before removing from the oven, open the foil and allow the bread to crisp and brown. Cut loaf in generous slices.

Variations:

Substitute feta (Greek) cheese for American cheese.
Substitute 1½ cups mincemeat for apple butter.
Add 1 cup of chopped raisins.
Add 1 cup of chopped walnuts or pecans.
Substitute 1 cup tart currant jelly for the apple butter.
Substitute Swiss cheese for the American cheese.

SWEDISH MEAT BALLS IN CRUSTS

½ pound ground beef
½ pound ground ham
1 cup instant flour
½ teaspoon salt
1 tablespoon vegetable shortening
⅛ cup milk
½ package dry yeast
2 eggs, beaten

Mix the ham and beef very thoroughly. Form into 20 little meat balls, using the large end of a melon-ball maker. Place the meat balls in a skillet over low heat and let them brown. Shake the pan back and forth so that they will remain round. When all are browned, set aside.

Put the flour in a mixing bowl, mix in the salt and cut in the shortening. Warm the milk just slightly, and stir in the yeast. Pour ⅔ of the beaten egg into the center of the flour, mix slightly and then add the yeast and milk mixture. Knead into a dough. Form dough into 20 little balls and place in a greased cookie tin. Put into a warm place for about 45 minutes, or until the balls have doubled in size. Brush them with the remaining ⅓ of the beaten egg. Place dough balls in a pre-heated 375° F. oven for 10 minutes. Remove and let cool until you are able to handle them.

With a very sharp knife, cut the bread balls in half. With the tip of a teaspoon remove the soft dough, leaving only the crusty part. In the center place a meat ball, cover with the other half of the bread ball and return the balls to the cookie tin. Place them in a 375° F. oven again, until the outsides are golden brown.

Chapter VI

DEPARTMENT OF
INTERIOR SURPRISES

MOST MEAT PIES call for left-over meat, but the pies in this chapter are all made with fresh hamburger. However, if you happen to have the lean remnants of a beef roast, do not hesitate to add them.

Meat pies could be considered one-dish meals, yet they are too distinctive to be allowed to lose their identity that way.

The pies available in frozen-food packages are usually either chicken, beef or turkey. So a hamburger meat pie can be a pleasant, tasty surprise.

TUCSON MEAT PIE

1½ pounds hamburger
3 tablespoons olive oil
1 large onion, chopped fine
1 large pepper, chopped fine
1 8-ounce can tomato sauce
¼ cup water
1 teaspoon salt
¼ teaspoon pepper
½ teaspoon chili powder
⅛ teaspoon sweet basil
1 teaspoon Accent

Topping

½ cup milk
1 cup Bisquick
2 tablespoons melted butter or margarine

Slowly sauté the hamburger in the olive oil till it is a light, even brown. Add the onion and the green pepper. Pour in the tomato sauce, rinse the can with the water and add this water to the mixture. Add the salt, pepper, chili powder, sweet basil and Accent, and simmer for 15 minutes. Put the entire mixture in a casserole big enough to leave room for the biscuits to rise.

Mix the milk with the Bisquick. On a floured board, knead until smooth and shiny. Roll out the dough until it is about

½" thick. Cut circles, squares or diamond shapes about 2" in diameter. Lay them in a design over the top of the meat mixture. Brush each circle with the melted butter. Place in a 325° F. oven for 30 minutes, or until the biscuits have turned golden brown.

Variations:

Add 1 #2 can niblet-style corn to the hamburger mixture.
Add 1 #2 can black-eyed peas to the hamburger mixture.
Add 1 #2 can butter beans to the hamburger mixture.
Add 1 package frozen lima beans to the hamburger mixture.
Add 1 package frozen carrots and peas to the hamburger mixture.
Add 2 potatoes, cubed in ½" pieces to the hamburger mixture (increase cooking time 10 minutes).
Add 1 #2 can boiled tiny potatoes to the hamburger mixture.

FLANK STEAK STUFFED WITH HAMBURGER

There was a time when flank steak was considered a comparatively cheap cut of meat, but those days are gone. However, the delicious taste of this particular cut is well worth the price. I used to stuff flank steaks with bread until I discovered that when I stuffed them with hamburger they were twice as good.

¾ pound hamburger
1 tablespoon dehydrated parsley
1 tablespoon dehydrated onion
1 cup moist bread crumbs
2 flank steaks, about 1 pound each
1 package dry onion soup mix

Mix the hamburger, parsley, onion, and bread crumbs together very well. Spread the flank steaks out on a cutting board and roll them flatter with your rolling pin.

Put half the hamburger mixture on each steak. Roll up the steaks tightly around the hamburger and fasten with metal skewers. Set out two squares of aluminum foil, each large enough to wrap one steak. Place half of the onion soup mixture and one steak, on each square. Wrap the steaks tightly in the foil and place in a shallow baking pan.

Roast at 375° F. for 1 hour. Slice in generous portions and serve. These steaks are delicious cold, too, and they make excellent sandwiches.

84

DE LUXE HAMBURGER PIE

2 pounds hamburger
2 tablespoons butter or margarine
1 cup chopped onion
1 can condensed cream of mushroom soup
½ pound cream cheese, at room temperature
½ cup heavy cream
½ teaspoon salt
¼ teaspoon pepper
1 teaspoon Accent
2 tablespoons tomato paste
24 pitted ripe olives, cut into halves
1 package oven-ready biscuits

Brown the hamburger in the butter or margarine, add the onion and continue to cook until the onion begins to get transparent. Meanwhile, with a large blending fork blend the soup, cream cheese and heavy cream. Stir in the salt, pepper, Accent and tomato paste. Add the olives to the meat mixture and then stir the meat mixture into the soup-cream cheese mixture.

Turn all into a greased casserole. Place the biscuits over the top, and put in a preheated 350° F. oven for 30 minutes, or until the biscuits are golden brown.

Variations:

Substitute 1 can cream of celery soup for the mushroom soup.
Substitute 1 can cream of chicken soup for the mushroom soup.
Substitute 1 can chicken gumbo soup for the mushroom soup.
Substitute 1 cup large-curd creamed cottage cheese for the cream cheese.
Substitute 1 cup Swiss cheese for the cream cheese.
Add 1 can niblet-style corn.
Add 1 package frozen lima beans.
Add 1 package frozen carrots and peas.

HAMBURGER PIZZA

1 pound hamburger
½ cup coarsely chopped onion
½ cup coarsely chopped ripe olives
½ cup mushroom stems and pieces
¾ pound mozzarella cheese, diced into ½" pieces
1 small can tomato paste
1 clove garlic, minced
½ teaspoon oregano
¼ teaspoon pepper
½ teaspoon salt
1 14-ounce package refrigerated hot roll mix
2 tablespoons olive oil
¼ cup grated Parmesan cheese

Into a 2-quart mixing bowl put the hamburger, onion, olives, mushrooms and cheese. Add the tomato paste, garlic, oregano, pepper and salt; mix well with a blending fork. At this point, preheat your oven to 450° F.

Divide the hot roll mix into two portions. Knead the biscuit sections together until you have 2 balls of dough about 3" in diameter. Place the balls of dough on a floured board and roll into 2 ⅛"-thick 10"-diameter circles. Place the circles on a floured and buttered cookie sheet. Flute the outer edges of the circles to prevent the pizza mixture from running out. (If it runs out it will stick to the pan.)

Divide the meat mixture in half and spread a half on each of the circles. Brush the olive oil around the fluted edges and over the top. Sprinkle with the cheese. Place in the preheated 450° F. oven and bake from 20 to 25 minutes, or until the edges of the crust are a rich golden brown.

NOGALES TAMALE PIE

4 cups slightly salted boiling water
1 cup yellow corn meal
1 tablespoon olive oil
1 pound hamburger
1 onion, chopped very fine
1 green pepper, chopped very fine
1 #2 can little Italian tomatoes
½ teaspoon salt
½ teaspoon chili powder
Dash Tabasco (optional)
1 package chopped frozen spinach

Put the four cups of boiling water in the top of the double boiler. Fill the bottom with water and turn on the heat. Slowly stir in the corn meal so that no lumps form. Stir until it begins to thicken and coat the spoon. Turn the heat down to simmer and cover the double boiler.

Heat the olive oil in a skillet and add the hamburger to it. Sauté the hamburger until it is golden brown; add the onion and green pepper and sauté for 5 minutes longer. Add the tomatoes, salt, chili powder and Tabasco, if your family likes spicy food. Continue cooking for 10 minutes longer. Then stir in the chopped spinach and remove from the fire.

Grease a 1½-quart casserole. Into the bottom pour half the corn meal mixture, and carefully spoon the meat mixture over it. Top the meat mixture with the remainder of the corn meal. Place in a preheated 350° F. oven for 30 minutes, or until the corn meal topping has turned to golden brown.

Variations:

Substitute 1 package frozen niblet-style corn for the spinach.
Add 1 package frozen lima beans.
Add 1 #2 can butter beans.
Add 1 #2 can lima beans, drained.
Add 1 #2 can red kidney beans.
Add 1 #2 can black-eyed peas.

VEAL BREAST STUFFED WITH HAMBURGER

My family's biggest complaint about economy dishes like stuffed veal breast is that they want more meat. Here is a recipe that has economy and plenty of meat, too.

1 3-pound veal breast
1 teaspoon salt
1 pound hamburger
2 cups moist bread crumbs
1 medium onion, chopped very fine
1 tablespoon paprika

Have your butcher make a pocket in the veal breast. If you purchase meats in a market where they are prepackaged, you can do this yourself with a very sharp paring knife. Just slice a pocket midway between the top and the bottom of the veal breast. It should be large enough to hold the meat and other stuffing ingredients.

Salt the interior of the veal breast. Mix the hamburger with the onions and bread crumbs, and stuff this mixture into the pocket. Fasten the end with skewers. Sprinkle the paprika all over the outside of the veal breast and place in a shallow roasting pan. Cover with foil for the first half of the cooking time. Roast at 350° F. for 1 hour. Then remove foil and bake uncovered for 45 minutes more. The veal should become a rich brown color.

You can make delicious gravy from the pan juices. Remove the meat to a heated platter. Add ½ cup water to the pan juices, and thicken with a heaping tablespoon of flour dissolved in another ¼ cup of water.

EGG-BURGER SURPRISES

1 pound hamburger
½ teaspoon salt
¼ teaspoon pepper
¼ cup instant flour
6 hard-cooked eggs, peeled and cooled
1 raw egg, slightly beaten
1 cup dry bread crumbs or 1 cup crushed shredded wheat
Vegetable oil for deep frying

Mix the hamburger, salt, pepper and flour until smooth. Form into 6 large patties, and place a hard-cooked egg in the center of each. Bring up the sides of each patty and form into a covering all around the egg. Brush with the slightly beaten egg and roll in the bread crumbs or shredded wheat.

Drop into hot fat and fry until the patties turn golden brown. Drain on paper toweling. Cut each patty in half when serving, leaving half of the egg in each section. These can be served hot or cold and create a sensation when used as hors d'oeuvres with cocktails.

HAMBURGER MEAT PUDDING

1 pound hamburger
3 eggs, separated
4 strips bacon, cut into ¼" pieces
¼ cup milk
1 cup soft bread crumbs
1 tablespoon brandy (optional)
¼ teaspoon lemon rind
1 tablespoon parsley, chopped fine
¼ teaspoon pepper
2 tablespoons butter

Place the hamburger in a mixing bowl and add the egg yolks. Add the bacon, milk and bread crumbs. Add the brandy, lemon rind, parsley and pepper. Mix all very well.

Beat the egg whites until they are stiff and dry. Fold them into the meat mixture. Brush a ring mold generously with the butter and carefully spoon in the meat mixture. Try not to pack it too tightly. Place the ring mold in a pan of water and bake in a 350° F. oven for 50 minutes, or until firmly set.

This goes well served with creamed green beans or peas. Mushrooms in cream sauce make it a more elegant dish.

HAMBURGER ONION PIE

Crust

2 cups flour
½ ounce dry yeast
¼ cup lukewarm water
2 eggs
¼ cup milk
1 tablespoon olive oil

Filling

1 pound hamburger
8 medium-sized onions, cut in ¼" slices
8 strips anchovy
10 black olives, pitted
1 cup canned tomatoes
2 tablespoons olive oil

Place the flour in a mixing bowl; dissolve the yeast in the water and set aside. Break the eggs into the flour, add the milk and olive oil. Stir and, when partially mixed, add the dissolved yeast. Stir and then knead until you have a smooth dough. Set aside to rise for 30 minutes.

Place 1 tablespoonful of olive oil in a skillet; add the hamburger and cook until slightly browned. Add the onions and continue to cook until they are transparent and glazed. Remove from heat and set aside to cool. Cut the anchovy into ¼" pieces; slice the olives. Reserve half of the olives for the top of the pie. Stir the anchovies, tomatoes and olives into the hamburger mixture.

Put the ball of dough on a floured board and roll out into a circle to fit a large pie tin. Place the dough in the tin, making sure it is well up around the edges. Brush the bottom and sides with the remaining olive oil. Put the hamburger mixture into the pie crust. Decorate the top with the remaining olive slices. Place in a 350° F. oven for 35 minutes, or until the crust is browned. Cut in wedges and serve piping hot.

HAMBURGER DUMPLINGS

6 strips bacon
½ pound hamburger
1 tablespoon dehydrated parsley
1 tablespoon chopped chives, or two scallions, cut very fine
½ teaspoon salt
¼ teaspoon pepper
6 slices white bread soaked in 1 cup milk
3 eggs, beaten until lemon yellow
3 tablespoons butter
¾ cup fine bread crumbs

Dice the bacon very fine and put into a skillet. Fry until it is golden brown and crisp. Remove the bacon from the pan with a slotted spoon and set aside. Now sauté the hamburger in the bacon fat until it is browned. Stir in the parsley, chives, salt and pepper. Remove from heat. Set aside to cool.

Squeeze the milk from the bread and add the bread to the hamburger; now stir in the beaten eggs and mix very well. Form the mixture into small balls about the size of golf balls. Drop into rapidly boiling water and cook for about 12 minutes. Meanwhile, melt the butter and brown the bread crumbs in it. Place the dumplings on a heated platter; sprinkle the browned bread crumbs over the top. Decorate with the tiny pieces of crisp bacon.

PIMENTOS WITH PAPRIKA HAMBURGER

8 fresh pimentos approximately 2-3" in diameter
1 pound hamburger
1 egg
1 tablespoon paprika
1 teaspoon salt
3 tablespoons olive oil

With a very sharp knife, cut around the stem of the pimentos. Scrape out all of the seeds and pulp. Rinse under running water and invert to drain. Mix the hamburger, egg, paprika and salt very thoroughly. Press the meat mixture into the hollow in each of the pimentos. Brush the olive oil over the bottom and sides of a shallow baking tin. Place the pimentos in the tin, cover with aluminum foil and bake in a 350° F. oven for 35 minutes.

This dish goes well with macaroni and cheese or with buttered noodles.

HAMBURGER STUFFING FOR TURKEY OR CHICKEN

2 pounds hamburger
½ cup raisins, chopped very fine
¼ cup chopped onion
¼ cup chopped celery
1 tart apple, chopped very fine
½ pound chestnuts, roasted, peeled and coarsely chopped
½ cup pine nuts
1 cup water
1 cup mincemeat
½ cup instant rice

Brown the hamburger until it is all separated and has lost its reddish color. Add the raisins, onion, celery and apple. Stir in the chestnuts and the pine nuts. Add the water and cook, tightly covered, over a low flame for 1 hour. Stir from time to time, and if it gets too dry add more water. Last, stir in the mincemeat and the rice and simmer for 5 minutes, or until the rice is tender. Let cool until you are able to handle it while stuffing the fowl.

This stuffing can be made the day before and refrigerated until you need it. Never stuff a bird the day before it is to be eaten. Prepare the stuffing separately, and stuff the fowl just before roasting it.

GROUND LAMB TURKEY STUFFING

2 tablespoons butter
½ cup chopped onion
2 pounds ground lean lamb
¼ teaspoon cloves
¼ teaspoon cinnamon
¼ teaspoon nutmeg
1 8-ounce can tomato sauce
1 cup dry bread crumbs
4 tablespoons chopped parsley
½ cup chopped walnuts
1 cup celery, cut into ¼" pieces
2 eggs, beaten to lemon yellow

Melt the butter in a large saucepan. Add the chopped onion and sauté until transparent. Add the ground lamb and continue to sauté until the lamb is a rich golden brown color. Add the cloves, cinnamon and nutmeg. Add the tomato sauce and simmer over low heat for 30 minutes. Add the bread crumbs, parsley and walnuts. Stir all very well and remove from heat. Let cool. Stir in the celery and then the eggs. Mix all very well. Stuff the turkey, and roast it immediately.

This is enough stuffing for a 12 to 15 pound turkey. For best results, spoon the stuffing in lightly.

HAMBURGER-STUFFED MUSHROOMS

24 very large mushrooms
½ pound very lean hamburger
2 tablespoons melted butter
1 tablespoon dehydrated parsley
1 clove garlic, chopped fine
2 beef bouillon cubes dissolved in ¼ cup hot water
½ teaspoon salt
¼ teaspoon pepper
½ cup soft bread crumbs

Wash the mushrooms in rapidly running water. Drain until they are dry. With a very sharp knife, remove the entire stem from each mushroom. Put these stems in a chopping bowl and chop until the pieces are as small as bread crumbs.

Place the hamburger in a mixing bowl. Add the chopped mushroom stems, 1 tablespoon of the melted butter, the parsley, garlic, bouillon cubes, salt, pepper and bread crumbs. Mix all very well.

Place the mushroom caps, hollow side down, in a baking tin. Brush with the remaining butter and place under the broiler for 10 minutes, or until they begin to get brown. Remove from heat and let them cool until you are able to handle them.

Now fill each hollowed-out mushroom with the meat mixture. Put them back in the baking tin, meat side up. Place in a 400° F. oven for 20 minutes, or until the meat begins to brown. Serve piping hot.

DANISH MEAT PIE

Filling

4 strips of bacon, cut into ¼" pieces
½ pound ground chuck
½ pound lean ground pork
½ pound ground veal
3 tablespoons instant onion flakes
1 clove garlic, chopped fine
¼ teaspoon dill seed
¼ teaspoon celery seed
⅛ teaspoon cloves
½ teaspoon salt
4 twists of pepper mill
1 #2 can apple sauce

Crust

2 cups biscuit mix
¾ cup milk
¼ teaspoon salt

Brown the diced bacon in a skillet. Add the beef, pork and veal and cook until the meat loses its reddish color. Drain off any excess fat. Add the onion flakes and garlic. Stir in the dill seed, celery seed, cloves, salt and pepper. Last, add the apple sauce. Bring to a simmer, cover and continue to simmer for 35 minutes. Remove from heat and set aside to cool.

Mix the biscuit mix with the milk and salt. Knead on a floured board until it is stiff enough to handle. Roll out two 9" circles. Place one circle in a 9" pie tin; flatten it out well, bringing it up over the edge for sealing. Put in the meat filling and top with the other circle of dough. Seal the edges to prevent dripping. Gash the top of the pie in six or seven places so the steam can come out.

Place in a preheated 425° F. oven for 20 minutes. Then reduce the heat to 375° F. and bake for 35 minutes longer, or until crust is golden brown.

Chapter VII

SOUP'S ON

MAKE SOUP FROM HAMBURGER? Impossible, most people would say. Well, I make soup from hamburger, and my family likes it. Hamburger, with its high protein content, is a very logical ingredient for soup. Surely it is more reasonable to make it from hamburger than to make it by boiling soup bones for hours, then cooling, straining, etc. Hamburger takes the labor out of homemade soups. We have instant coffee, instant tea, instant almost everything—why not instant soup?

If you still make soup the old-fashioned way, and like to work hard, there's nothing wrong with that. But if you want delicious quick soups, try the ones in this chapter.

BASIC BROTH FROM HAMBURGER

2 pounds lean hamburger
4 quarts cold water
2 large carrots, diced
1 small onion, diced
1 stalk celery, diced
4 sprigs parsley, minced
½ teaspoon pepper
1 teaspoon salt

Slowly sauté the hamburger in the bottom of a soup kettle. Pour off any fat which may accumulate. Add the water and bring to a boil. Simmer for 1 hour. Skim off any froth which may gather during this time. At the end of the hour, add the vegetables, pepper and salt; cook for another 30 minutes.

This is a delicious light soup to use at the beginning of a hearty meal. It can also be made up, frozen, and later used as the base for other, richer soups.

HAMBURGER FRENCH ONION SOUP

1 tablespoon butter
½ pound hamburger
10 medium-sized onions, sliced very thin
1 can beef consommé or stock
1 cup water
2 beef bouillon cubes

Brown the butter in the bottom of your soup kettle. Add the hamburger and fry until very brown and well separated. Add the sliced onions, consommé, water and bouillon cubes and simmer for 30 minutes.

Serve with squares of buttered toast topped with Parmesan cheese.

HAMBURGER MINESTRONE

1 pound hamburger
2 tablespoons olive oil
2 medium-sized onions, sliced thin
⅛ teaspoon sweet marjoram
1 clove garlic
½ bay leaf
2 #2 cans red kidney beans
1 #2 can tomatoes
2 cups shredded white cabbage
1 cup cooked rice
1 cup water (optional)
1 teaspoon salt
¼ teaspoon pepper
½ teaspoon Accent

Sauté the hamburger in the olive oil until it is broken up. Add the onions, marjoram, garlic and bay leaf and sauté for 5 minutes longer. Mash the kidney beans in their own liquid with a potato masher, or put them through your food blender. Add the beans to the meat mixture, along with the tomatoes. Continue to cook over a very low flame for 45 minutes. Keep tightly covered during this period.

Ten minutes before serving time, add the shredded cabbage and the rice. Simmer for 10 minutes. At this point if you feel that this soup is too thick for your family, add the optional cup of water and simmer for a few minutes longer. Add the salt, pepper and Accent. Let stand for a few seconds and then serve.

This soup is excellent if garnished with a heaping teaspoonful of grated Parmesan cheese on each bowl. A very thin slice of lemon floated on top of the soup is also an excellent garnish.

HAMBURGER CHOWDER

1 pound hamburger
1 tablespoon butter
3 large onions, sliced thin
4 stalks celery, cut into ¼" pieces
3 cups water
4 medium raw potatoes, cut into ½" cubes
1 teaspoon salt
4 peppercorns
1 teaspoon Accent
2 packages frozen mixed garden vegetables

Use a 1½ quart or larger saucepan for this soup. Slowly sauté the hamburger in the butter until it is a rich dark brown in color. Add the onions and celery and cook until the onions are slightly glazed.

Add the water and the diced potatoes and cook until the edges of the potatoes are slightly transparent. Now add the salt, peppercorns and Accent. Simmer for 5 minutes.

Add the two packages of frozen vegetables and cook *uncovered* for ten minutes, or until the green beans in the vegetable mixture are easily pierced with a fork.

It is very important that you leave off the cover for the last ten minutes of cooking; this insures that your soup will have that magazine-picture look when you serve it. Covering changes the color of fresh vegetables from bright to drab.

Served with saltines, this is a meal in itself.

Variations:

Add 2 fresh tomatoes, cubed in ¼" pieces.
Add 1 #2 can tomatoes.
Add ½ package chopped spinach.
Substitute 1 package frozen peas and carrots for the mixed vegetables.
Substitute 2 packages frozen baby limas for the mixed vegetables.

97

HAMBURGER-RED BEAN SOUP

1 pound hamburger
3 tablespoons butter or margarine
2 #2 cans red kidney beans
2 medium-sized onions, sliced very thin
2 medium-sized potatoes, washed but not peeled, cut into
½" cubes
4 cups water
1 teaspoon monosodium glutamate
1 teaspoon salt
¼ teaspoon pepper
1 cup heavy cream
1 egg, beaten to a lemon yellow

Sauté the hamburger in the butter or margarine until slightly browned and fairly well separated. Add the kidney beans just as they come from the cans, liquid and all. Add the onions and potatoes. Add the water, and bring to a boil for 10 minutes. Add the monosodium glutamate, salt and pepper. Remove soup from the stove and let cool for a few minutes.

Combine the cream and egg, and add about a half cup of the broth from the soup. Stir well; then add this mixture to the soup, stirring constantly while doing so. Return to heat for 5 minutes.

Serve piping hot. Garnish with grated Parmesan-Romano cheese, if desired.

HAMBURGER CAULIFLOWER SOUP

1 small head cauliflower or 1 package frozen cauliflower
3 tablespoons butter
1 pound hamburger
¼ cup chopped onion
1 small tomato, diced
8 cups hot water
1 teaspoon salt
¼ teaspoon pepper
1 teaspoon Accent
1 cup elbow macaroni

Thoroughly wash the cauliflower under rapidly running water. Break into blossom pieces, and stand aside in a dish of salted water. (If you use frozen cauliflower, this is not necessary.)

Heat the butter in the bottom of a soup kettle and add the hamburger. Brown the hamburger slightly and then add the onion and the diced tomato. Drain the cauliflower and add to the meat mixture, along with two cups of hot water. Cover tightly and simmer for 30 minutes, then add the salt, pepper and Accent. Now add the remainder of the water and the dry macaroni.

Cook until the macaroni is tender. Serve with a sprinkle of Parmesan cheese over each bowl.

RICHER HAMBURGER CAULIFLOWER SOUP

1 pound hamburger
3 tablespoons butter
8 cups water
1 large head cauliflower or 3 packages frozen cauliflower
3 tablespoons cornstarch
3 cups milk
¼ cup grated Parmesan-Romano cheese
1 teaspoon salt
¼ teaspoon pepper
½ teaspoon Accent
2 egg yolks

Sauté the hamburger in the butter until slightly browned. Add the water and bring to a rolling boil. Meanwhile, clean the fresh cauliflower under running water. Break up into flowers and, with your salad chopping knife, chop very fine. Add the chopped cauliflower to the hamburger broth. Turn flame down to simmer.

Meanwhile, put water in the bottom of the double boiler and bring to a boil. Stir the cornstarch into the milk until all is dissolved. Put the milk and cornstarch in the top of the double boiler and cook until the mixture begins to coat the spoon. Stir constantly during this time. As soon as it has thickened, add the cheese. Turn the flame down low enough just to keep the mixture warm.

Add the salt, pepper and Accent to the hamburger-cauliflower mixture. Now take ½ cup of this mixture and stir it into the thickened milk mixture. This is to prevent curdling when you add the milk mixture to the soup.

Add all of the milk mixture to the hamburger-cauliflower broth. Remove from the stove and, after it has cooled for a few minutes, stir in the beaten egg yolks. Serve immediately. Garnish with grated Parmesan cheese if desired.

HAMBURGER BEAN SOUP

1 pound hamburger
1 tablespoon butter or margarine
¼ teaspoon rosemary
¼ cup chopped parsley
3 cloves garlic, minced
1 tablespoon flour
1 small tomato, diced, or ¼ cup tomato sauce
½ teaspoon salt
¼ teaspoon pepper
1 teaspoon Accent
8 cups water
1 cup navy or northern beans, soaked overnight

Sauté the hamburger in the butter or margarine until slightly browned. Add the rosemary, parsley and garlic and sauté five minutes longer. Sprinkle the flour over the sautéed meat and herbs, stirring well. Add the diced tomato, salt, pepper and Accent. Slowly add the water. Bring to a rolling boil and turn the heat down to simmer.

Now add the drained beans and simmer for two hours. If the soup is too thick, add a little more water. The beans should break easily against the side of the kettle when the soup is done.

Serve with croutons.

Variations:

Add 1 package frozen mixed vegetables
Add 1 package baby lima beans

HAMBURGER-POTATO SOUP

4 slices lean bacon, cut into ¼" pieces
1 pound hamburger
3 cups boiling water
½ teaspoon salt
¼ teaspoon pepper
1 teaspoon monosodium glutamate
2 medium-sized onions, sliced very thin
8 medium-sized potatoes, washed but not peeled, diced in
  ½" squares
1 tablespoon cornstarch
2 cups milk
2 sprigs of parsley, minced, or 1 tablespoon dehydrated parsley

Put the small pieces of bacon into the bottom of a soup kettle; place over a low flame and sauté until the bacon is golden brown. Drain off any excess fat. Add the hamburger and cook and stir until it is all uniformly broken into small pieces and is just beginning to get brown.

Add the water, salt, pepper and monosodium glutamate. When all comes to a rapid boil, add the onions and potatoes. Turn the heat down to simmer and cook slowly for 30 minutes. Do not overcook the potatoes, for half the joy of potato soup is being able to bite into a piece of potato with its own good flavor. Remove from the heat when the edges of the potatoes begin to look slightly transparent.

Stir the cornstarch into the milk, making sure all is dissolved. Slowly, stirring all the while, add the cornstarch-milk mixture to the soup. Cook for 5 minutes longer. Just before serving, stir in the parsley.

Variations:

Add 1 package frozen mixed vegetables.
Add 1 package frozen baby lima beans.
Add 1 package frozen cream-style corn.
Add 1 package frozen peas and carrots.

HAMBURGER-SPINACH SOUP

1 pound lean ground chuck
1 tablespoon butter
2 packages chopped frozen spinach
2 cups milk or half milk and half cream, if you like it rich
½ teaspoon salt
4 twists of pepper mill
¼ teaspoon nutmeg
2 tablespoons cornstarch
¼ cup water

Brown the chuck in the butter. Add the frozen spinach and cook till thoroughly defrosted. Do not cover. Stir in the milk, add the salt, pepper and nutmeg. Simmer for 5 minutes. Thoroughly mix the cornstarch and water. Very slowly, add to the spinach-meat mixture. Stir until thickened. Serve with a dash of nutmeg over each bowl, if desired.

SPINACH SOUP WITH HAMBURGER

1 tablespoon butter
1 pound hamburger
1 cup water
1 package frozen shredded spinach
4 tablespoons cornstarch
1 quart milk
½ teaspoon salt
¼ teaspoon pepper
1 teaspoon monosodium glutamate

Place the butter in the bottom of a soup kettle and melt slowly. Add the hamburger and sauté until it is browned and broken up. Add the water, along with the frozen spinach, and simmer, uncovered, until the spinach is thawed and tender.

Stir the cornstarch into the milk and place over a very low flame. Stir constantly until the mixture begins to thicken. Add several spoonfuls of the meat-spinach mixture to the cornstarch and milk. Then turn the entire milk mixture into the meat-spinach mixture. Now add the salt, pepper and monosodium glutamate; cook for 5 minutes longer, uncovered, over a low flame.

Serve piping hot, with croutons.

HAMBURGER-FRENCH PEA SOUP

1 tablespoon butter
1 medium onion, cut in ⅛″ slices
1 pound ground chuck
1 #2 can baby green peas, not drained
1 small head lettuce, shredded very fine
1 medium-sized leek, cut sliver thin
3 tablespoons parsley, chopped very fine
1 teaspoon sugar
½ teaspoon salt
¼ teaspoon pepper
2 cups beef stock or 2 cups water with 4 bouillon cubes dissolved in it
2 cups half and half cream

Melt the butter in a skillet and cook the onion until it is glazed. Add the meat and cook until it loses its reddish color. Set aside.

In a soup kettle place the green peas, liquid and all; add the lettuce, leek, parsley, sugar, salt and pepper. Add the meat stock and bring to a rolling boil; cook, uncovered, for

10 minutes, or until the vegetables can be mashed with a fork.

Strain the vegetable mixture through a fine sieve. Work the vegetables through the sieve until they are reduced to a smooth paste. Return to the soup kettle and add the hamburger. Bring to a simmer for 5 minutes. Now take a half cup of the mixture and stir it into the cream; then add the cream to the vegetables and simmer for 5 minutes longer. This is to prevent curdling and to give the soup a creamy consistency.

Serve with toasted croutons.

GREEK LAMB SOUP

2 tablespoons butter or magarine
1 pound ground lean lamb
4 cups water
½ teaspoon salt
¼ teaspoon pepper
1 bay leaf
1 tablespoon dehydrated parsley
1 leek, sliced fine
1 large carrot, peeled and diced
3 stalks of celery, diced
1 small celery root, diced
1 large parsnip, peeled and diced
3 tablespoons instant flour
1 cup frozen peas

Melt the butter or margarine in a skillet and brown the lamb until it is all broken apart. Place the water in a kettle along with the salt, pepper, bay leaf and parsley. Bring to a rolling boil. Strain the browned lamb, saving the fat. Place the strained lamb in the boiling water. Turn the heat down to simmer.

Return the lamb drippings to the skillet and brown the leek, carrot, celery, celery root and parsnip. Sprinkle the flour over the vegetables and stir and turn until the flour is browned too.

Take 1 cup of the simmering meat broth and pour it over the vegetables. Continue to cook until the parsnip cubes are tender; then add the vegetables to the meat broth. Stir in the frozen peas and cook for 5 minutes longer.

Serve with rounds of toast topped with Parmesan cheese.

HUNGARIAN MEAT BALL SOUP

4 strips of bacon cut into ¼" squares
1 large onion, sliced
1 pound hamburger
½ teaspoon salt
4 twists of pepper mill
2 teaspoons paprika
⅛ teaspoon thyme
⅛ teaspoon marjoram
1 clove garlic, minced
4 cups stock
2 tablespoons flour
¼ cup water
3 cooked potatoes, diced in ½" pieces

Place the diced bacon in the bottom of the soup kettle and fry until it is a crisp golden brown. Add the onion to the bacon and its drippings. Sauté it until it is transparent and just turning brown.

Form the hamburger into tiny meat balls about ¾" in diameter. As you form them, add them to the onion-bacon mixture. Shake the pan back and forth between additions so that the meat balls brown on all sides; add the salt, pepper, paprika, thyme, marjoram and garlic. Add one cup of the stock, and let simmer for about 20 minutes. Mix the flour in the water, being careful that there are no lumps. Slowly add this to the meat mixture. Bring to a simmer again. Gradually add the rest of the soup stock and simmer for 20 minutes longer. Put in the diced potatoes just before serving.

HAMBURGER, POTATO AND LEEK SOUP

2 tablespoons butter
1 pound ground chuck
6 to 8 leeks, white part only, sliced in ⅛" pieces
½ cup celery, chopped fine
3 cups sliced raw potatoes
3 cups meat stock, or 3 cups water with 3 bouillon cubes
   dissolved in it
½ teaspoon salt
5 whole black peppercorns
2 cups half and half cream
1 tablespoon chopped parsley
1 tablespoon chopped chives

Melt the butter in a large saucepan. Add the chuck and cook until it loses its reddish color. Add the leeks, celery, potatoes and stock. Add the salt and peppercorns. Cover and simmer until the potatoes can be mashed with a fork against the side of the kettle. Add about a half cup of the soup broth to the cream. Mix well, then add to the soup. Stir while you are adding the cream. Simmer for an additional 10 minutes.

Serve in a large soup tureen garnished with chopped parsley and chives. Serve piping hot, with saltines.

LAMB SOUP

1 pound ground lean lamb
3 tablespoons butter
1 package frozen chopped spinach
6 green onions (shallots)
½ teaspoon paprika
1 quart water
½ cup precooked rice
8 peppercorns
3 egg yolks
½ cup sour cream

Brown the lamb in the butter until it is separated and about the size of large peas. Add the spinach. Slice the shallots into ¼" pieces; do not use too much of the green portion, as this will make the flavor very harsh. Add the shallots to the spinach and the lamb. Add the paprika and water and then stir in the rice. Add the peppercorns. Cook for about 14 minutes longer, or until the rice is tender.

Beat the egg yolks until they are golden yellow; add the sour cream to the eggs and beat again. Remove the soup from the heat and let cool for a few minutes. Take about a half cup of the soup stock and add to the cream and egg mixture. Stir well; then add the cream and egg mixture to the soup. Return to the heat for 5 minutes more. Stir continuously during this time. Serve with croutons.

BELGIAN HAMBURGER SOUP

4 potatoes, scrubbed very clean
1 cup celery, chopped
1 small can tomato paste
¾ cup chopped onion
2 cloves garlic, cut in small pieces
⅛ teaspoon thyme
½ teaspoon salt
4 twists of pepper mill
1½ quarts water
1 pound hamburger

Chop the whole potatoes (unpeeled) very fine. Place potatoes, celery, tomato paste, onion, garlic, thyme, salt and pepper in the water. Bring to a rapid boil, and then turn heat down to simmer. Simmer for about 1½ hours, stirring occasionally. Brown the hamburger over moderate heat. When it is all separated and about the size of peas, remove from heat and drain off all accumulated fat.

Place the vegetable mixture in a large colander or a Foley food mill. Save the liquid in a separate bowl. Force the vegetables through the colander. Add the hamburger and the puréed vegetables to the stock. Reheat all together and serve.

HAMBURGER-PEA SOUP

2 cups dried whole peas
1 pound hamburger
¼ cup chopped onion
2 tablespoons butter or margarine
1 tablespoon dehydrated parsley flakes
½ teaspoon salt
¼ teaspoon ground pepper or 4 twists of pepper mill
¼ cup cream or condensed milk
6-8 pieces of rosemary

Soak the peas overnight in water; drain and cover again with cold water. Bring to a rolling boil and then turn heat down to simmer until the peas are tender. Brown the hamburger in the butter or margarine, add the onion, parsley flakes, salt and pepper and continue to cook until the onion is glazed and transparent.

Add the hamburger mixture to the peas, stir in the cream and add the rosemary. Simmer for 10 minutes longer. Serve with toasted croutons.

CHILI

1 pound hamburger
2 tablespoons butter or margarine
½ cup celery, chopped fine
½ cup onion, chopped fine
1 teaspoon salt
4 twists of pepper mill
1 teaspoon chili powder
2 #2 cans of tomatoes
1 cup water
1 8-ounce package elbow macaroni

Brown the hamburger in the butter or margarine. Add the celery and onion and cook until tender. Add the salt, pepper and chili powder. Stir in the tomatoes and water. Add the elbow macaroni as it comes from the package. Simmer for 1 hour, or until the macaroni is tender. Serve piping hot with saltines.

CHILI CON CARNE

1 tablespoon butter or margarine
2 large onions, diced in ¼" pieces
1 pound ground chuck
1 teaspoon salt
1 teaspoon chili powder
1 cup diced raw potatoes
1 small green pepper, diced in ¼" pieces
½ cup chopped celery
1 #2 can tomatoes
1 10½-ounce can condensed tomato soup
2 #2 cans kidney beans (do not drain)

Melt the butter or margarine in the bottom of a large saucepan. Add the onions and cook until they are tender and transparent. Add the chopped meat and continue to cook until the meat loses its reddish color. Add the salt and chili powder. Continue to cook for a few seconds longer.

Add the potatoes, green pepper, celery, tomatoes and tomato soup. Simmer for 15 minutes longer, or until the edges of the potato cubes become transparent. Last, add the kidney beans and simmer for 15 minutes longer. If the chili is too thick for your taste, add a little tomato juice.

Serve with crisp crackers.

Chapter VIII
QUICKIES

QUICKIE CUTLETS

½ pound ground chuck
½ pound ground veal
½ teaspoon salt
4 twists of pepper mill
4 slices American process cheese
2 eggs, well beaten
1 cup dry bread crumbs
Vegetable oil for deep frying

Mix the chuck, veal, salt and pepper very well. Form into 8 patties. Fold the pieces of cheese in four, place on one of the patties, then cover with another patty. Press the edges together so the cheese is well sealed inside.

Brush each side of the patty with the beaten egg and then dip into the bread crumbs. If necessary, press the bread crumbs into the surface. Drop into deep oil and fry until they are golden brown. Serve with hashed brown potatoes and creamed green beans.

HAMBURGER BREAKFAST SURPRISE

The hue and cry for high-protein breakfasts can be met with this delicious dish.

1 pound ground chuck
½ pound lean ground pork
1 tablespoon dehydrated parsley
½ teaspoon salt
½ teaspoon pepper
1 cup white bread, soaked in milk to cover
1 cup dry bread crumbs, rolled fine
3 tablespoons butter
6 eggs

Mix the chuck, pork, parsley, salt and pepper very well. Squeeze the milk out of the bread and add the bread to the meat mixture. Discard what little milk is left. Mix all well, and form into 6 4″ diameter patties. Dip each patty into the fine bread crumbs.

Melt the butter in a skillet with a tight-fitting cover. Sauté the patties on one side until golden brown. Turn the patties over and, with the back of a tablespoon, make an indentation large enough to hold an egg. Carefully break an egg into each hollow. Cover the pan and cook for 5 minutes, or until the eggs are completely set and firm.

TOMATOES WITH FILLING

8 3" diameter tomatoes
1 pound hamburger
1 cup instant rice
½ teaspoon salt
4 twists of pepper mill
1 onion, minced
⅛ teaspoon thyme
⅛ teaspoon marjoram
⅛ teaspoon oregano
1 tablespoon olive oil

With a very sharp knife, cut away the stem portion and scoop out the inside of each tomato. Place the pulp in a bowl, and add to it the hamburger, the rice just as it comes from the package, the salt, pepper, onion and herbs.

Mix all very well. Stuff each of the tomato shells with the meat mixture and place in an oiled flat baking dish or in individual casseroles. Bake for 35 minutes in a 350° F. oven.

It is wise to allow two stuffed tomatoes per person, as this dish is very tasty and one apiece will not be enough.

QUICK MEAT PIE

1 pound hamburger
1 can deviled ham (4-ounce size)
1 8-ounce package cream cheese, at room temperature
1 can chicken gumbo soup
1 package frozen corn
1 onion, minced
10 ripe olives, pitted and sliced
1 can oven-ready biscuits

Brown the hamburger in a skillet. Remove from heat and stir in the deviled ham, cheese and soup. Break up the frozen corn so that the kernels are separated, and add to the meat mixture. Stir in the onion and the olives. Place all in a deep casserole and top with the biscuits.

Bake at 375° F. for 30 minutes, or until the biscuits are golden brown. Serve with a parsley garnish, if you like.

SAGE AND RICE HAMBURGER

1 pound hamburger
1 egg, slightly beaten
½ cup soft bread crumbs
4 tablespoons butter
1 medium-sized onion, cut into ¼" pieces
1 clove garlic, sliced very thin
2 cups warm water with 3 beef bouillon cubes dissolved in it
2 cups precooked rice
½ teaspoon powdered sage
½ cup Parmesan-Romano cheese

Mix the hamburger with the slightly beaten egg and the bread crumbs. Form into 8 small patties about 2" in diameter. Melt the butter in a large skillet with a tight-fitting cover. Brown the meat patties on both sides in the butter. Remove the patties with a spatula and set in a warm place. Reserve the remaining butter.

Sauté the onion and garlic in the remaining butter until the onion is slightly transparent. Add the bouillon to the onion. Add the rice just as it comes from the package; then add the sage. Stir very well. Cook over low heat, tightly covered, for 10 minutes, or until all of the rice has doubled in size and is tender and separated.

Place the sage rice on a heated platter with the hamburger patties around the edge. Sprinkle the rice with the cheese. Place under the broiler for 3 or 4 minutes, or until the cheese begins to brown. Serve piping hot.

GREEN RICE WITH HAMBURGER

2 tablespoons butter
1 pound hamburger
1 onion, chopped fine
2 cups water
2 cups instant rice
½ teaspoon salt
1 can strained baby food spinach
2 tablespoons parsley, chopped fine

Melt the butter in a skillet and brown the hamburger. Add the onion and continue to cook until it is transparent.

Place the water in a saucepan and bring to a rapid boil. Stir in the rice and add the salt. Cover tightly and cook for 5 minutes, or until all the kernels are separated. Then stir in the strained spinach. Add the hamburger and onion. Place on a heated platter and garnish with the parsley.

110

QUICK MEAT SAUCE OVER RICE

1 pound hamburger
2 tablespoons cornstarch
2 cups V-8 vegetable juice cocktail
1 beef bouillon cube
½ teaspoon salt
2 cups precooked rice
2 cups water

Brown the hamburger in a skillet until it loses its reddish color. Stir the cornstarch into the V-8 juice and pour over the hamburger. Add the bouillon cube and salt. Cook for 8 minutes, or until thickened.

Put the rice in a saucepan with the water and cook until all the liquid has been absorbed and the rice is tender. Place the rice in a large serving bowl, make a hollow in the center and pour in the thickened meat sauce.

Ten Variations for the Meat Sauce:

1. Stir in #2 can drained niblet-style corn 5 minutes before serving.
2. Substitute 1 8-ounce package broad cooked noodles for the rice.
3. Add 2 packages frozen lima beans 5 minutes before serving.
4. Add 2 packages frozen peas with little onions 5 minutes before serving.
5. Omit the rice and stir into the meat sauce 1 #2½ can pork and beans.
6. Add 2 packages frozen zucchini squash 5 minutes before serving.
7. Add 2 packages frozen green beans 5 minutes before serving.
8. Add 1 #2 can mushroom stems and pieces, drained, 5 minutes before serving.
9. Add #2 can yellow butter beans 5 minutes before serving.
10. Omit the rice and add 2 #2 cans macaroni and cheese 5 minutes before serving.

HAMBURGER NESTS

1 pound ground chuck
½ teaspoon salt
¼ teaspoon pepper
1 tablespoon minced onion
1 tablespoon olive oil
2 tablespoons dehydrated parsley
8 eggs
1 cup heavy cream sauce
4 tablespoons Parmesan cheese

Mix the chuck very thoroughly with the salt, pepper and minced onion. Grease 4 individual casserole dishes with the olive oil. After dipping your fingers in ice water, divide the meat into 4 equal portions. Line the sides and bottoms of the casseroles with the meat. Place the casseroles on a cookie sheet under the broiler for 5 minutes, or until the tops begin to brown. Then remove from the oven. Turn oven from broil down to 350° F. and close door to keep hot.

Very carefully, break 2 eggs into each of the casseroles; sprinkle with dehydrated parsley. Return casseroles to the oven (still at 350° F.) for 8 minutes, or until egg whites have set firmly. Remove from oven, but leave heat at 350° F.

Place 3 tablespoonfuls of the cream sauce on each of the casseroles, then sprinkle with cheese. Return to oven for 5 minutes longer. Serve piping hot with wedges of toast and a tossed green salad. If you have oven-to-table dishes you can serve direct from the casseroles; otherwise, invert onto plates.

Chapter IX
MEAT BALLS GALORE

MEAT BALLS made out of ground meat is a universal dish; you can find variations of it wherever there are people. India has its meat ball dishes, Japan offers its contributions and the European countries have given us innumerable variations. In this chapter we hope you find a few new ones to add to your list of meat ball favorites. A whole book could be written on meat balls alone, so I am giving you only the most unique ones I know.

A friend has passed on to me a trick for successful meat ball cookery that you might like to try. After the meat balls have been formed, plunging them momentarily into rapidly boiling water keeps them from losing their round shape during the remainder of the cooking time. The boiling water does not change the taste; indeed, it actually seals in the flavor of the meat.

If you like to make small meat balls about the size of walnuts, there is one kitchen gadget which is a timesaver—the melon-ball maker. This is a ladlelike gadget with two sizes of round scoops, small on one end and large on the other. This type of melon-ball maker can be found in almost any housewares department or variety store. Invest in one; you will find it indispensable. For larger meat balls, you will find an ice cream scoop a boon.

So here are my most unusual meat ball recipes. I have a lot more favorites, but you probably already have many of the more common ones in your own recipe file.

SWEET AND SOUR MEAT BALLS WITH RICE

1 pound ground beef
½ pound ground lean pork
2 eggs
1 teaspoon Accent
½ teaspoon salt
4 twists of pepper mill
3 onions, sliced very thin
1 cup celery, sliced very thin
½ cup water
¼ cup lemon juice (or you may substitute vinegar if you like)
¼ cup light brown sugar
1 teaspoon bead molasses
1 tablespoon soy sauce
2 cups instant rice
2 cups water
2 tablespoons chopped almonds (optional)
1 tablespoon chopped pimento (optional)

Mix the beef, pork, eggs, Accent, salt and pepper very thoroughly. Form into meat balls about the size of walnuts. Plunge the meat balls into very rapidly boiling water, one at a time; remove them to drain as soon as they are firm. This will help them stay nice and round during the remainder of the cooking time. Brown the meat balls in a large frying pan. Instead of turning with a spatula, move the pan back and forth so that they roll while frying and browning. After they are all a golden brown, add the onions and celery. Continue to cook until the onions are transparent and the celery is tender.

Mix the water, lemon juice, sugar, molasses and soy sauce and pour over the meat balls. Bring to a boil, then turn the heat down to simmer for 20 minutes.

Cook the rice in the water in an uncovered pan for 3 to 5 minutes. Cover tightly and set aside for 5 minutes. Serve mounds of fluffy rice with the meat ball mixture poured over it. Garnish with almonds and pimento for a gourmet touch, if desired.

MEAT BALLS IN RED WINE

2 pounds ground chuck
1 egg, slightly beaten
3 tablespoons flour
½ teaspoon paprika
3 tablespoons butter
3 cups red wine (Burgundy or claret)
1 clove garlic, sliced
¼ cup warm water with 2 bouillon cubes dissolved in it
1 bay leaf
¼ teaspoon thyme
1 stalk celery, cut very fine
1 #2 can small onions
1 #2 can mushroom stems and pieces
1 8-ounce package wide noodles
3 quarts rapidly boiling slightly salted water
1 tablespoon butter or margarine

Mix the ground meat with the egg. Form into meat balls about the size of golf balls. Mix the flour and paprika and roll the meat balls in the mixture. Melt the 3 tablespoons of butter in a skillet and brown the meat balls on all sides. Remove them from the skillet, saving the drippings. Place the meat balls in a 1½-quart casserole. Over them, pour the red wine; add the garlic, bouillon, bay leaf, thyme and celery. Cover and place in a 350° F. oven for 45 minutes.

Reheat the drippings in the skillet and add the drained onions and mushrooms. Sauté until they are slightly browned. Add to the meat ball mixture and continue to braise at 350° F. for 15 minutes longer.

Boil the noodles in the 3 quarts of water. Drain, and add the butter or margarine. Place the noodles on a large heated serving platter; cover with the meat balls. Serve at once. This is enough for 8 servings.

MEAT BALLS WITH SAUERBRATEN GRAVY

2 pounds hamburger
1 egg
1 teaspoon salt
¼ teaspoon pepper
¼ cup onion, chopped fine
1 tablespoon dehydrated parsley
1 cup soft bread crumbs
¼ cup flour
2 tablespoons butter or margarine
1 cup meat stock, or 2 bouillon cubes dissolved in 1 cup water
¼ cup water
2 tablespoons cider vinegar
2 tablespoons sugar
¼ teaspoon nutmeg
⅛ teaspoon ground cloves
1 bay leaf
3-4 2″ diameter ginger snaps

Mix the hamburger with the egg, salt, pepper, onion and parsley. Add the bread crumbs. Mix and knead very well. Form into meat balls about the size of golf balls. Plunge into boiling water momentarily to seal in the flavor and help the meat balls retain their shape. Then roll them in the flour. (This acts as a browning agent.)

Melt the butter in a large skillet and brown the meat balls in it. When they are golden brown, add the stock and simmer for 5 minutes. Mix the water, vinegar, sugar, nutmeg and cloves and add to the meat. Break up the bay leaf into 3 or 4 pieces and add. Let simmer for 10 minutes longer. Crush the ginger snaps and add. Turn each meat ball over so that it is thoroughly coated with gravy. If you would like a more sour gravy, add another tablespoonful of cider vinegar. Simmer for an additional 10 minutes. Should the gravy get too thick, add more water.

Serve on a heated platter over buttered noodles or dumplings.

MEAT BALLS IN CARAWAY

2 potatoes, scrubbed but not peeled
1 medium-sized onion
1 pound ground chuck
1 teaspoon seasoned salt
4 twists of pepper mill
2 eggs, beaten to a lemon yellow
1 tablespoon dehydrated parsley
3 tablespoons flour
1 teaspoon paprika
3 cups water
3 beef bouillon cubes
½ teaspoon caraway seeds
½ teaspoon grated lemon peel

Cut the potato into chunks and put it into your food blender. When it is chopped very fine, add the onion and continue to blend for a few seconds longer. Add the blended potato and onion to the ground meat, along with the salt, pepper, eggs and parsley. Mix all very well and form into meat balls about the size of golf balls. Mix the flour and paprika thoroughly and roll the meat balls in it. Make sure they are thoroughly coated with flour.

Bring the water to a rolling boil and carefully drop in the meat balls. Add the bouillon cubes and turn the heat down to simmer. Cover tightly and simmer for 35 minutes.

At the end of this time, stir in the caraway seeds and the lemon peel. Continue to simmer for 10 minutes longer. If the gravy is not thick enough, leave the cover off during this last ten minutes.

This dish goes well with noodles, rice or plain boiled potatoes.

SERBIAN MEAT BALLS

½ pound ground lamb
½ pound ground beef
½ teaspoon salt
¼ teaspoon pepper
1 tablespoon olive oil
3 eggs, separated
1 teaspoon yoghurt
Dash of salt
Dash of pepper
1 teaspoon paprika

Mix the lamb and beef together thoroughly. Season with the ½ teaspoon salt and ¼ teaspoon pepper and form into meat balls about the size of golf balls. Heat the olive oil in a deep skillet and brown the meat balls on all sides.

Meanwhile, beat the egg yolks until they are light and lemon colored. Stir the yoghurt into the egg yolks, mixing very well. Add a dash of salt, a dash of pepper, and the paprika. Mix again. Beat the egg whites until they stand in peaks. Fold into the yoghurt-egg yolk mixture.

Remove the meat balls from the skillet and place them in a deep baking dish. Pour over this the yoghurt-egg mixture. Cook at 350° F. for about 20 minutes, or until the sauce is thickened.

Serve with mashed or plain boiled potatoes.

MEAT BALLS IN MUSTARD SAUCE

1 pound hamburger
2 tablespoons flour
1 teaspoon salt
4 twists of pepper mill
1 teaspoon Accent
1 tablespoon butter or margarine
3 cups meat stock
2 tablespoons dry mustard
1 tablespoon brown sugar
½ teaspoon cocoa

Mix the hamburger with the flour, salt and pepper. Add the Accent and mix thoroughly. Melt the butter or margarine in a deep skillet. Form the ground meat into meat balls about the size of golf balls. Place in the skillet and cook until they are golden brown.

Add the meat stock and simmer for 10 minutes. Then remove approximately ¾ cup of the broth and stir the mustard, brown sugar and cocoa in it. Return to the meat mixture and simmer again. Baste the meat balls with the sauce so that they will be evenly flavored. If you like a sweet-sour mustard sauce, add 1 tablespoon cider vinegar just before serving.

Serve with plain boiled potatoes or with boiled rice. This also goes well with buttered noodles.

CHICK PEAS AND MEAT BALLS

1 pound (approximately) soup bone
4 strips lean bacon, cut into ¼" pieces
3 cups water
1 cup dried chick peas, soaked overnight in 3 cups water
1 stalk leek, cut into fine pieces
1 large carrot, cut into ⅛" slices
2 medium-sized raw potatoes, scrubbed but not peeled, diced in ½" pieces
1 pound hamburger
1 small green pepper, chopped very fine
1 small onion, chopped very fine
½ teaspoon salt
¼ teaspoon pepper
2 eggs, beaten until they are lemon yellow

Place the soup bone and bacon in the water and bring to a rolling boil. Drain the soaked chick peas and add them. Skim the froth from time to time as it rises to the top. Boil for 1 hour, or until the chick peas are tender. Remove the soup bone and discard. Add the leek, carrot, and raw potatoes. Simmer for an additional 30 minutes.

Meanwhile, mix the hamburger, green pepper, onion, salt, pepper and eggs very well. Form into meat balls about the size of golf balls and drop into the simmering chick pea mixture. Simmer for 30 minutes longer. Turn the mixture from time to time to keep it from sticking to the bottom of the pan and to insure even cooking of the meat balls.

Serve in a large tureen, garnished with paprika.

SWEDISH MEAT BALLS

½ cup soft bread crumbs
½ cup light sweet cream
¼ pound ground veal
¼ pound pork (can be fat)
1 pound ground beef
1 tablespoon onion juice
1 teaspoon salt
¼ teaspoon nutmeg
4 twists of pepper mill
½ teaspoon white sugar
1 tablespoon melted butter
2 tablespoons butter for frying

Soak the bread crumbs in the cream. Meanwhile, mix all of the meat together very well. Add the onion juice, salt, nutmeg, pepper and sugar. Finally stir the melted butter into the milk-bread crumb mixture.

Using the large end of a melon-ball maker, form the meat mixture into little balls and place in a skillet in the butter. From time to time, shake the skillet back and forth to brown the meat balls on all sides. This shaking action will brown them more evenly than turning them over with a spatula.

This is a dish that can be served either hot or cold.

SWEDISH MEAT BALLS #2

½ cup bread crumbs
1 tablespoon onion flakes
½ cup milk
1 pound ground chuck
1 teaspoon salt
4 twists of pepper mill
⅛ teaspoon ginger
¼ teaspoon nutmeg
5 tablespoons cream cheese (softened at room temperature)
2 tablespoons butter or margarine
1 can cream of mushroom soup

Soak the bread crumbs and onion flakes in the milk. Meanwhile, mix the meat with the salt, pepper, ginger and nutmeg. Add the milk, onion and bread crumb mixture to the meat and stir lightly. Last, stir in the cream cheese.

Using the large end of a melon-ball maker, form into little meat balls and place in a skillet with the melted butter. Shake the pan back and forth while browning. This will keep the meat balls nice and round. After all of the meat balls have become golden brown, pour the mushroom soup over them. Turn the heat down to a very low simmer until the soup is all melted and thoroughly distributed.

Serve with plain boiled potatoes.

SWEDISH MEAT BALLS #3

1 pound ground chuck
1 pound ground lean pork
2 eggs, beaten to a lemon yellow
1 cup bread crumbs
¾ cup mashed potatoes
1 teaspoon salt
1 cup condensed milk
1 teaspoon brown sugar
¼ teaspoon cloves
¼ teaspoon ginger
¼ teaspoon nutmeg
¼ teaspoon allspice
4 twists of pepper mill
3 tablespoons butter for frying
2 cups half and half cream

Mix very well all of the ingredients—except the butter for frying and the cream—in the order in which they are listed. Using the large end of a melon-ball maker, form into tiny meat balls. Sauté the meat balls in the butter until they are well browned. Shake the pan from side to side so that they roll and brown evenly on all sides. Pour off any excess drippings which may accumulate during the frying. Stir in the cream and simmer for 20 minutes, or until the sauce is thickened.

Serve with boiled potatoes or with broad noodles.

MEAT BALLS WITH SWEET AND SOUR MUSHROOMS

Meat balls

1 pound ground chuck
1 egg
½ teaspoon salt
¼ teaspoon pepper
½ cup soft bread crumbs
¼ cup milk
3 tablespoons butter

Mushroom sauce

3 cups small fresh mushrooms
1 tablespoon flour
1 10½-ounce can beef consommé
1 tablespoon sugar
Juice of 1 lemon

Thoroughly mix all the meat ball ingredients except the butter and form into balls about 1″ in diameter. Using a large skillet, melt the butter and place the meat balls in it. To brown them evenly, gently shake the pan back and forth so that they roll and turn. When all are evenly browned, remove them from the skillet to a platter and make the sauce.

Clean the mushrooms under running water, and drain. Stir the flour into the butter left in the skillet. When it is blended, add the consommé. Cook for 5 minutes over moderate heat until thickened. Add the sugar and lemon juice. Stir in the mushrooms, being careful not to break them. Simmer for 10 minutes, turning frequently so that the mushrooms are all coated and tender. Add the meat balls and simmer for 5 minutes longer.

Arrange on a heated platter, garnished with parsley. If you want an especially festive dish, sprinkle toasted chopped almonds and pimento over the top.

DUTCH KLOPSE

1 pound ground lean pork
1 pound ground lean veal
2 eggs
½ cup moist bread crumbs
½ teaspoon salt
4 twists of pepper mill
2 quarts water
2 tablespoons cider vinegar
1 teaspoon mixed pickling spices
4 tablespoons butter or margarine
3 tablespoons flour
3 cups meat stock or 3 cups water with 6 bouillon cubes
dissolved in it
1 tablespoon capers

Mix the pork and veal, eggs and bread crumbs together. Add the salt and pepper. Bring the water to a rolling boil; add the vinegar and spices. Form the meat into balls about the size of golf balls and drop one by one into the boiling water. Cover and simmer for 10 minutes.

Melt the butter in a deep skillet and stir in the flour until it is smooth. Add the meat stock and stir until it is thickened. Remove the meat balls from the boiling spiced water and put them into the thickened sauce. Add the capers and simmer for 15 minutes longer.

Serve piping hot with plain boiled potatoes.

MEAT BALLS WITH PINE NUTS

1 pound hamburger
1 cup mashed potatoes
¼ cup pine nuts
1 tablespoon dried black currants
¼ teaspoon thyme
¼ teaspoon dill seeds
1 tablespoon dehydrated parsley
½ teaspoon salt
4 twists of pepper mill
Oil for deep frying

Mix all of the ingredients very thoroughly. Form into meat balls about the size of golf balls. Drop into deep-frying oil one at a time and fry until they are golden brown. Remove to paper toweling to drain. Serve with chili sauce or catsup.

123

HAMBURGER SHISH KABOBS

1 pound ground round steak
½ cup mild Cheddar cheese, grated
1 teaspoon salt
1 teaspoon garlic powder
¼ teaspoon pepper
½ teaspoon cinnamon
1 #2 can small potatoes
8 cherry tomatoes or 4 very small tomatoes, halved
1 #2 can boiled onions
2 green peppers, sliced in 4 pieces the long way

Mix the ground meat, cheese, salt, garlic powder, pepper and cinnamon very well. Form into 16 meat balls about 1½" in diameter.

On shish kabob skewers put a potato first, then a meat ball, then a cherry tomato or tomato wedge, then an onion, another meat ball, and last a piece of green pepper, folded in half. Repeat until all the ingredients are used up. Place on a broiling rack under the broiler and cook until the meat is browned on all sides. Serve immediately.

WESTERN-STYLE MEAT BALLS

¾ cup quick-cooking oatmeal
½ pound ground chuck, mixed with ½ pound ground veal (if possible, have the butcher put the meat through the grinder two or three times)
1 teaspoon salt
4 twists of pepper mill
¾ cup condensed milk
3 tablespoons flour
1 teaspoon paprika
3 tablespoons olive oil
½ cup onion, diced into ¼" pieces
¼ cup barbecue sauce
1 can condensed tomato soup
1 soup can water
1 package frozen niblet-style corn

Mix the oatmeal with the ground meat, add the salt, pepper and milk. Form into meat balls about the size of golf balls. Mix the flour and paprika thoroughly, and roll each of the meat balls in this mixture until they are coated on all sides.

Heat the olive oil in a deep skillet with a tight-fitting cover. Sauté the meat balls until they are a rich brown. Add the onion, and continue to cook until it is transparent. Drain off any excess oil left in the pan.

Mix the barbecue sauce with the tomato soup and water. Pour this sauce over the meat balls and let simmer, tightly covered, for 30 minutes. Spoon the sauce over the meat balls from time to time during this period.

Break up the frozen corn and add to the meat balls. Simmer for 10 minutes longer. Serve immediately, piping hot.

NOTE: Lima beans, baked beans, French-style green beans, black-eyed peas or frozen succotash may be used for variety instead of the corn.

MEAT BALLS WITH CORN AND BEANS

2 pounds hamburger
1 teaspoon monosodium glutamate
1 teaspoon salt
¼ teaspoon pepper
1 egg, slightly beaten
2 tablespoons butter or margarine
¼ cup chopped onion
2 cloves of garlic, minced very fine, or 1 tablespoon garlic juice
½ teaspoon chili powder
1 #2 can niblet-style corn
1 #2 can red kidney beans, not drained
1 cup canned tomatoes

Mix the hamburger with the monosodium glutamate, salt, pepper and egg. Dipping your hands in cold water, form this mixture into meat balls about the size of golf balls. Melt the butter in a large skillet; add the onion and garlic. Cook for 5 minutes and then add the meat balls. Sprinkle the chili powder over the meat balls; continue to sauté the meat balls until they are well browned. Drain off any excess grease after they are done.

Place the browned meat balls in the bottom of a 1½-quart casserole. Mix the corn, kidney beans and tomatoes together and pour over the meat balls. Place in a 375° F. oven for 25 minutes. Serve piping hot.

Chapter X

LAMBURGERS

LAMB has long been a favorite of Middle Eastern peoples. Here in the United States it is not used as much as it should be, which is unfortunate, because it is a meat that is high in protein and low in fat.

Most supermarkets now have lamb patties made up in packages of four, six or eight. Occasionally you can convince the butcher to sell you a pound of ground lamb not made up into patties. If you can't get it ground by the pound, buy the patties; it takes little effort to break them up and use them instead. Besides, since a leg of spring lamb rivals porterhouse steak in price most of the time, getting the patties may be less expensive than having a whole piece ground for yourself. The patties are usually about equal in price to ground chuck.

Many people say they dislike lamb because, without being aware of it, they were once served mutton when they thought they were getting lamb—and mutton is a very tasteless meat. Today, however, when a package is labeled lamb, it is truly lamb.

If there is anyone in your household who claims he dislikes lamb, sneak in one of the following recipes. You may make a convert to the cause of this nutritious and healthful food.

LAMB SOUP

1 pound ground lamb
1 medium-sized onion, sliced very thin
1 box frozen shredded spinach
¼ cup chopped parsley
¼ teaspoon paprika
3 cups water
¼ cup precooked rice
1 teaspoon salt
¼ teaspoon pepper
1 egg yolk
1 cup sour cream

126

Put the ground lamb into a soup kettle over a low flame. Sauté slowly until the lamb is golden brown. Drain off any accumulation of fat. Add the onion and the frozen spinach and cook, uncovered, for 5 minutes more, or until the spinach is thawed and separated. Add the parsley, paprika, water and rice. Add the salt and pepper; bring to a rolling boil and then turn the heat down to simmer. Simmer for 10 minutes.

Beat the egg yolk until it is lemon yellow; add the sour cream and beat together until very smooth. Remove the soup from the stove. Stir several spoonfuls of the hot soup into the sour cream and egg and then add the cream and egg mixture to the soup. Cook for a few seconds longer before serving.

Garnish with sprigs of parsley if you wish additional color.

LAMB PILAF

3 tablespoons butter or margarine
1 pound ground lamb
1 onion, diced
2 tablespoons dried black currants
1 tablespoon pine nuts (optional)
1 tablespoon dehydrated parsley
¼ teaspoon allspice
2 cups precooked rice
1 teaspoon salt
¼ teaspoon pepper
1 cup canned tomatoes
2 cups meat stock or 2 cups warm water with 4 bouillon cubes dissolved in it

Place the butter or margarine in the bottom of a kettle which has a tight-fitting cover. Melt, and brown the ground lamb in it. Add the onion, and continue to cook until it is transparent. Add the black currants, pine nuts, parsley, allspice and rice. Continue to cook for 8 minutes longer. Stir constantly so that there is no scorching or sticking. Add the salt and pepper, the tomatoes and meat stock. Stir all very well.

Cook over low heat for about 20 minutes. At this point all of the liquid should have been absorbed by the rice. If there is still too much, turn the heat down to simmer, take off the cover of the kettle and place a clean dish towel (folded in two thicknesses) over the opening of the kettle. Replace the cover on top of the towel and cook for 5 minutes longer. The towel will absorb all of the unwanted liquid and leave the rice in beautiful separate grains.

Serve on a hot platter.

LAMB-EGGPLANT CASSEROLE

If you mention lamb and eggplant to anyone of Turkish or Greek extraction, they light up like a neon sign and start describing how delicious it is. Try it!

1 pound ground lamb
2 tablespoons olive oil
4 medium-sized onions, chopped fine
¼ cup parsley
1 teaspoon monosodium glutamate
½ teaspoon salt
¼ teaspoon pepper
2 eggs, separated
1 cup soft bread crumbs
4 cups whole milk
6 tablespoons cornstarch
1 2-pound eggplant, or 2 smaller ones, peeled and cut in ½″ slices
6 tablespoons olive oil for frying
½ cup Parmesan or Parmesan-Romano cheese

Sauté the lamb in the olive oil until golden brown. Add the onions, parsley, monosodium glutamate, salt and pepper and continue to cook for 5 minutes longer. Beat the egg whites until they stand in peaks. Fold in the bread crumbs. Remove the meat mixture from the stove and set aside to cool. When cool, fold in the egg white and bread crumb mixture.

In the top of your double boiler, mix the milk with the cornstarch and cook over rapidly boiling water until it coats the spoon. Stir frequently during cooking. Beat the egg yolks until light Add a few spoonfuls of the thickened white sauce to the egg yolks. Then add the egg yolks to the white sauce. (This prevents curdling.) Cook for 3 minutes longer.

Heat the olive oil in a large skillet and gently fry the eggplant slices until they are slightly browned. Into a greased 1½-quart casserole, place a layer of the browned eggplant. Follow this with half of the meat mixture. Place another layer of eggplant over this and follow with half of the cream sauce. Now place remainder of the meat mixture over the cream sauce and follow with another layer of eggplant. Pour the remainder of the cream sauce over the entire casserole, and sprinkle with the cheese. Place in a 425° F. oven for 45 minutes.

LAMB IN GRAPE LEAVES

This is a famous Greek delicacy, time consuming to make but wonderful to eat. It is used in most Greek households for festive occasions; try it for one of your special dinners.

½ pound ground lamb
½ cup rice
2 onions, chopped very fine
5 tablespoons olive oil
1 can beef bouillon
1 teaspoon Accent
½ teaspoon salt
¼ teaspoon pepper
40 grape leaves*
6 tablespoons butter

Put the lamb into a skillet over low heat and sauté until it is golden brown. Add the rice, onions and olive oil. Continue to sauté until the rice kernels turn snow white. Add the bouillon, Accent, salt and pepper. Simmer until the rice has absorbed all of the liquid.

If using fresh grape leaves, wash them thoroughly in warm water, then plunge into boiling water for a few seconds. Drain the leaves and place a tablespoonful of the meat-rice mixture in the center of each leaf. Roll the leaf up tightly, folding in the ends as you would do when wrapping a package. Place the grape leaf rolls side by side in the bottom of a heavy saucepan. Additional leaves go between the layers. Dot the tops of the rolled-up leaves with pieces of butter, and add enough water to cover. Cover the saucepan tightly and simmer for 1½ hours. Serve with Egg-Lemon Sauce, below.

Egg-Lemon Sauce

2 eggs
Juice of 2 lemons

Drain the excess liquid from the saucepan containing the grape leaves and set them aside to cool slightly. Beat the eggs until they are lemon colored. While still beating, add the lemon juice and the liquid from the grape leaf-lamb mixture. Pour this sauce over the grape leaves, and serve.

* If you know anyone who grows grapes, you may be able to get leaves fresh from the vine. But be careful; some grape leaves are too harsh in flavor to be palatable. If fresh leaves are unobtainable, prepared ones may be purchased in any international food store.

LAMB AND RICE

1½ pounds ground lamb
1 medium onion, sliced thin
1 #2 can tomato juice
1½ cups uncooked rice
1 teaspoon Accent
½ teaspoon salt
¼ teaspoon pepper
⅛ teaspoon cinnamon
⅛ teaspoon nutmeg

Brown the ground lamb in the bottom of a large kettle. Pour off any accumulated fat. Add the onion and cook until it is slightly glazed. Add the tomato juice and rice, then the Accent, salt, pepper, cinnamon and nutmeg. Stir all together thoroughly.

If there is not enough liquid to cover, add some warm water. Simmer slowly for 20 minutes. When cooking is done, the rice should be doubled in size. If any liquid remains, cook without a cover for a few minutes until the liquid disappears.

GYPSY LAMB STEW

1 pound ground lamb
3 carrots, peeled and sliced very thin
3 onions, sliced very thin
⅛ teaspoon aniseed
½ teaspoon salt
¼ teaspoon pepper
2 cups precooked rice
2 cups water
4 shallots (green onions), sliced very thin
1 green pepper, diced into ¼" pieces

Place the ground lamb in a 2-quart kettle which has a tight-fitting cover. Brown the lamb until it is all broken apart and a golden brown in color. Add the carrots and onions, and continue to cook until the onion slices are clear and transparent. Add the aniseed, salt and pepper and mix well.

Place the rice over the lamb mixture and cover with the water. With cover on kettle, cook over low heat until all of the liquid is absorbed and the rice is fluffy. Mix lightly before placing on a heated platter. Garnish with the shallots and green pepper.

LAMB STEW, TURKISH STYLE

1½ pounds ground lamb
1 tablespoon olive oil
4 large potatoes, peeled and diced
6 small onions
2 green peppers, seeded and sliced in rings
4 cloves garlic, sliced very thin
1 bay leaf
1 teaspoon sage leaves or ½ teaspoon ground sage
1 teaspoon fennel, chopped very fine (optional)
1 teaspoon dill seed
1 #2 can tomatoes
2 cups meat stock or 2 cups warm water with 4 bouillon cubes dissolved in it
1 tablespoon flour

Place the lamb and olive oil in a large cooking kettle. Brown the lamb until it is all separated. Add the potatoes, onions, peppers, garlic, bay leaf, sage, fennel (if you want to use it) and dill seed. Last, stir in the tomatoes and meat stock. Cover tightly and simmer for 1 hour.

Just before serving, remove ½ cup of the gravy, let cool, and stir in the flour. Return this flour-gravy mixture to the kettle and stir until the stew is thickened.

OKRA WITH LAMB

1 pound ground lamb
1 onion, chopped fine
½ cup water
½ teaspoon salt
¼ teaspoon pepper
¾ cup canned tomato sauce
½ cup rice
2 packages frozen okra

Brown the lamb in the bottom of a kettle with a tight-fitting cover. Pour off any grease accumulation after the lamb has browned. Add the onion, water, salt, pepper and tomato sauce. Bring to a boil.

Stir in the rice and okra. Simmer over a very low flame for 45 minutes with the cover on tight. If at the end of this time there is still moisture, continue to cook for a few minutes longer without the cover.

Garnish with very thin slices of lemon, if desired.

LAMB WITH POMEGRANATES

1 pound ground lamb
1 egg
1 tablespoon minced or instant onion
½ teaspoon salt
1 teaspoon Accent
⅛ teaspoon thyme
¼ teaspoon pepper
½ cup moist bread crumbs
1 tablespoon butter or margarine
2 large pomegranates
1 cup water
2 cups instant rice

Mix the lamb with the egg, onion, salt, Accent, thyme, pepper and bread crumbs. Form into meat patties about 3″ in diameter and ¾″ thick. Melt the butter or margarine in a large skillet and brown the lamb patties until they are golden brown.

Peel the pomegranates and remove all the fibrous pith. Put the pulp into a chopping bowl and chop until very fine. Add this to the lamb; then add the water. Cover and cook over low heat for 25 minutes. Turn the patties several times during the cooking so that the pomegranate flavor is evenly distributed.

Cook the rice according to the directions on the package and serve with the meat balls and gravy poured over.

LAMBURGERS WITH EGGPLANT

1 pound ground lamb
½ teaspoon salt
¼ teaspoon pepper
¼ cup olive oil
4 large onions, sliced
1 medium-sized eggplant
1 cup stock or 1 10½-ounce can consommé
1 #2 can tomatoes
2 eggs
¼ cup milk

Season the ground lamb with the salt and pepper. Put the olive oil in a skillet and sauté the lamb in it until it is golden brown and all broken apart. Strain the lamb from the olive oil and set aside. Slice the eggplant in ½″ slices; do not peel. Sauté the eggplant in the olive oil until it begins to brown. Then remove from the olive oil and set aside.

Pour the olive oil left in the skillet into a large baking dish; swirl it around so that it will coat the sides and bottom. Place a layer of the eggplant on the bottom. Follow this with a layer of meat, and then a layer of the sliced onions. Repeat until all the ingredients are used up.

Mix the stock with the tomatoes and pour over the ingredients in the baking dish. Cover and bake in a 350° F. oven for 35 minutes. The liquid should be reduced to half by this time; if it is not, bake for a few minutes longer without a cover.

Beat the eggs until they are lemon colored, add the milk and beat again. Pour this over the lamb and eggplant. Reduce the oven heat to 250° F. and bake for an additional 35 minutes, or until the eggs have formed a custard on top of the dish. Serve piping hot.

LAMB CAKES

1 pound ground lamb
½ cup cooked rice
1 tablespoon dehydrated onion
1 tablespoon dehydrated parsley
½ teaspoon celery seed
½ teaspoon salt
4 twists of pepper mill
1 teaspoon dried mint leaves, crushed
2 eggs
½ cup flour
1 teaspoon water
Deep fat for frying

Mix the lamb, rice, onion, parsley, celery seed, salt, pepper and mint leaves very thoroughly. Set aside while you prepare the following dough:

Break the eggs into the flour, add the water, and knead and work until you have a stiff dough. If the eggs are large you may have to add a little more flour. On a floured pastry cloth, roll out the dough until it is about 1/16" thick. With a tumbler or round cookie cutter, cut circles. Place a tablespoonful of the lamb mixture in the center of half the circles, then place another circle on top of each. Press the edges tightly to seal each double circle.

Meanwhile, heat the frying oil to 350° F. Drop in each little cake individually. As soon as each is golden brown, remove it and place it in a warm oven until the others are fried. These cakes are delicious served with a salad. They can also be prepared in advance and refrigerated or frozen.

LAMBURGERS WITH LEMON SAUCE

4 large carrots
2 stalks celery
2 large onions
½ teaspoon salt
¼ teaspoon pepper
2 pounds ground lamb
1 egg (for the meat balls)
2 tablespoons flour
3 egg yolks
1 tablespoon cold water
⅓ cup fresh lemon juice

Chop the carrots, celery and onions until they are about the consistency of cole slaw. Cover with water and place over low heat to simmer. Add the salt and pepper to the lamb; stir in the unbeaten egg; mix very well. Dipping hands in cold water, form into meat balls about the size of a walnut.

When the vegetables have simmered so that the celery and onions are clear and transparent, drop in the meat balls one at a time. Raise the heat if necessary so that the balls will not lose their shape upon contact with the liquid. Continue to simmer for 30 minutes.

Drain the liquid from the meat balls and vegetables and place them on a heated platter in a 200° F. oven. Take 2 tablespoons of the liquid and stir the flour into it until it is a smooth paste; gradually stir the flour mixture into the remainder of the meat-vegetable liquid. Cook until it is thickened.

Beat the egg yolks until they are lemon colored; gradually add the water and the lemon juice and continue to beat until frothy. Pour into the thickened sauce very gradually; stir constantly while adding. Remove from the heat and pour over the meat balls and vegetables.

Serve with plain boiled potatoes.

LAMB SHISH KABOBS

Meat Balls

2 pounds ground lamb
2 eggs, well beaten
2 cloves garlic or 1 tablespoon garlic juice
1 teaspoon salt
¼ teaspoon pepper

Marinade

2 tablespoons grated onion
1 tablespoon vinegar
Juice of 1 lemon
1 teaspoon grated lemon rind
¼ teaspoon cloves
2 bay leaves
½ cup water
½ cup red wine (preferably Burgundy)

Accompaniments

1 #2 can boiled potatoes, drained
1 #2 can boiled onions, drained
4 tomatoes, cut into wedges
2 green peppers, sliced lengthwise

Mix the lamb with the eggs, garlic, salt and pepper. Form into 1½" meat balls. Have a kettle of boiling water ready; as you finish each meat ball, drop it into the boiling water for a few seconds. This will make the meat balls firm enough to put on the skewers.

Put all of the marinade ingredients except the wine in a small saucepan. Bring to a boil and remove from stove to cool. Then add the wine. Strain the marinade into a shallow dish large enough to hold all the meat balls. Add the meat balls to the marinade and roll them back and forth gently so that they all become well coated. Let them stand in the marinade in a cool place for 1 hour.

Slip a meat ball on the skewer; follow with a potato, an onion, a tomato and a slice of green pepper, folded in half. Repeat until all of the ingredients are used up. Place skewers on a broiling rack and broil. Turn during the broiling so that all the meat is evenly browned. Serve immediately.

LAMBURGERS WITH FRESH CRANBERRIES

2 pounds ground lamb
1 egg, beaten slightly
½ teaspoon salt
4 twists of pepper mill
⅛ teaspoon rosemary
2 cups fresh cranberries
½ cup sugar
2 tablespoons lemon juice
1 teaspoon grated lemon rind
1 small onion, minced
2 cups precooked rice
2 cups water

Mix the ground lamb with the egg, salt, pepper and rosemary. Form into 8 patties, and sauté in a deep skillet until they are brown on both sides. Drain off any excess drippings.

In a separate saucepan place the cranberries, sugar, lemon juice, lemon rind and onion. Cook over low heat until the cranberries are tender. Add this mixture to the lamb patties and simmer for 8 minutes longer.

Bring the water to a boil and add the rice. Cook for 5 minutes or until all the kernels are separated and tender. Place the hot rice on a platter and top with the lamb patty-cranberry mixture.

LAMBURGERS, INDIAN STYLE

1½ pounds ground lamb
1 teaspoon salt
1 tablespoon olive oil
2 onions, cut into ⅛" slices
¼ teaspoon cumin
¼ teaspoon ginger
¼ teaspoon paprika
½ teaspoon coriander
¼ teaspoon tumeric
¼ teaspoon nutmeg
1 #2 can tomatoes
½ cup sour cream

Mix the ground lamb and the salt thoroughly. Form into 2" diameter meat patties, and brown in the olive oil until a rich deep brown. Turn down the heat and add the onions, all of the spices and the tomatoes. Simmer for 45 minutes. Cover during this time.

Stir 2 tablespoons of the gravy from the meat balls into the sour cream, then mix the sour cream with the rest of the gravy. Simmer for an additional 8 minutes. Turn the meat patties over from time to time so that they are all coated with the gravy. Serve with noodles, rice or riced potatoes.

PATLIJAN A LA NAZ

2 medium-sized eggplants
2 tablespoons salt
1 pound ground lamb
½ cup chopped parsley
½ teaspoon salt
¼ teaspoon pepper
10 slices onion ¼" thick
5 slices bacon, cut in half
1 #2 can tomatoes

Do not peel the eggplants. Cut 1" off the bottom and the top and discard. Cut each eggplant into 5 uniform slices. Place the eggplant slices in a shallow dish and sprinkle with the salt. Let stand for at least 1 hour, or until the slices are soft.

Mix the lamb with the parsley, salt and pepper. Form into 10 uniform patties about the same size as the eggplant slices. Drain the water accumulation from the eggplant. Wipe each slice with a cloth and then place in a flat greased baking dish. On top of each slice of eggplant put a slice of onion. Place a lamb patty on top of the onion. Press down the edges on the eggplant. Put a half slice of bacon over each lamb patty. Distribute the tomatoes and their juice around the eggplant-lamb rings. Bake in a 350° F. oven for 1 hour and 45 minutes.

Chapter XI

VIVA ITALIA

THE UNITED STATES owes Italy many debts of gratitude. Among other things, they have sent us wonderful people, wonderful music—and wonderful food. Every American housewife has at least one prized recipe for a macaroni dish; and the impact pizza has had on American eating habits is a phenomenon of the postwar period.

Most Italian recipes feature *pasta,* or macaroni, a generic term which includes spaghetti and noodles as well as many different varieties of macaroni itself. By last count there were about 160 types of macaroni. Naturally even the larger supermarkets do not handle them all; they feature only the types that are most popular. If you want to go all out for Italian cooking, and need the more unusual shapes of macaroni, you can probably find them in an Italian specialty store.

Cooking macaroni is an art. Nothing in the world can ruin a good Italian dish more than overcooked macaroni. You should use 3 quarts of slightly salted water to each half pound of macaroni. Have the water boiling rapidly before adding the macaroni; boil for 5 minutes, and then start testing. The macaroni should be firm when you bite it. Naturally, the thinner the shape of the particular variety of macaroni you are using, the shorter the cooking time. For instance, spaghettini (thin spaghetti) will require less cooking time than a heavier kind of *pasta.*

Many cooks ruin good macaroni by rinsing it in cold water after cooking. Never, never do this. The macaroni will get chilled, and when you mix it with the sauce there will be a congealing action that will destroy the flavor of the whole dish. If you want to stop the cooking action, pour a cup or two of cold water into the boiling macaroni. Then drain at once and cover with the proper sauce.

RICE, HAMBURGER AND ZUCCHINI

1 tablespoon olive oil
1 pound ground chuck
1 small onion, chopped very fine
3 potatoes, peeled and diced
4 medium zucchini squash, cut in ¼" slices
2 stalks celery, sliced fine
2 cups precooked rice
2 cups water
1 #2 can kidney beans, drained
½ cup Parmesan cheese

Put the olive oil in a deep saucepan with a tight-fitting cover. Sauté the ground meat until it is brown, then add the onion, potatoes, squash and celery. Cover tightly and cook for 8 minutes, or until the potatoes are done. Add the rice and the water; stir so that all is well mixed. Cover tightly and place over low heat for 8 minutes. Then remove from the heat and stir in the kidney beans. Set aside for 5 minutes. There will be enough heat in the rice mixture to heat the beans.

Place on a heated platter and sprinkle the cheese over the top. Serve immediately.

ITALIAN RICE

3 tablespoons butter
½ pound ground chuck
1 tablespoon dehydrated onion
2 cups precooked rice
2 cups beef bouillon
Pinch of saffron
½ teaspoon salt
¼ teaspoon pepper
Butter for dotting
½ cup Parmesan cheese

Place the 3 tablespoons of butter in the bottom of a deep saucepan with a tight-fitting cover. Melt the butter and add the meat. Sauté until the meat is brown. Add the onion, and stir in the rice just as it comes from the package. Cook, uncovered, for 5 minutes.

Add the bouillon, saffron, salt and pepper. Turn the heat to low and cook, covered, for 5 minutes, or until all the liquid is absorbed. Put the rice and meat on a hot platter, dot with a little butter and sprinkle the cheese over the top.

Serve piping hot, garnished with sprigs of parsley.

HAMBURGER SCALLOPINE

1 pound ground chuck
1 pound ground veal
1 egg, slightly beaten
½ cup bread crumbs
½ teaspoon salt
¼ teaspoon nutmeg
1 teaspoon sugar
¼ teaspoon pepper
1 tablespoon paprika
2 tablespoons butter or margarine
1 clove garlic, minced
2 medium-sized onions, sliced
1 4-ounce can mushroom stems and pieces
Juice of 1 lemon
1 8-ounce can tomato sauce
1 teaspoon dry mustard
¼ teaspoon thyme
2 tablespoons parsley, chopped

Mix the chuck and veal; add the slightly beaten egg and the bread crumbs. Add the salt, nutmeg, sugar and pepper. Mix all very well. Form into 8 meat patties. Sprinkle each side of the patties with paprika. Melt the butter in a large skillet. Brown the meat patties on each side. Then add the garlic, onions and mushrooms; continue to cook until the onions are glazed and transparent.

Mix the lemon juice with the tomato sauce; add the mustard and thyme. Pour the sauce over the meat patties and cook for 35 minutes. Keep the skillet covered during this period. If the sauce gets too thick, add a little water from time to time.

Garnish with the parsley and serve with boiled potatoes.

MACARONI AND MEAT BALLS

3 tablespoons butter
1 pound ground chuck
1 tablespoon dehydrated onion
3 tablespoons flour
1½ cups milk
½ teaspoon salt
¼ teaspoon nutmeg
3 tablespoons Parmesan-Romano cheese
2 egg yolks, beaten with 1 tablespoon water
1 8-ounce package elbow macaroni
3 quarts rapidly boiling slightly salted water

Melt the butter in a skillet; add the ground meat and the dehydrated onion. Cook until the meat is slightly browned and well separated. Remove the meat from the butter by straining it. Return the butter to the skillet.

Over very low heat, add the flour to the butter and stir until it is smooth. Add the milk, salt and nutmeg. Cook over low heat, stirring constantly until it is thick. This should be a rather heavy-bodied cream sauce. Remove from the heat and allow to cool. Then stir in the egg yolks and cheese. Add the browned meat to the sauce.

Put the macaroni in the water. Cook for 10 minutes, or until tender. Drain and place in a greased casserole dish. Pour the meat sauce over the macaroni and place in a 350° F. oven for 20 minutes. Serve immediately.

PIZZA WITH HAMBURGER

1 pound hamburger
1 onion, cut into ¼" slices
1 can tomato paste
2 tablespoons water
½ teaspoon salt
¼ teaspoon pepper
½ teaspoon oregano

Dough

2 cups biscuit mix
¾ cup milk
⅛ teaspoon salt
½ cup grated Parmesan cheese
2 tablespoons olive oil

Mix the hamburger with the onion, tomato paste, water, salt, pepper and oregano. Set aside for a few minutes to allow flavors to blend.

Mix the biscuit dough with the milk and ⅛ teaspoon salt. Divide the dough in half. On a floured board, roll out the 2 pieces of dough large enough to fit 9" cake tins. Grease the cake tins, place the dough in them and cover the tops with forkfuls of the meat mixture. Sprinkle the cheese over the top, and sprinkle a tablespoonful of olive oil on each pie. Bake in a preheated 400° F. oven for 25 minutes, or until the crust is golden brown. Serve piping hot.

LASAGNE #1

2 tablespoons olive oil
1 pound ground chuck
½ cup minced onion
1 #2 can tomatoes
1 6-ounce can tomato paste
1 cup water
½ teaspoon salt
¼ teaspoon pepper
1 teaspoon light brown sugar
1 pound lasagne
6 quarts rapidly boiling slightly salted water
1 cup large-curd creamed cottage cheese
6 3" slices mozzarella cheese, cut into 1" squares
½ cup grated Parmesan cheese

Place the olive oil in the bottom of a deep kettle with a tight-fitting cover. Heat oil and add the chuck. Sauté until the meat is brown and well separated. Add the onion and continue to cook until it becomes transparent. Add the tomatoes, tomato paste, water, salt, pepper and sugar. Stir all very well and bring to a simmer. Let simmer for 35 minutes. Stir from time to time to prevent any sticking to the bottom of the pan.

Meanwhile, cook the lasagne in the 6 quarts of water for about 15 minutes, or until you can break off a piece of the lasagne with the side of a fork. Remove from heat and drain. Allow to cool. Grease an oblong, 3" deep baking dish. Remove meat sauce from stove. Allow to cool.

Cover the bottom of the baking dish with a couple of spoonfuls of the meat sauce; top with strips of lasagne. Place 3 or 4 tablespoonfuls of the cottage cheese on next; distribute a few squares of the mozzarella, sprinkle on a little of the Parmesan. Now add 3 more tablespoonfuls of the meat sauce. Cover with a layer of lasagne, and continue layering in the same sequence until all the ingredients are used up. The final layer should be meat sauce.

Place the baking dish, uncovered, in a 350° F. oven for 40 minutes. After removing from oven, allow lasagne to cool for at least 15 minutes; otherwise all the layers will run together.

This dish can be made ahead of time and reheated by placing in a 350° F. oven for 30 minutes. It freezes well, too.

LASAGNE #2

1 pound Italian sausage
1 pound ground chuck
1 clove garlic, minced
½ teaspoon sweet basil
2 large onions, diced
2 stalks celery, diced
1 10½-ounce can minestrone soup
1 6-ounce can tomato paste
1½ cups water
½ teaspoon salt
¼ teaspoon pepper
1 pound lasagne
6 quarts rapidly boiling slightly salted water
½ pound white goat's milk cheese (cream style), or substitute ½ pound large-curd creamed cottage cheese, broken up
1 cup grated Parmesan cheese

Remove the casings from the sausage and place it in a deep kettle. Sauté the sausage meat until it is golden brown; then add the chuck. Cook together until the chuck loses its reddish color. Add the garlic, basil, onions and celery and continue to cook until the onion is transparent. Add the soup, tomato paste, water, salt and pepper. Simmer for 30 minutes.

Meanwhile, cook the lasagne in the water until it is tender enough for you to cut it against the side of the kettle with a fork. Remove from the heat and drain, but do not rinse.

Place a layer of lasagne over the bottom of a large rectangular buttered baking dish about 3″ deep. On this sprinkle 2 tablespoonfuls of each cheese. Add a few spoonfuls of the hot meat sauce, then another layer of lasagne. Continue to repeat these layers until you have used up all of the lasagne. End with meat sauce on top; do not top with lasagne or the top layer will become tough in the baking.

Place in a 350° F. oven for 40 minutes. Remove from the oven and let cool for at least 15 minutes so that the cheese can set firmly. Cut into squares and serve.

HAMBURGER AND RICE WITH ARTICHOKES

3 tablespoons butter
½ pound ground chuck
½ pound Italian sausage
1 large onion, chopped very fine
1 8-ounce can mushroom stems and pieces
1 package frozen artichoke hearts
1 package frozen peas
1 tablespoon dehydrated parsley
½ teaspoon salt
¼ teaspoon pepper
1 cup precooked rice
1 can chicken gumbo soup
1 soup can water
½ cup buttered bread crumbs
½ cup Parmesan cheese

Melt the butter in a deep kettle with a tight-fitting cover. Add the ground meat and the sausage, after removing its casings. Sauté until the meat is golden brown. Add the onion, mushrooms, artichoke hearts, peas, parsley, salt and pepper Cover and simmer for 8 minutes. Remove from heat.

Stir in the rice, soup and water. Place all in a greased casserole and cover with aluminum foil. Bake in a 375° F. oven for 20 minutes. All the liquid should be absorbed by this time. If it is not, return the casserole to the oven for a few minutes longer.

Mix the bread crumbs and the cheese together. Remove the foil from the casserole and sprinkle the bread crumbs and cheese over the top. Return to the oven for 5 minutes longer, or until the bread crumb and cheese mixture has turned golden brown. Serve immediately.

PASTITSO

Although Pastitso is really a Greek dish, because of its ingredients, it fits perfectly into the "Viva Italia" category.

2 pounds ground chuck
¾ pound butter
¼ cup diced onion
1 cup warm water
4 tablespoons tomato paste
1 12-ounce package macaroni
6 quarts rapidly boiling, slightly salted water
½ pound grated cheese; feta if you can get it, but mild American may be substituted
4 cups scalded milk
2 tablespoons cornstarch
2 tablespoons water
9 eggs, beaten until they are lemon colored
1 teaspoon salt
¼ teaspoon pepper
¼ teaspoon cinnamon

Brown the ground meat in two tablespoons of the butter. Add the onion and continue to cook until slightly glazed. Add the cup of water and tomato paste; cook for 5 minutes longer. Set aside to cool.

Boil the macaroni in the slightly salted water. Cook until it is nearly done. It should be a little on the tough side. Drain, and add ¼ pound of butter to the hot macaroni; stir in 5 tablespoonfuls of the cheese. Set aside until you make the sauce.

Melt the remaining butter in the hot milk. Mix the cornstarch with the two tablespoons of water and work into a paste. Stir this into the hot milk and butter and cook over a very low heat until thickened. Set aside to cool. Stir the eggs into the cooled cream sauce. Add the rest of the grated cheese, the salt, pepper and cinnamon.

Mix the hamburger and the macaroni together. Put half of this mixture into a 2-quart casserole. Pour half of the cream sauce and cheese over it. Add the rest of the macaroni and meat. Pour the remainder of the cream sauce over the top. Bake in a 350° F. oven for 1 hour. Serve piping hot.

SPAGHETTI WITH MEAT BALLS

Meat Balls

1 pound ground chuck (double ground, if your butcher will do it)
1 cup white-bread crumbs (do not use crusts), soaked in ½ cup water
1 tablespoon minced onion
1 clove garlic, minced
1 tablespoon chopped fresh parsley or 1 tablespoon dehydrated parsley
2 teaspoons salt
2 eggs
4 tablespoons olive oil

Sauce

2 medium-sized onions, peeled and sliced very thin
1 #2 can small Italian tomatoes
1 6-ounce can tomato paste
¾ cup warm water
2 tablespoons light brown sugar
¼ teaspoon basil
Pinch of thyme
Pinch of rosemary
Pinch of oregano
½ teaspoon salt
¼ teaspoon pepper

Spaghetti

1 pound spaghetti or spaghettini
6 quarts rapidly boiling slightly salted water
½ cup Parmesan cheese

Place the ground meat in a good-sized mixing bowl. Add the soaked bread crumbs (do not squeeze or drain). Add the onion, garlic, parsley and salt. Beat the eggs until they are lemon colored, and stir into the meat mixture. After dipping your hands in flour, form meat into balls about the size of golf balls. You should have about 12 of them.

Heat the olive oil in a skillet and brown the meat balls. (If you shake the pan from time to time they will stay nice and round.) After they are all browned, remove from the oil with a slotted spoon and set aside in a warm place.

To the olive oil which remains in the pan, add the slices of onion and cook until they are transparent. Then add the tomatoes, tomato paste, warm water and brown sugar. Stir and bring up to a simmer. Now add the basil, thyme, rosemary, oregano, salt and pepper and cover tightly. Let simmer for 45 minutes. At the end of this time, add the meat balls and cook for another 20 minutes.

Cook the spaghetti in the 6 quarts of water. Be sure it does not overcook. When done to the bite test, drain and place on a heated platter. Pour the meat balls and sauce over the mound of spaghetti. Serve the Parmesan cheese on the side as an additional garnish.

SPAGHETTI

4 strips very lean bacon, cut in ¼" pieces
1 pound ground chuck
3 onions, cut into ¼" slices
2 stalks celery, cut into ¼" pieces
2 carrots, diced
1 6-ounce can tomato paste
1 can chicken gumbo soup
½ cup white wine (optional)
2 cloves garlic, sliced very thin
½ teaspoon salt
4 twists of pepper mill
1 pinch of thyme
1 cup water or meat stock
1 pound spaghetti
6 quarts of rapidly boiling, slightly salted water
½ cup grated Parmesan-Romano cheese

Place the diced bacon in a deep skillet and brown. Add the ground chuck and continue to cook until it loses its reddish color. Add the onions, celery and carrots and continue to sauté until the onions and celery are glazed and transparent.

Add the tomato paste and soup. Then add the wine, garlic, salt, pepper, thyme and water or meat stock. Stir all very well, and let simmer for 45 minutes.

Cook the spaghetti in the 6 quarts of water. After 5 minutes of cooking, test spaghetti by biting one of the strands. Do not overcook. Drain the spaghetti, place on a heated platter, and pour the meat sauce over it. Sprinkle the cheese over the top. Serve immediately.

SPAGHETTI #2

This dish can be prepared far ahead of time and popped into the oven when needed. It freezes well, too, so it is a good one to have on hand when you're pressed for time.

1 tablespoon olive oil
1 pound ground chuck
1 small onion, chopped very fine
2 tablespoons catsup
1 8-ounce can mushroom stems and pieces (do not drain)
12 pitted black olives, sliced
1 can cream of mushroom soup
1 cup water
1 pound spaghetti
6 quarts rapidly boiling slightly salted water
½ cup buttered bread crumbs
3 tablespoons grated Parmesan cheese

Place the olive oil in a large skillet and sauté the ground chuck until it loses its red color. Add the onion, catsup, mushrooms with their liquid, black olives, soup and 1 cup of water. Bring to a simmer and continue to simmer while you are cooking the spaghetti.

Put the spaghetti in the 6 quarts of water. Cook for 5 minutes, then test by biting one of the strands. When the spaghetti has become slightly glazed and just a little tough to the taste, drain it and place it in a large mixing bowl. Pour the meat sauce over the spaghetti and mix together. Place all in a greased casserole dish. Mix the bread crumbs with the grated cheese and spread over the top.

Bake in a 350° F. oven for 40 minutes. The spaghetti finishes cooking during this time; if there is too much liquid left, return to the oven for a little while longer.

SPAGHETTI #3

Meat Balls

1 pound ground chuck
1 pound Italian sausage
2 cloves garlic, minced
½ cup bread crumbs
3 eggs, beaten to a lemon yellow
¼ cup flour
4 tablespoons olive oil

Sauce

2 cans tomato soup
3 tablespoons dehydrated onion flakes
1 cup water
1 teaspoon white sugar
Pinch of basil
½ teaspoon salt
¼ teaspoon pepper

Spaghetti

1 pound spaghetti
6 quarts rapidly boiling slightly salted water

Place the ground chuck in a large mixing bowl. Remove the sausages from their casings and add to the chuck. Add the garlic. Mix the bread crumbs with the eggs and let stand for a few minutes, until they are very soft. Add the bread crumbs and eggs to the meat mixture and mix thoroughly.

Form the meat mixture into small balls, using approximately a teaspoonful of meat for each. Roll them in the flour until they are coated. Heat the olive oil in a skillet and put in the meat balls. Shake the pan back and forth so they brown evenly on all sides. Add the tomato soup, onion flakes, water, sugar and basil. Add the salt and pepper and simmer for 30 minutes.

Cook the spaghetti in the 6 quarts of water. Do not overcook. Test by biting one of the strands after the first 5 minutes of cooking. When the spaghetti is done to your taste, put it on a heated platter and pour the meat balls and sauce over it. Serve immediately.

SPAGHETTI #4

¼ pound salt pork, cut into ¼" cubes
½ pound ground chuck
1 clove garlic
1 medium onion, chopped fine
1 tablespoon dehydrated parsley
1 stalk celery, chopped fine
1 #2 can tomatoes
½ teaspoon salt
¼ teaspoon pepper
2 packages frozen green peas
1 pound vermacelli spaghetti
6 quarts rapidly boiling slightly salted water

Place the diced salt pork in a skillet and sauté until it is golden brown. Add the ground meat and continue to cook for 5 minutes. Add the garlic, onion, parsley and celery. Cook until the onion is glazed. Add the tomatoes, salt and pepper. Bring to a simmer and cook for 30 minutes.

Cook the spaghetti in the water. Test by biting a strand to see if it is done to your taste. When it is, remove from heat and add the frozen peas. Let the peas remain in the hot spaghetti and water for 5 minutes, then strain through a collander. Place the spaghetti and peas in a deep serving dish and pour the hot meat mixture over it. Mix lightly and serve.

SPAGHETTI #5

½ pound ground chuck
1 tablespoon olive oil
4 cups water
½ teaspoon salt
½ cup onion, diced into ¼" pieces
1 8-ounce package thin spaghetti elbows
¼ teaspoon pepper
1 10½-ounce can condensed tomato soup

Brown the ground meat in the olive oil and set aside. Meanwhile, bring the water to a rolling boil, add the salt and onion. Add the spaghetti and continue to cook until it is almost done. Do not drain.

Add the browned meat to the spaghetti. Add the pepper. Continue to cook until the spaghetti is tender. Stir in the tomato soup. Simmer for 5 more minutes and then serve.

150

½ pound ground chuck
½ pound ground veal
½ pound ground lean pork
½ cup pignolia nuts, chopped (you can get them from an
  Italian specialty store)
½ cup seedless raisins, chopped very fine
3 eggs, beaten to a lemon yellow
2 tablespoons olive oil
1 onion, diced in ½" pieces
1 clove garlic, cut very fine
1 #2 can Italian tomatoes
1 can tomato paste
¼ cup sugar
1 teaspoon salt
¼ teaspoon pepper
1 pound vermicelli spaghetti
12 quarts rapidly boiling slightly salted water

Mix the chuck, veal, pork, pignolia nuts, raisins and beaten eggs very thoroughly. Form into 1" diameter meat balls. Heat the olive oil in a large skillet; add the onion and garlic. Sauté for 5 minutes. Now brown the meat balls in the olive oil. Shake the pan from side to side to retain their shape and to assure even browning. When all the meat balls are browned, remove to a platter. Set aside.

Remove the onion and garlic from the olive oil with a slotted spoon and discard. Add the Italian tomatoes to the olive oil. Stir in the tomato paste, sugar, salt and pepper. Simmer over low heat for 1 hour. If the sauce gets too thick, add a little water. Twenty minutes before serving time, return the meat balls to the sauce and continue to simmer.

Cook the spaghetti in the water. Do not overcook; the spaghetti should be just tender enough to cut with a fork. Drain and place on a heated platter. Make an indentation in the center of the spaghetti and pour in the meat balls and sauce.

SPICED MEAT BALLS

½ pound ground chuck*
½ pound ground veal
½ pound ground pork
3 slices bread soaked in ½ cup milk
1 egg, slightly beaten
½ teaspoon salt
¼ teaspoon pepper
½ teaspoon allspice
¼ teaspoon nutmeg
2 tablespoons olive oil
1 24-ounce can V-8 vegetable juice
2 tablespoons cornstarch
¼ cup water
6 quarts rapidly boiling slightly salted water
1 pound spaghetti
¼ cup grated Parmesan-Romano cheese

Mix the beef, veal and pork thoroughly. When the bread has absorbed all of the milk, add the egg to it and mix into a thick paste. Add this to the meat and again mix well. Add the salt, pepper, allspice and nutmeg. Mix again. Form into meat balls about the size of golf balls.

Heat the olive oil in a skillet and brown the meat balls evenly on all sides. Add the V-8 juice and bring to a simmer. Let simmer for 30 minutes. Mix the cornstarch with the ¼ cup water and stir into the meat ball mixture to make it thicken. Be careful not to let it stick to the bottom of the pan.

Boil the spaghetti in the 6 quarts of water. Do not overcook; test the spaghetti by biting one of the strands after the first 5 minutes of cooking. When it is done to your taste, drain it and place it on a heated platter. Pour the meat balls and sauce over all. Sprinkle the cheese over the top, and serve.

* You can sometimes find chuck, veal and pork already mixed and sold in a package at the supermarket. If your local store sells it, you can buy it this way and save the trouble of mixing it yourself.

MEAT AND MACARONI PIE ITALIAN STYLE

1 package pie crust mix (enough for a 10″ double crust)
1 cup dry macaroni elbows
1 tablespoon olive oil
½ pound lean ground hamburger
½ teaspoon salt
¼ teaspoon freshly ground pepper
¼ teaspoon pulverized sweet basil
½ cup grated Romano cheese
1 15–ounce can tomato sauce
3 eggs, beaten until lemon yellow

Prepare the pie crust mix according to package directions; line the bottom of a 10″ deep pie plate with half of the mix; set the remainder aside until later.

Cook the macaroni according to package directions; drain and set aside.

Place the olive oil in a large skillet over moderate heat. Add the ground meat and saute until a rich shade of brown. Remove from the heat.

Add the salt, pepper, basil, Romano cheese and tomato sauce. Mix well, and then stir in the cooked macaroni. Mix again and then stir in the beaten eggs. Pour the mixture into the waiting pie crust.

Roll out the remaining top pie crust; make several decorative gashes and place over the meat mixture. Seal the edges well and flute with a fork.

Place in a 350° F. oven for ½ hour or until the crust is a delicate shade of brown. Cool slightly and serve in wedges. Serves 4 to 6.

ITALIAN ESCAROLE

¾ pound lean ground beef
¼ cup olive oil
1 tablespoon pine nuts
1 tablespoon finely chopped raisins
1 tablespoon chopped parsley
¼ cup chopped ripe olives
5 filets of anchovy, finely chopped
½ cup soft bread crumbs
¼ teaspoon nutmeg
2 medium sized heads escarole

Place the ground meat in a skillet with 2 tablespoons of the olive oil over moderate heat. Saute the meat until it breaks apart and is a delicate shade of brown. Remove from the heat and add the pine nuts, raisins, parsley, chopped olives, chopped anchovy, bread crumbs and nutmeg. Mix thoroughly.

Remove any tough outer leaves from the escarole and discard; wash heads thoroughly. Flatten them out, tops down, on paper toweling to drain. Pat them dry after draining.

Divide the meat mixture in half. Place one half in the center of each head of escarole. Bring up the leaves around the meat mixture and tie with white kitchen string to keep the meat intact.

Place the remainder of the olive oil in a saucepan with a tight fitting cover. Place the escarole in the olive oil over low heat. Cover and cook for 10 minutes; then turn the heads over and cook for an additional 10 minutes. Avoid scorching by adding more olive oil if necessary. Serves 4.

RICOTTA AND GROUND MEAT LOAF

1 pound Ricotta (Italian Cottage Cheese)
2 teaspoons finely chopped parsley
¼ teaspoon grated nutmeg
1 egg, beaten until lemon yellow
½ pound ground beef
½ pound ground veal
1 cup fine bread crumbs
¼ cup cold water
2 (additional) eggs beaten until lemon yellow
¼ cup finely chopped onion
2 teaspoons (additional) finely chopped parsley
¼ cup grated Parmesan cheese
¼ cup grated Romano cheese
1 teaspoon salt
¼ teaspoon freshly ground pepper
¼ cup olive oil

Mix the Ricotta cheese, parsley, nutmeg and egg together thoroughly and set aside.

Place the ground meat in a mixing bowl; add ¾ cup of the bread crumbs, water, beaten eggs, chopped onion and parsley. Mix together thoroughly. Add the Parmesan and Romano cheese, salt and pepper and mix again until all is evenly blended. Divide into two portions.

Pour half of the olive oil in the bottom of an oblong baking dish; brush it up along the sides. Sprinkle the bottom of the dish with the remaining bread crumbs. Place half of the meat mixture over the bottom of the dish, making an indentation in the middle to hold the cheese.

Place the cheese mixture in the middle of the layer of meat. Do not get it out to the edges, leave about ¾" border around all the sides.

Place the remaining meat mixture over the cheese; bring it down to meet the first layer. Press tightly all around the edges to seal in the cheese mixture and to prevent it from oozing out during baking. Drizzle the remainder of the olive oil over the top of the loaf.

Bake in a 375° F. oven for 30 minutes or until the surface is a delicate golden brown. Loosen the edges with a sharp knife and invert on a heated platter. Slice in 1" slices and serve. Serves 4 to 6.

ITALIAN MEAT LOAF #2

1 pound lean ground meat (half beef and half veal is good)
1 cup soft bread crumbs
½ cup cold water
2 eggs beaten until lemon yellow
2 tablespoons grated onion
¼ cup grated Parmesan cheese
¼ cup grated Romano cheese
1 teaspoon salt
¼ teaspoon freshly ground pepper
¼ cup olive oil
1 teaspoon fennel seeds (optional)
2 cups mashed potatoes (may be left-overs)
1 tablespoon finely chopped parsley
4 slices Mozzarella cheese 3" x 3" x ⅛"

Place the ground meat, ¾ cup of the bread crumbs in a mixing bowl along with the cold water, beaten eggs and onion. Mix thoroughly. Add the grated cheeses, salt and pepper. Again mix thoroughly. Divide into two equal parts.

Pour half of the olive oil in the bottom of an oblong baking dish. Brush the oil up along the sides slightly. Sprinkle the remaining bread crumbs over the bottom; sprinkle the fennel seeds over the bread crumbs. Press one half of the meat mixture into the bottom of the dish making a slight indentation in the center.

Mix the mashed potatoes and parsley together thoroughly.

155

Place the mashed potato mixture on top of the first layer of meat. Cut the Mozzarella cheese slices in half and place them on top of the mashed potatoes shingle fashion.

Place the second portion of meat over the mashed potatoes. Press the top layer of meat down around the edges to form a seal so that the mashed potatoes and cheese will not ooze out during baking. Brush the top of the loaf with the remaining olive oil.

Bake in a 350° F. oven for 35 minutes or until the top is delicately browned. Remove from the oven and loosen the edges with a sharp knife. Invert the loaf on to a heated platter and slice in 1 inch slices. Serves 4 to 6.

ITALIAN MEAT LOAF (LAYERED)

¾ pound lean ground beef
½ pound lean ground pork
2 tablespoons finely chopped parsley
2 eggs, slightly beaten
1 teaspoon salt
¼ teaspoon pepper
¼ cup olive oil
¼ cup grated Romano cheese
4 slices Mozzarella cheese 3″ x 3″ x ⅛″ thick
2 hard cooked eggs, chilled, peeled and sliced

Combine the beef, pork, parsley, eggs, salt and pepper together in a mixing bowl. Mix thoroughly and divide in half.

Pour half of the olive oil into an oblong baking dish. Brush it up along the sides of the dish to prevent the loaf from sticking. Place half of the meat mixture in the oiled dish; press it flat, making a slight indentation in the center. Sprinkle with the grated Romano cheese. Cut two of the slices of Mozzarella in half and place in the center. Place the sliced eggs, shingle fashion, on the cheese and then top the sliced eggs with the remaining slices of cheese cut in half.

Place the remainder of the meat on top of the eggs and cheese. Press the meat down to seal the edges all around the loaf. Drizzle the remaining olive oil over the top.

Place in a 350° F. oven and bake for 35 minutes or until it is delicately browned. Slice and serve. Serves 6.

ITALIAN MEAT BALLS, CHICKEN LIVER AND GREEN BEAN CASSEROLE

4 tablespoons butter
2 tablespoons flour
1½ cups milk
½ teaspoon salt
2 tablespoons grated Parmesan cheese
1 egg yolk, beaten until lemon yellow
⅛ teaspoon freshly grated nutmeg
¾ pound ground sirloin
½ (additional) teaspoon salt
¼ teaspoon freshly ground pepper
¼ cup olive oil
¼ pound butter divided in 3 equal parts
1 cup chicken livers cut in halves
2 cups fresh mushrooms, sliced
2 10–ounce packages frozen green beans cooked according to package directions and drained well
½ cup coarsely crushed saltine cracker crumbs

Melt the butter in a 2–quart sauce pan over low heat; stir in the flour and continue to stir until a smooth paste. Gradually add the milk and continue to cook and stir until the consistency of thick cream. Remove from the heat and stir in the salt and grated cheese. Gradually add the egg yolk, stirring and beating until thoroughly mixed. Add the grated nutmeg and mix again. Set aside in the sauce pan.

Place the ground sirloin in a bowl and add the salt and pepper. Mix and knead until the seasonings are well distributed. Form into meatballs ¾″ in diameter. Heat the olive oil in a large skillet and saute the meatballs until a rich shade of brown. Turn them with a spoon while browning so that they do not lose their shape. Remove from the skillet with a slotted spoon and add them to the sauce.

Place one of the thirds of butter in the skillet in which you sauteed the meatballs. Place over moderate heat and add the chicken livers. Saute, turning frequently, for 8 to 10 minutes or until delicately browned. Remove with a slotted spoon and add to the sauce.

Place the second piece of butter in the same skillet over moderate heat; add the mushrooms and saute until they are delicately browned. Remove with a slotted spoon and add to the sauce.

Place the last and remaining third piece of butter in the same skillet and add the cooked beans. Saute over moderate heat, turning gently and frequently, until the beans are very delicately browned. Remove the beans with a slotted spoon and add to the sauce and other ingredients. Save any butter remaining in the skillet until later for browning the cracker crumbs.

Gently mix all of the ingredients that you have added to the sauce by turning over and over until the sauce is evenly distributed. Pour the entire mixture into a suitable, lightly buttered casserole. Smooth the top.

Place the cracker crumbs in the butter left in the skillet and saute them over moderate heat until they are delicately browned. Sprinkle the browned crumbs over the top of the casserole. Bake in a 375° F. oven for ½ hour. Serves 6.

PIZZA MEAT PIE *SANS* CRUST

2 pounds lean ground beef
1¾ cups fresh bread crumbs
½ cup finely chopped onion
½ cup finely chopped green pepper
1 egg, beaten until lemon yellow
1 teaspoon pulverized basil
½ teaspoon pulverized oregano
¼ teaspoon pulverized thyme
1 teaspoon salt
¼ teaspoon freshly ground pepper
1 15–ounce can tomato sauce with herbs
4 slices Mozzarella cheese 3″ x 3″ x ⅛″ thick

Place the ground beef in a mixing bowl; add the bread crumbs, chopped onion, green pepper, egg, basil, oregano, thyme, salt and pepper. Mix lightly and add 1 cup of the tomato sauce; reserve the remainder of the tomato sauce until later. Mix until all is thoroughly blended.

Lightly grease a 10″ pie plate. Pat the meat mixture into the pie plate bringing up the outer edges slightly. Drizzle the remaining tomato sauce over the surface. Place, uncovered, in a 350° F. oven for 45 minutes or until the surface has become lightly browned.

Cut the slices of cheese diagonally into triangles and place them over the surface of the meat pie. Return to the 350° F. oven for an additional 8 to 10 minutes or until the cheese has melted and become bubbly. Remove from the oven; allow to cool slightly and then cut into wedges like a pie and serve. Serves 4 to 6.

ITALIAN MEAT BALLS *ALLA* ROMANA

1½ pounds lean ground beef
2 slices enriched white bread cut into ½″ cubes
½ cup milk
1 teaspoon salt
¼ teaspoon freshly ground pepper
¼ teaspoon grated nutmeg
1 egg beaten until lemon yellow
¼ cup grated Parmesan cheese
36 large raisins
¼ cup pine nuts
1 tablespoon olive oil
1 10½–ounce can of beef broth
1 tablespoon lemon juice
½ teaspoon sugar
2 tablespoons cornstarch dissolved in ¼ cup tepid water

Place the ground beef in a mixing bowl. In another bowl, place the bread cubes and pour the milk over them. Mix and beat with a fork until thoroughly moistened and broken up. Add to the ground beef. Add the salt, pepper, nutmeg and the beaten egg. Stir slightly and then add the Parmesan cheese. Mix all together and then knead until the mixture is smooth and evenly colored. Divide into twelve equal portions.

Flatten each portion, and place three raisins and three or four pine nuts in the middle. Bring up the sides and form into a meatball enclosing the raisins and nuts.

Heat the olive oil in a large skillet over moderate heat; add the meatballs and saute until a rich brown on all sides. Turn the meatballs with a spoon so that they retain their round shape. Add the lemon juice and sugar to the beef broth; mix well and then add to the meatballs. Bring to a rolling boil and then reduce the heat to simmer. Cook at simmer for 15 minutes.

Remove the meatballs with a slotted spoon to a deep oven proof platter. Place in a moderate 350° F. oven to keep warm.

Add the cornstarch and water to the remaining broth; stir constantly until thickened. If the mixture becomes too thick, add a little water. When the sauce has become thickened and clear, pour over the waiting meatballs.

If desired, ¼ cup of raisins and a tablespoon of pine nuts may be added to the sauce along with the cornstarch mixture. Serve with plain boiled vermicelli spaghetti or with fluffy mashed potatoes. Serves 4 to 6.

PONTI POLENTA

½ pound seasoned Italian sausage
½ pound lean ground beef
2 tablespoons olive oil
2 cups sliced fresh mushrooms
1 #2 can tomatoes (2½ cups)
½ teaspoon salt
¼ teaspoon freshly ground pepper
¼ teaspoon pulverized oregano
3 cups boiling water
1 cup yellow corn meal
1 cup cold water
1 (additional) teaspoon salt
2 tablespoons melted butter
¼ cup Parmesan cheese

Skin the Italian sausages and break up into bite sized pieces. Break up the ground meat into bite sized dabs. Heat the olive oil in a large skillet and add the sausage and ground meat. Saute over moderate heat until the meat is slightly browned. Add the mushrooms and continue to saute until the mushrooms are slightly browned.

Add the tomatoes, salt, pepper and oregano; mix thoroughly but try not to break up the pieces of meat. Cook over moderate heat until it reaches a bubbling boil. Reduce heat to simmer, cover and cook at simmer for 30 minutes. Stir from time to time to prevent scorching. If the sauce becomes too thick and begins to stick to the bottom of the pan, add a small amount of water or tomato juice.

Meanwhile, bring the three cups of water to a bubbling boil in the top of a double boiler. Mix the corn meal, cold water and salt together thoroughly. Slowly add the corn meal mixture to the boiling water, stirring constantly. Cook until thick; stir frequently. Cover when thickened and smooth.

Bring approximately 2 cups of water to a boil in the bottom of the double boiler. Place the corn meal mixture in the top of the double boiler over the boiling water and continue to cook for 15 minutes.

Spoon the cooked corn meal mixture on to an oven-proof platter; using the back of the spoon, form a well in the center. Drizzle the melted butter over the corn meal and place under the broiler about 5″ from the heat for 5 minutes or until the peaks and ridges just begin to brown.

Remove the corn meal from the oven and spoon the meat-tomato-mushroom mixture into the center well. Sprinkle with the Parmesan cheese and serve at once. Serves 4 to 6.

PARMESAN BEEF SANDWICHES

2 pounds ground beef
2 medium sized eggs, beaten until lemon yellow
¼ cup finely chopped onion
1 teaspoon salt
¼ teaspoon pulverized oregano
⅛ teaspoon freshly ground pepper
1 6–ounce can tomato paste
2 tablespoons grated Parmesan cheese
6 slices Mozzarella cheese 3″ x 3″ x ⅛″ thick
6 ¾″ thick uniform slices Italian bread
2 tablespoons melted butter
¼ teaspoon garlic powder

Mix the ground beef, beaten eggs, onion, salt, oregano and pepper together thoroughly. Form into six patties which are approximately the size of the slices of Italian bread.

Place the patties on a broiler pan and broil about 3″ away from the heat until the top side begins to brown slightly.

Mix the tomato paste and the Parmesan cheese together by beating with a fork. Remove the patties from the broiler and turn them over, browned side down. Place a generous spoonful of the tomato paste-cheese mixture on the top of the raw side of each pattie. Return to the oven for 5 minutes or until the tomato sauce has begun to bubble. Then top each pattie with a slice of the Mozzarella cheese. Turn the oven to 350° F. and return the patties to the oven.

Combine the melted butter and garlic powder; brush the slices of bread with the butter mixture and also place in the 350° F. oven. Bake both the patties and bread at 350° F. for 10 minutes or until the cheese has melted and the bread has been warmed thoroughly.

Place the cheese topped patties on the slices of bread and serve while piping hot. Serves 6.

ITALIAN HAMBURGER AND CABBAGE LOAF

2 pounds lean ground beef
2 cups finely shredded cabbage (cut as finely as you would for cole slaw)
½ cup finely chopped green pepper
1 teaspoon finely chopped garlic
3 eggs
1 teaspoon salt
¼ teaspoon freshly ground pepper
¼ teaspoon sweet basil, pulverized
4 10″ strips thick style bacon
1 6-ounce can tomato paste

Place the ground meat in a mixing bowl; add the shredded cabbage, green pepper and garlic. Mix all thoroughly.

Add the eggs, one at a time, and mix well after adding each egg. Add the salt, pepper and basil. Mix thoroughly.

Pack the meat mixture into a 9″ x 5″ x 3″ loaf pan. Pat down well to expel any air bubbles. Cut the strips of bacon in half the short way and place them diagonally across the top of the meat loaf.

Bake, without covering, in a 350° F. oven for 1 hour. At the end of this baking time, spread the tomato paste, just as it comes from the can, over the surface of the meat loaf. Again place in the 350° F. oven and bake for 30 minutes longer. Remove the loaf to a heated platter and slice into ¾″ slices. Serves 4 to 6.

Note: This loaf is moist and juicy—it's the cabbage that does it. This loaf is excellent hot, and even better cold as sandwich material.

GREEN-RIPE OLIVE AND HAMBURGER BAKE

1 pound lean hamburger
½ cup coarsely chopped onion
1 6-ounce can of mushrooms and steak gravy
1 10½-ounce can cream of mushroom soup
⅔ cup pitted, coarsely chopped green-ripe olives
1 4-ounce can mushroom stems and pieces, drained
1 8-ounce package thin egg noodles, cooked according to package directions and drained
2 cups coarsely grated Mozzarella cheese
½ cup coarsely chopped mixed nuts or pine nuts

Place the hamburger in a large skillet over moderate heat. Saute until it loses its reddish color and breaks apart. Add the chopped onion and saute until transparent. Remove the skillet from the heat and allow to cool slightly.

Add the mushroom and steak gravy, mushroom soup, olives and mushrooms. Mix all thoroughly.

Place half of the cooked noodles over the bottom of a 2–quart buttered casserole. Follow this with half of the hamburger mixture and half of the Mozzarella cheese. Repeat the layers, ending up with the cheese. Cover tightly with foil and bake at 350° F. for 20 minutes. At the end of this 20 minutes, remove the cover, and sprinkle the nuts over the surface. Bake for an additional 20 minutes without covering until the cheese is bubbly and slightly golden brown. Serves 4 to 6.

PART II

INTRODUCTION

TO THE HOT DOG

WIENERS, FRANKFURTERS, franks or hot dogs are the all-encompassing titles given to this most delicious and best-known sausage. Though no one in America needs an introduction to the hot dog, to many people it simply means a wiener in a long bun with mustard and relish oozing from its open side. That is one way to serve this delicious sausage. There are many other ways to use delicious, tasty wieners in cooking; this book will give them to you.

Seasoned ground meat held captive in a casing goes way back into ancient history. Who invented the wiener or hot dog as we know it today is open to claim and debate. One school of thought maintains that it was invented in the 1850's by an enterprising Austrian. He named his sausage "Wien" after Vienna, Austria. There is another school of thought which maintains that the hot dog was invented by an ambitious butcher in Frankfort on Main in Germany at about the same time. He called his tasty sausages "Frankfurters."

The fellow who put the long bun around the wiener came from St. Louis. His brother-in-law was selling hot wieners sans bun at the St. Louis Exposition in 1904. In order to facilitate eating these hot wieners, he furnished his customers with sanitary white cotton gloves. The customers were supposed to return the gloves for laundering so that they could be used over and over again. You know human nature and forgetfulness. The gloves walked.

The wiener salesman took up the problem with his brother-in-law who was a baker. No doubt one hot summer evening they were discussing the pitfalls of owning a business and free enterprise. The dilemma of the walking gloves was brought up, and the baker-brother-in-law came forth with the idea of a long bun to exactly fit that wiener. They tried it, and it worked. Soon after, beautifully-gowned ladies and cut-away-coated gentlemen were strolling arm in arm chomping away on America's new lunch on-the-go—the hot dog.

Where the wiener in a bun really made its big mark, of course, was at Coney Island in New York. The gentleman who put the hot dog into the everyday vocabulary of the U. S. A. was Mr. Nathan Handwerker. When he started his very first "Nathan's Famous Coney Island Hot Dog Stand," people were dubious of a sandwich that cost a mere five cents.

Legend has it that Mr. Handwerker hired a group of handsome, wholesome-looking young men, dressed them in starched white coats, put a stethoscope in each outside breast pocket with just enough of the instrument showing to identify the young man possibly as an intern or young doctor. The legend goes on to relate that all these young men had to do for their wages was to cheerfully munch Nathan's five-cent wiener sandwiches in front of his stand. Naturally, people noticed these young wiener-munching "doctors" and the rumor got around that if the doctors ate and liked the five-cent wiener sandwiches, they had to be good and be good for you.

The rest of the story reads like a success epic. Mr. Handwerker had his special mixture of good beef, spices and garlic. To this day, Nathan's wieners are some of the most delicious and best known in the world.

The wiener is just about 115 years old, and it continues to grow in popularity with each new generation. In the United States we consume 80 wieners yearly per person on the average. That comes to enough wieners to make about three round trips to the moon if they were laid end to end.

When buying hot dogs, always purchase those that have the name of a reputable meat packer on them. Off brands can be off flavor. There are many makers of wieners in the U. S. A. When you find a nationally known or regional brand that is to your complete liking, stay with it to avoid disappointment.

Each meat packer has his own secret formula for making his particular brand of wieners. Flavors vary from brand to brand, often due to the amount and kinds of spices used. They may also vary in the actual type of meat content. One packer may use all beef; another may use a mixture of beef and pork; still another may use portions of beef, pork and veal. However, all packers use only Government-inspected meats and all wieners are made under the most rigid conditions of their particular formula.

The fresh, lean meat that goes into wieners is carefully weighed; then it is finely ground. It is automatically measured after grinding so that each hot dog in your package is uniform. The finely ground, seasoned and measured meat is then put into casings or molds. Then the sausages are smoked for many hours over hardwood fires which often contain hickory wood and apple wood. It is through this slow, patient smoking that the wiener takes on its succulent flavor and wonderful appetizing color.

After smoking, the wieners are cooked again in either hot water or live steam. After this second thorough cooking, the wieners are rapidly chilled and then packaged. Immediately after this chilling and packaging, they are rushed to your local market so that you will always be able to purchase them at their flavor peak. Rest assured that when you buy that package of wieners in your market, you are buying thoroughly cooked meat without a fraction of an ounce of waste.

Hail to the Hot Dog! It is wonderful protein food, equally good for young and old. Wieners contain the same top protein and meat value as very lean steaks and roasts. To be sure you are getting this pure meat, always read the labels on the wieners you purchase. If there has been any filler such as corn meal, wheat or soybean flour used, the packer's label, according to Federal law, must state this fact.

If you have only eaten wieners in the usual bun, mustard and relish manner, try some of the wonderful recipes in this book. Wieners are made from only the purest ground lean meat. They are delicately seasoned and delicately smoked. Above all, wieners are always fully cooked before they reach your shopping cart making them a truly time-saving, economical, delicious source of protein and energy for your family.

Chapter XII

HOT DOG HORS D'OEUVRES

BECAUSE OF THEIR ruddy, inviting color and delicate flavor, hot dogs make some of the most delicious hors d'oeuvres you'll ever have the pleasure of serving.

Since all hot dogs come to you already cooked, preparation time for hors d'oeuvres is cut down to a minimum. Your tray can take on the hues and tones of a painting by the simple addition of olives, parsley, cheese and pimientos.

If you want to tease and please appetites, use hot dogs in making your appetizers; you will rate an accolade of praise from your family and guests.

HOT DOG AND CUKE SPREAD

6 hot dogs
1 5-inch cucumber
¼ cup chili sauce
½ cup mayonnaise
12 slices enriched white bread, crusts removed

Chop the hot dogs until they are the consistency of coarse corn meal. Peel the cucumber, leaving on a bit of the green skin. Cut the cucumber in half lengthwise. Using a teaspoon, scrape away the seeds and center pulp, discard. Cut up the cucumber halves into ½-inch pieces and then chop until the consistency of coarse corn meal.

Combine the chopped hot dogs, chopped cucumber, chili sauce and mayonnaise. Mix well, then spread on six slices of the white bread; top each with another slice of bread. Cut into "finger" sandwiches. Arrange on a tray in layers with wax paper between the layers and place in the refrigerator at least 2 hours before serving. Makes 24 finger sandwiches.

HOT DOG SAUERKRAUT APPETIZERS

¼ cup butter
½ cup onion, finely chopped
1 clove garlic, finely chopped
2 tablespoons parsley, finely chopped
6 hot dogs, chopped to hamburger consistency
1 beef bouillon cube dissolved in ½ cup hot water
¼ cup all-purpose flour
1 #2 can sauerkraut
½ cup all-purpose flour (additional)
2 eggs, beaten until lemon yellow
¼ cup half-and-half cream
2 cups pretzel crumbs, made from crushed cocktail
    pretzel sticks
Vegetable oil for deep frying

Melt the butter in a suitable saucepan. Add the onion, garlic and minced parsley. Saute over low heat until the onion is tender and transparent. Stir in the chopped hot dogs. Mix ¼ cup flour and the bouillon water until it is smooth and free of lumps. Add to the hot dog mixture and stir until well blended.

Drain the sauerkraut; using a sharp chopping blade or a food chopper, chop the sauerkraut until it is very fine and equal in consistency to the chopped hot dogs. Add the chopped sauerkraut to the hot dog mixture. Cook over low heat, stirring frequently, until the mixture is thick and glossy. Remove from heat and cool to room temperature; then place in the coldest part of the refrigerator for at least 1 hour or until firm enough to form into firm balls.

Using the large end of a melon-ball maker, scoop up equal portions of the mixture and form into balls. Roll the balls in the ½ cup flour. Mix the eggs and cream together and dip each ball into it; then roll in the pretzel crumbs until evenly coated. Drop into vegetable oil which has been heated to 375° F. Fry for 5 minutes or until a rich golden brown. Drain on paper toweling. Insert a toothpick or cocktail pick into each ball for easier serving.

These appetizers can be made and fried in advance and then kept warm in the oven without impairing their flavor. Makes approximately 50 appetizers.

GLAZED HOT DOGS

8 hot dogs
1 tablespoon unflavored gelatin
2 tablespoons cold water
1 cup creamy-style French dressing
½ teaspoon salt
¼ teaspoon pepper
1 very large orange or grapefruit (optional)

Cut the hot dogs into 1-inch pieces crosswise and put a toothpick into the center of the 1-inch side of each piece of hot dog. Set aside on waxed paper.

Soak the gelatin in the cold water for 5 minutes or until softened. Place the softened gelatin in the top of a double boiler over rapidly boiling water. Cook over the hot water until the gelatin is completely dissolved. Add the cup of French dressing to the dissolved gelatin, stirring well. Add the salt and pepper. Remove from heat and allow the mixture to cool until it is slightly thickened.

Dip each hot dog piece into the thickened dressing; allow it to drip. Place the glazed hot dog pieces on a flat plate and chill in the refrigerator for about 1½ hours.

To serve, cut the orange or grapefruit in half, and place the halves cut side down on a serving platter. Stick the picks with the glazed hot dog pieces into the orange or grapefruit skin. The red-orange of the hot dogs and the orange or yellow of the fruit makes a very colorful dish. Makes about 30 appetizers.

HOT DOG AND OLIVE SPREAD

½ cup green, pimiento-stuffed olives, sliced 1/16 inch thick
8 hot dogs, finely chopped
½ cup mayonnaise
½ teaspoon powdered mustard
½ teaspoon celery seed

Mix all the ingredients thoroughly. Spread on 2-inch rounds of white bread. This is good as a cold appetizer. If you wish to serve hot, place the spread rounds of bread in the broiler about 4 inches away from the heat until the mixture is bubbly and just beginning to brown. Serve piping hot. Makes approximately 24 appetizers.

HOT DOGS IN EDAM FONDUE

8 hot dogs
1 Edam cheese (approximately ½ pound)
2 tablespoons brandy
1 teaspoon prepared yellow mustard
½ teaspoon horseradish
½ teaspoon Worcestershire sauce
⅛ teaspoon nutmeg
2 drops Tabasco

Cut the hot dogs into 1-inch pieces. Spear each hot dog piece with a colorful cocktail pick and place them in the bottom of a chafing dish or a candle-heated serving dish. Set aside, allowing the hot dogs to warm through.

Meanwhile, peel the wax coating from the ball of Edam cheese. Cut the cheese into wedges approximately ½ inch thick. Place the wedges in the top of a double boiler over very slowly boiling water. Cook until the cheese has melted, stirring occasionally.

After the cheese has melted, add the brandy, mustard, horseradish, Worcestershire sauce, nutmeg and Tabasco. Mix all well and pour over and around the hot dog pieces. Serve at once, keeping the cheese soft and melted over the chafing-dish burner or candle. Serve with rounds of Melba toast or toasted rounds of caraway rye bread. Makes about 36 appetizers.

PINK AND GOLD CLOVER LEAVES

½ cup mayonnaise
1 tablespoon prepared yellow mustard
32 cocktail crackers, approximately 2½ inches in diameter
8 slices American cheese, cut in quarters
4 hot dogs, cut in 8 slices per wiener

Mix the mustard and mayonnaise together well. Place a dab of mayonnaise in the center of each cracker. Place three slices of wiener clover-leaf fashion on top of the mayonnaise.

Place a quarter piece of the cheese on top of the hot dog slices. Put the crackers on a large cooky sheet; bake in a 400° F. oven until the cheese has melted. Serve at once, piping hot. Makes 32 hors d'oeuvres.

HOT DOG CANAPE #1

4 hot dogs
¼ cup grated Cheddar cheese
¼ cup condensed tomato soup
1 tablespoon grated onion
½ teaspoon horseradish
¼ teaspoon prepared mustard
1 tablespoon minced parsley
24 2-inch rounds toasted bread

Chop the hot dogs until they are the consistency of coarse corn meal. Add the Cheddar cheese, tomato soup, grated onion, horseradish, mustard and parsley. Blend all together until well mixed.

Spread on toasted bread rounds. Place on a cooky sheet; broil 6 inches from heat for 5 minutes or until the mixture begins to get bubbly and brown. Serve piping hot. Makes 24 canapes.

HOT DOG CANAPE #2

6 hot dogs
¾ cup grated sharp Cheddar cheese
¼ cup onion, finely chopped
1 egg, beaten until lemon yellow
1 teaspoon Dusseldorf-style prepared mustard
1 loaf snack rye bread

Chop the hot dogs until they are the consistency of coarse corn meal. Add the grated cheese, onion, beaten egg and mustard. Mix all thoroughly.

Spread the mixture on the slices of snack rye and place in a 375° F. oven for 15 minutes or until the cheese begins to melt and the tops are slightly browned and bubbly. Serve piping hot. Makes approximately 36 canapes.

HOT DOG OLIVES

30 very large pimiento-stuffed olives
3 hot dogs
1 3-ounce package cream cheese, at room temperature
1 drop Tabasco

174

Cut the stuffed olives in half lengthwise. Remove the pimiento stuffing and put in a chopping bowl along with the hot dogs. Chop the hot dogs and pimiento until the consistency of coarse corn meal.

Add the cream cheese to the hot dogs and pimiento. Mix together well. Add the Tabasco and mix again. Fill the olive halves with the mixture and fasten together with colored cocktail picks. Chill in the refrigerator for at least 1 hour before serving. Makes 30 appetizers.

HOT DOG SURPRISE #1

6 hot dogs
1 10-ounce can cream of celery soup
1 8-ounce package cream cheese, at room temperature
36 Melba toast rounds or cocktail rye slices

Chop the hot dogs until they are the consistency of coarse corn meal. Add the hot dogs and softened cream cheese to the condensed celery soup; mix thoroughly. Place in the refrigerator for 1 hour to firm up.

Spread the mixture on the Melba toast rounds; place on a cooky sheet. Broil 6 inches from heat until a delicate golden brown. Makes 36 appetizers.

HOT DOG SURPRISE #2

6 hot dogs
1 10-ounce can tomato soup
1 cup grated sharp Cheddar cheese
1 teaspoon horseradish, pressed dry
1 teaspoon prepared mustard
cocktail crackers

Chop the hot dogs until they are the consistency of coarse corn meal. Add the condensed tomato soup to the chopped hot dogs, then stir in the grated cheese, horseradish and mustard. Mix all well. Spread on cocktail crackers. Place on a cooky sheet; broil 6 inches from heat until they are a delicate shade of brown. Serve at once, piping hot. Makes 48 appetizers.

175

HOT DOG DOLLIES

12 slices lean bacon, about 10 inches in length
24 large pimiento-stuffed olives
8 hot dogs
24 round wooden picks
24 small sprigs parsley

Cut the bacon slices in half. Wrap each olive in a half slice of bacon so that the pimiento end is peeking out. Secure with one of the wooden picks by going through from the top to where the two ends of bacon overlap. Set aside.

Cut the hot dogs into thirds crosswise. On one cut end, make four cuts about 1 inch deep into the hot dog so that when it is set on this cut end, the four sections spread out like a skirt. Insert the bacon-wrapped olive in the uncut end. The "dolly" will stand up on the four skirt sections and the toothpick.

Place the dollies, standing upright, on a cooky sheet in a 400° F. oven for 10 minutes or until the bacon is crisp and golden. Insert the sprig of parsley where the bacon and the hot dog meet, like a bouquet.

These appetizers are good either hot or cold and create a real conversation piece at parties. If you want to be especially gay, insert an additional sprig of parsley in the bonnet of crisp bacon. Makes 24 dollies.

CUCUMBER INTRO

1 medium-sized cucumber
4 hot dogs, coarsely chopped
½ cup mayonnaise
1 tablespoon grated horseradish
1 tablespoon minced onion
1 teaspoon paprika

Using the saw-toothed edge of a potato peeler, score the sides of the cucumber leaving it half white and half green. Slice the cucumber into ¼-inch slices.

Mix the mayonnaise, horseradish and onion together. Put a dab of this flavored mayonnaise in the center of each cucumber slice; top the mayonnaise with some of the chopped hot dogs. Sprinkle with the paprika for color. Makes approximately 15 hors d'oeuvres.

DEVILED EGGS SUPREME

6 hard-boiled eggs, peeled and chilled
¼ cup mayonnaise
3 hot dogs, finely chopped
1 teaspoon Dusseldorf-style prepared mustard
6 pimiento-stuffed green olives, cut in half

Cut the eggs in half lengthwise; slip out the yolks and mash with a fork. Add the mayonnaise, the chopped hot dogs and the mustard; mix well.

Using a spatula, refill each egg white half with a heaping portion of the yolk mixture. Place one of the olive halves, pimiento side up, on the top of each egg. Chill in the refrigerator for 1 hour before serving.

If you want to be especially fancy, place the yolk mixture in a pastry tube with a serrated end. Force out the yolk mixture in a wavy design, and then top with the slice of olive. Makes 12 hors d'oeuvres.

PEANUT ROLL-UPS

6 slices fresh white enriched bread
6 hot dogs, cut in half horizontally
½ cup chunk-style peanut butter
½ cup Virginia-style peanuts, finely chopped
½ cup melted butter

Remove the crusts from the slices of bread. Cut the slices diagonally so that you end up with 12 triangles of bread. Spread each piece with peanut butter; sprinkle the chopped peanuts over the peanut butter.

Place a ½ hot dog on top of the peanuts and peanut butter. Bring up two corners of the bread and fasten them around the hot dog with a toothpick. Brush the outside of each roll-up with the melted butter. Broil about 6 inches from heat for 5 minutes or until the outside of the bread is a golden brown. Serve piping hot. Makes 12 hors d'oeuvres.

DOGGIE PUFFS

1 cup boiling water
½ cup soft butter
¼ teaspoon salt
1 cup all-purpose flour
4 eggs
8 hot dogs
¼ cup hot dog mustard relish
1 tablespoon onion, finely chopped
1 tablespoon dehydrated parsley

Bring the water to a rolling boil and add the soft butter. Continue cooking for 1 minute longer or until all of the butter has melted. Remove from heat and allow to cool slightly.

Mix the salt with the flour and add to the butter-water mixture. Beat with a slotted spoon until smooth. Add the eggs, one at a time; beat vigorously after each addition. Drop by spoonfuls, in circles about the size of a quarter, onto a lightly greased cooky sheet. Leave about a ¾-inch space between each circle. Bake in a 350° F. oven for 25 minutes or until they are just slightly browned and puffed up.

Chop the hot dogs until they are about the same consistency as the hot dog mustard relish. Add the chopped onion and parsley and mix all well with the relish.

Halve each puff horizontally and place about a teaspoonful of the hot dog mixture in the center of the bottom half. Replace the top and return the puffs to the cooky sheet. Place in a 400° F. oven for 3 minutes or until the tops are a rich golden brown. Serve at once. Makes about 40 appetizers.

Chapter XIII

HOT DOG SOUPS

WHEN YOU LOOK at hot dogs with cold logic, there is no reason why they shouldn't augment the flavors of soup. After all, they are pure meat, delicately flavored, with nary a speck of waste.

Every soup does not lend itself to using hot dogs, but there are many that do. Some soups are just too strongly flavored and overwhelm the hot dogs. The blander flavored soups seem to be most compatible with hot dogs.

Try some of the recipes in this chapter if you've never "souped up" a hot dog. Then start experimenting with some of your own favorite soup recipes—you will be pleasantly surprised.

The soups in this chapter are all "made from scratch." However, hot dogs can be added to many of the wonderful canned soups one finds on the supermarket shelves. If you are a canned soup fan for those hurry-up lunches, try adding hot dogs the next time. This is an excellent way to up the protein content and enhance the flavor of the soup. Active children with their innate love of hot dogs will especially enjoy the addition.

POLISH BREAD SOUP WITH HOT DOGS

6 cups hot beef stock
6 slices enriched white bread, toasted lightly
6 eggs, poached until just firm
6 hot dogs, cut in ¼-inch slices

The soup stock in this recipe would be seasoned to taste and boiling hot.

Place a slice of the toast in the bottom of each soup bowl. Place a poached egg on top of the toast, and distribute a portion of the hot dog slices around the edge of the bread.

Pour 1 cup of the boiling hot soup stock over the toast, egg and hot dog pieces. Serve at once. Serves 6.

BEAN SOUP WITH HOT DOGS

1 cup dried Navy beans, soaked overnight in water to cover
1 ham bone from the hock end of a ham
1½ quarts water
6 whole cloves
6 whole allspice
6 peppercorns
1 clove garlic, sliced paper thin
1 cup onion, coarsely chopped
½ teaspoon salt
½ cup sliced, pitted ripe olives
8 hot dogs, cut in ½-inch circles
¼ cup parsley, finely chopped

Drain the soaked beans and rinse under cold running water. Place the beans and the ham bone in a 3-quart soup kettle. Add the water. Place the cloves, allspice, peppercorns and garlic slices in a little cloth bag and add to the beans and the hambone. Add the chopped onion and salt. Cook over moderate heat for 2 hours or until the beans mash easily against the side of the kettle.

Remove the bag of spices and the ham bone and discard. Strain the soup through a coarse sieve. Force half of the beans through the sieve and return the remainder to the soup stock.

Add the sliced olives and the hot dog circles. Place over moderate heat for 8 minutes longer, to warm the hot dog pieces thoroughly. Stir in the chopped parsley just before serving. Serve with saltines or croutons. Serves 6.

CORN CHOWDER WITH HOT DOGS

½ cup diced bacon
½ cup diced onion
1 cup water
1 cup raw potatoes, peeled and diced
1 #2 can creamed corn
2 cups milk
4 hot dogs, diced in ¼-inch cubes

Saute the bacon in the bottom of a soup kettle until it is a golden brown. Add the onion and continue to saute until it is transparent and tender. Pour off any excess bacon fat. Add the water and the potatoes and bring to a rolling boil. Turn the heat down to simmer and continue to cook for 15 minutes or until the edges of the potato are transparent.

Add the creamed corn and milk. Simmer for an additional 8 minutes, stirring occasionally to prevent sticking. Add the hot dog cubes just before serving. Serve with saltines. Serves 4.

KIDNEY BEAN SOUP WITH HOT DOGS

2 #2 cans red kidney beans
1½ cups Burgundy wine
1 cup sliced onion
¼ teaspoon ground cloves
½ teaspoon salt
¼ teaspoon pepper
½ teaspoon Accent
1 cup warm water
6 hot dogs, cut in ⅛-inch circles
2 tablespoons parsley, very finely chopped
6 slices enriched white bread
½ teaspoon savory
½ cup melted butter

Drain the kidney beans and place their liquid in a large saucepan along with the Burgundy wine and the sliced onion. Stir in the ground cloves, salt, pepper and Accent. Simmer over low heat for 8 minutes.

Meanwhile puree the kidney beans in a food blender or force them through a fine sieve.

Strain the bean liquid and wine mixture and return to the saucepan. Discard the onions. Add the pureed beans, sliced hot dogs and water. Simmer for an additional 8 minutes.

Brush both sides of the bread with the melted butter and then sprinkle lightly with the savory. Stack the bread slices together and cut up into ½-inch cubes. Spread the buttered bread cubes over the bottom of a shallow baking pan and place in a 450° F. oven for 10 minutes or until they are a golden brown. Stir the parsley into the hot soup and serve piping hot with the toasted croutons. Serves 6.

POTATO SOUP WITH HOT DOGS #1

2 cups raw potatoes, peeled and diced in ½-inch cubes
2 cups onions, diced in ½-inch cubes
2 beef bouillon cubes
½ teaspoon salt
¼ teaspoon pepper
2 cups milk, scalded
1 cup half-and-half cream, scalded along with the milk
3 tablespoons dehydrated parsley
6 hot dogs, cut in ¼-inch circles

Place the diced potatoes and diced onions in a saucepan with enough water to cover. Cook over moderate heat until the potatoes are fork tender. Drain off 1 cup of the potato water and dissolve the bouillon cubes in it. Discard the remainder of the potato stock.

Force the boiled potatoes and onions through a coarse sieve and then add the bouillon water to them; add the salt and pepper and mix well. Gradually stir this mixture into the scalded milk and half-and-half cream.

Place over very low heat; stir in the parsley and the sliced hot dogs; heat for 5 more minutes. Serve piping hot with oyster crackers. Serves 6.

POTATO SOUP WITH HOT DOGS #2

6 hot dogs, cut in ½-inch circles
6 medium-sized Idaho potatoes
3 cups cold water
½ cup flour
4 cups milk
1 teaspoon salt
¼ teaspoon pepper
½ teaspoon pulverized thyme
⅛ teaspoon oregano
½ cup butter
3 cups onion, finely chopped
1 cup half-and-half cream
¼ cup cooking sherry

Peel the potatoes and dice them into ½-inch cubes. Place in a kettle with the cold water and bring to a boil over moderate heat. Cook until the edges are transparent and glazed. Remove from heat and mash the potatoes coarsely in their liquid.

Mix the flour and milk together until smoothly blended. Add to the potato mixture along with the salt, pepper, thyme and oregano. Mix all well and place over very low heat, stirring frequently to prevent sticking. Cook for 8 minutes or until slightly thickened.

Place the butter in a saucepan over moderate heat. When melted, add the chopped onion and cook until onion is limp and transparent. Add the onion and its butter to the potato mixture.

Add the half-and-half; add the sherry, stirring rapidly to prevent curdling. Add the hot dog circles and continue to cook over very low heat for an additional 5 minutes or until the hot dogs are heated through. Serves 6 generously.

BEAN AND HOT DOG CHOWDER

6 hot dogs, cut in ¼-inch slices
2 tablespoons butter or margarine
½ cup celery, diagonally sliced ⅛ inch thick
¾ cup onion, thinly sliced
¼ cup green pepper, finely chopped
2 #300 cans pork and beans (approximately 3½ cups)
2 8-ounce cans tomato sauce
½ teaspoon salt
¼ teaspoon pepper
1 teaspoon brown sugar

Place the sliced hot dogs and margarine in a large soup kettle over moderate heat. Saute the hot dogs until they just begin to get brown. Add the celery, onion and green pepper and continue to saute until the onion is limp and transparent.

Remove the pieces of pork from the beans and discard. Add the beans, juice and all, to the hot dog mixture. Continue to cook over moderate heat. Add the tomato sauce, salt, pepper and brown sugar and mix all well. Cook for 5 to 8 minutes longer or until all is heated through.

Serve in bowls, just as you would thick chili con carne. Serve with saltines. Serves 6.

183

PEA SOUP WITH HOT DOGS

2 cups dried peas
1 large ham bone
12 cups water
½ teaspoon salt
¼ teaspoon pepper
2 cups diced celery
2 cups onions, thinly sliced
1 cup raw potatoes, peeled and diced
¼ cup parsley, finely chopped
8 hot dogs, cut in ⅛-inch circles

Soak the peas overnight in cold water to cover. The next day, drain away the water in which the peas were soaked. Place the peas, ham bone, water, salt and pepper in a soup kettle with a tightly fitting cover. Bring to a rolling boil and skim off any froth which may gather.

Add the celery, onions, potatoes and parsley. Again bring to a rolling boil, then reduce the heat to simmer. Cook for 1 hour or until the peas can be crushed against the side of the kettle.

Remove the ham bone and discard, then puree the soup by forcing through a fine sieve. Return the pureed soup to the heat and add the hot dogs. Cook for an additional 5 minutes. Serve piping hot with saltines or croutons. Serves 6.

SPLIT PEA SOUP WITH HOT DOGS

1 cup quick-cook split peas
4 cups water
1 large bay leaf
½ cup celery, diced in ¼-inch cubes
1 carrot, finely shredded
½ cup onion, diced in ¼-inch cubes
1 clove garlic, cut in half
¼ cup butter
1 teaspoon salt
¼ teaspoon pepper
1½ cups milk
8 hot dogs

Place the quick-cook split peas in a 2½-quart saucepan with the water, bay leaf, celery, carrot, onion and garlic.

Cook over low heat for 40 minutes or until the peas can be mashed against the side of the kettle with ease.

Remove the bay leaf and the two pieces of garlic. Strain the mixture through a sieve, and then force the peas and vegetables through the sieve. Add the butter, salt, pepper and milk.

Mix well and place over very low heat. Cut the hot dogs into quarters the long way, and then cut in half crosswise. Add the hot dog pieces to the soup and continue to cook over very low heat for 5 minutes longer or until piping hot. Serve with croutons. Serves 6.

GERMAN BEEF AND HOT DOG SOUP

1½ pounds beef stew meat, cut in 1-inch cubes
1 tablespoon paprika
2 tablespoons butter
2 cups onion, diced in ½-inch cubes
6 cups water
1 teaspoon salt
¼ teaspoon pepper
1 #303 can tomatoes (2 cups)
3 cups raw potatoes, peeled and diced in ½-inch cubes
6 hot dogs, cut in ½-inch slices
2 tablespoons parsley, finely chopped

Sprinkle the beef cubes with the paprika. Melt the butter in the bottom of a large soup kettle which has a tightly fitting cover. Add the beef cubes and saute them until they are a rich brown color.

Add the diced onion and continue to saute until the onion is transparent and tender. Add the water, salt, pepper and tomatoes. Cover tightly and simmer for 1 hour or until the beef is tender enough to cut with a fork.

Add the diced raw potatoes and cook for 15 minutes or until the edges of the potatoes are transparent and they are fork tender. If the soup has become too thick, add a little more water.

Add the hot dog slices and cook for 5 minutes longer. Serve at once, piping hot. Garnish each bowl with a sprinkle of parsley. Serve with saltines. Serves 6.

HOT DOG AND ONION SOUP

6 hot dogs
2 tablespoons butter
2 cups sweet onion, sliced ⅛ inch thick
¼ cup grated carrot
2 tablespoons all-purpose flour
4 beef bouillon cubes, dissolved in 2 cups boiling water
¼ teaspoon pepper
1½ cups half-and-half cream, heated to just below the
   boiling point

Melt the butter in a 2-quart saucepan. Add the chopped onion and grated carrot. Saute over low heat until the onion becomes transparent and soft. Stir in the flour and blend until smooth. Add the 2 cups of boiling water with the bouillon cubes dissolved in it. Cover tightly and simmer for 35 minutes.

Cut the hot dogs into ¼-inch slices; add to the simmering bouillon and onion. Cook for 6 minutes longer. Take several spoonfuls of the bouillon mixture and stir into the hot cream, then add the hot cream to the bouillon mixture. Add pepper. Mix well and serve piping hot. Serve with saltines. Serves 6.

HOT DOG BARLEY SOUP

8 hot dogs, cut in ⅛-inch circles
⅔ cup barley
6 cups water
½ teaspoon salt
¼ teaspoon pepper
¾ cup carrots, diced in ¼-inch cubes
¾ cup onion, diced in ¼-inch cubes
¾ cup turnip, diced in ¼-inch cubes
¾ cup celery, diced in ¼-inch cubes
¼ cup parsley, finely chopped

Place the hot dog slices, barley and water in a saucepan with a tightly fitting cover. Cook over moderate heat for 20 minutes.

Add the salt, pepper, carrots, onion, turnip, celery and parsley and continue to cook over moderate heat for another

40 minutes or until the carrots are soft and tender. Serve piping hot with saltines. Serves 4. (If this soup is too thick for your family's tastes, a little hot water may be added.)

QUICK HOT DOG SOUP

8 hot dogs, diced in ¼-inch cubes
2 tablespoons butter
2 tablespoons onion, finely chopped
1 10-ounce can cream of celery soup
1 10-ounce can cream of chicken soup
2 cups mashed potatoes; these can be leftovers or the instant type prepared according to package directions
2 cups milk
½ teaspoon salt
¼ teaspoon pepper
½ cup chopped water cress or ½ cup chopped fresh spinach

Melt the butter in a 2-quart saucepan over moderate heat. Add the chopped onion and saute until the onion is limp and transparent. Add the celery and chicken soup. Mix all well.

Stir in the mashed potatoes and add the milk. Again mix all well. Add the salt and pepper and cook over very low heat for 10 minutes or until the mixture is steaming hot, stirring frequently.

Add the hot dog cubes and the chopped water cress. Continue to cook for 3 minutes longer or until the hot dogs are heated through. Do not cover during this last 3 minutes of cooking or the bright green of the water cress or spinach will be lost.

Serve piping hot with saltines. Serves 6.

HOT DOG LENTIL SOUP

1 large ham bone or 2 cups diced lean ham
8 cups cold water
1 cup lentils
1 cup celery, diced in ¼-inch cubes
1 cup onion, diced in ¼-inch cubes
1 bay leaf
½ teaspoon salt
6 peppercorns
2 tablespoons cider vinegar
8 wieners, cut in ⅛-inch circles

Place the ham bone or ham in a large soup kettle with a tightly fitting cover. Add the water, lentils, celery, onion, bay leaf, salt and peppercorns and bring to a rolling boil. Turn the heat back to simmer and cook for 1½ hours or until the lentils can be crushed against the side of the kettle.

Stir in the cider vinegar and the wieners and cook for an additional 5 minutes. Serve piping hot with saltines. Serves 6.

Chapter XIV

SALADS MADE WITH HOT DOGS

SINCE ALL HOT DOGS are completely cooked when you purchase them at your supermarket, isn't it a good idea to use them in salads? If you're tired of adding canned fish or cold chicken or ham to your salads, try adding hot dogs. Not only are they far more economical, but the new taste will please everyone who tries it.

Salads made with hot dogs are a natural for summertime feasting. In summer, most of us are more active than in winter and protein is needed to sustain muscles. You can become a first-class "protein sneaker" if you make your salads with delicious, economical hot dogs. Children who are sometimes very adept at skipping vegetables will become avid salad eaters if you perk those salads up with the addition of hot dogs.

This chapter contains both hearty he-man salads and lighter ones. Again we urge you to experiment by using hot dogs in your own favorite salad recipes.

HOT DOG SHOESTRING SALAD

10 hot dogs
¼ cup onion, finely chopped
1½ cups celery, finely chopped
¼ cup grated raw carrots
¾ cup salad dressing or mayonnaise
1 large can shoestring potatoes
6 large lettuce leaves

Cut the hot dogs up into thirds and then cut each third into shoestring-sized strips. Place the shoestring hot dogs in a mixing bowl which has a tightly fitting cover. Add the onion, celery, carrots and half of the salad dressing. Toss to mix and chill in the refrigerator for at least a ½ hour.

When ready to serve, add the remainder of the salad dressing, the can of shoestring potatoes and again toss to mix. Place a portion of the salad on each of the lettuce leaves. Serves 6.

TOSSED HOT DOG SALAD

10 hot dogs
1 medium-sized head iceberg lettuce
¾ cup chopped tart apple, cored but not peeled
½ cup dill pickle, diced in ¼-inch cubes
¾ cup pitted, sliced ripe olives
¼ cup mayonnaise
¼ cup dairy sour cream
1 teaspoon lemon juice

Slice each hot dog into quarters the long way and then cut the quarters in half crosswise. Each hot dog will yield 8 strips. Break the lettuce up into bite-sized pieces and place in a large salad bowl along with the hot dog strips, the apple, dill pickle and the sliced ripe olives.

Whip the mayonnaise, sour cream and lemon juice together until light and fluffy. Add to the salad greens and the hot dogs. Toss all lightly and serve. Serves 6.

Variations:

Use French dressing instead of mayonnaise for a nippier flavor.
Garnish with 4 hard-boiled, sliced eggs for added flavor.
Add 1 tablespoon drained capers for a flavor variation.
Add ¾ cup American cheese cut in ¼-inch cubes for flavor variation.
Add ¾ cup commercial croutons at the last minute for crunchiness.

REFRIGERATOR HOT DOG AND POTATO SALAD

12 medium-sized salad potatoes
12 hot dogs
2 tablespoons vinegar
1 tablespoon water
¼ teaspoon celery seed
1 tablespoon onion juice
½ teaspoon salt
¼ teaspoon pepper
¼ cup mayonnaise
6 lettuce cups

190

Cook the unpeeled salad potatoes in slightly salted water until they are tender enough to be pierced with a fork. Drain and peel. Slice the potatoes while still hot into ¼-inch slices. Slice the hot dogs into ¼-inch slices and toss lightly with the potato slices.

Mix the vinegar, water, celery seed, onion juice, salt and pepper together. Drizzle this mixture over the potatoes and hot dogs. Turn the mixture over several times so that the flavors are evenly distributed. When cooled to room temperature, cover tightly and place in the refrigerator for at least 2 hours to chill thoroughly.

Before serving add the mayonnaise and mix well. Serve in lettuce cups. Garnish with sprigs of parsley or strips of pimiento for added color. Serves 6.

HOT DOG APPLE SALAD

2 cups elbow macaroni, cooked according to package directions
6 hot dogs
4 medium-sized McIntosh Apples
2 tablespoons lemon juice
4 stalks pascal celery
1 tablespoon onion, finely chopped
1 teaspoon celery seed
¼ cup parsley, finely chopped
1 cup dairy sour cream
½ teaspoon salt
1 teaspoon prepared mustard
6 lettuce cups

Drain the macaroni and set aside. Cut the hot dogs up into ¼-inch cubes. Add to the macaroni and mix well.

Peel and core the apples. Cut up into ½-inch cubes. Drench with lemon juice and set aside for 5 minutes; then add to the macaroni mixture. Cut the celery diagonally into 1/16-inch slices. Add to the macaroni mixture. Add the chopped onion, celery seed and the parsley. Mix all well.

In a separate bowl, mix the sour cream, salt and mustard until well blended. Pour this mixture over the hot dog-macaroni mixture. Turn the mixture over several times until all is well mixed and evenly flavored. Chill in the refrigerator for at least 2 hours. Serve in lettuce cups. Serves 6.

HOT DOG ASPIC

1 tablespoon unflavored gelatin
¼ cup cold water
1½ cups hot beef bouillon or stock
10 hot dogs
½ cup celery, diced in ¼-inch cubes
¼ cup parsley, finely chopped
5 hard-boiled eggs, chilled and peeled
shredded lettuce

Soften the gelatin in the ¼ cup cold water. Dissolve the softened gelatin in the hot beef stock. Stir well until all of the gelatin granules are dissolved.

Cut the hot dogs in half and stand them on end, cut side down, in a 10-inch circular tube mold. Sprinkle the diced celery and the parsley over the bottom of the mold.

Cut the hard-boiled eggs lengthwise and place them around the center "tube" of the mold. Pour the gelatin mixture carefully into the mold.

Place in the refrigerator for at least 4 hours. Unmold on a bed of shredded lettuce. Serve in generous slices. Serves 6.

HOT DOG AND MACARONI SALAD #1

2 cups elbow macaroni, cooked according to package directions
1 8-inch cucumber
½ cup chopped onion
½ cup chopped green pepper
½ cup chopped celery
8 hot dogs, cut in ½-inch cubes
½ teaspoon salt
¼ teaspoon pepper
¼ teaspoon paprika
2 cups mayonnaise
4 hard-boiled eggs, peeled and sliced

Drain and rinse the macaroni in cold running water. Set aside to drain thoroughly.

Scrape the sides of the cucumber with a sharp fork or with the saw-tooth side of a potato peeler, removing just a portion of the peeling. Remove the cucumber ends and slice lengthwise into quarters. Using a teaspoon, scrape away the seeds and pulp and discard. Cut the cucumber into ⅛-inch pieces.

Add the cucumber pieces to the drained macaroni; add the onion, green pepper, celery and hot dogs. Mix all lightly.

Add the salt, pepper and paprika to the mayonnaise. Dice two of the sliced eggs and add to the mayonnaise. Reserve the other two sliced eggs for garnish. Add the mayonnaise to the macaroni-hot dog mixture. Fold and mix lightly. Place in a large serving bowl and garnish the top with slices of egg. Chill in the refrigerator at least 2 hours before serving. Serves 6 generously.

HOT DOG AND MACARONI SALAD #2

1 cup elbow macaroni, cooked according to package directions
1 cup American cheese, cut in ¼-inch cubes
½ cup celery, diced in ¼-inch pieces
1 canned pimiento, cut in ¼-inch pieces
¼ cup green pepper, diced in ¼-inch cubes
8 hot dogs, diced in ¼-inch cubes
1 cup mayonnaise
2 teaspoons cider vinegar
1 teaspoon Worcestershire sauce
1 tablespoon chopped parsley
6 lettuce cups

Rinse the cooked macaroni under cold running water and allow to drain thoroughly.

Place the drained macaroni in a mixing bowl; add the cubed cheese, celery, pimiento, green pepper and diced hot dogs. Mix all thoroughly.

Mix the mayonnaise, vinegar, Worcestershire sauce and parsley together well. Pour this mixture over the hot dog and macaroni mixture. Fold together with a light hand.

Place a portion of the salad in each of the lettuce cups. Chill in the refrigerator for ½ hour and serve. Serves 6.

FRESH SPINACH SALAD WITH HOT DOGS

1 pound fresh spinach, washed and thoroughly drained
2 cups cabbage, finely chopped
1 orange, peeled, seeded and sliced ¼ inch thick
¾ cup celery, diagonally sliced ⅛ inch thick
1 tablespoon grated onion
1 tablespoon parsley, finely chopped
1 tablespoon green pepper, finely chopped
⅓ cup salad oil
¼ cup cider vinegar
½ teaspoon salt
⅛ teaspoon pepper
8 hot dogs, diced in ¼-inch cubes

Using a kitchen shears, cut the spinach into ¼-inch ribbons. Add the cabbage and the sliced orange segments. Toss lightly to mix.

Mix the celery, onion, parsley, green pepper, salad oil vinegar, salt and pepper together. Pour over the spinach and cabbage. Add the diced hot dogs and toss all lightly so that the salad ingredients are coated with the salad oil, vinegar and seasonings. Serves 6.

Variation:

Eliminate the oil and vinegar and use ½ cup French dressing instead.

HOT DOG AND FOUR BEAN SALAD

1 #303 can green beans, undrained
1 #303 can yellow wax beans, undrained
1 #303 can green lima beans, drained
1 #303 can red kidney beans, drained
½ cup onion, thinly sliced
½ cup green pepper, diced in ¼-inch cubes
6 hot dogs, diced in ¼-inch cubes
1 cup cider vinegar
1½ cups granulated sugar
½ cup peanut oil

Place the green beans and their liquid and the wax beans

and their liquid in a large mixing bowl which has a tightly fitting cover.

After draining the lima beans and the kidney beans, rinse them well under cold running water to eliminate all of the cloudy liquid. Let them drain in a collander until completely free of liquid and then add them to the other beans in the mixing bowl. Add the onion, green pepper and the diced hot dogs. Set aside.

Place the vinegar and the sugar in a saucepan and bring to a rolling boil for 2 minutes. Remove from the heat and add the peanut oil. Pour this mixture over the mixture of beans and hot dogs. Mix all well and chill in the refrigerator, tightly covered, for 2 hours. Serves 6 generously.

Note: This is an excellent salad for buffet suppers or for cookouts because it can be made the day before and still taste delicious.

HOT DOG AND LENTIL SALAD

1½ cups lentils, cooked according to package directions
½ cup red Italian onion, thinly sliced
½ cup cubed tart baking apple; cored but unpeeled
¼ cup canned pimiento, cut in ¼-inch cubes
½ cup celery, cut in ¼-inch cubes
8 hot dogs, cut in ¼-inch circles
¼ cup fresh lemon juice
½ cup salad oil
¼ teaspoon black pepper
¼ teaspoon powdered mustard
2 tablespoons dehydrated parsley
12 large sprigs of water cress or 6 lettuce cups

Drain the cooked lentils and allow them to cool to room temperature. Add the sliced onion, cubed apple, pimiento and celery. Add the sliced hot dogs and toss all lightly to mix well.

Mix the lemon juice, salad oil, black pepper, mustard and parsley together well. Pour this mixture over the other ingredients and mix lightly.

Cover and place in the refrigerator for at least 4 hours or overnight. Serve on the sprigs of water cress or in a lettuce cup. Serves 6.

MIXED UP HOT DOG SALAD #1

1 8-inch diameter cauliflower (it should be young and
   tender)
6 hot dogs, diced in ¼-inch cubes
1 clove garlic, finely minced
1 3-inch diameter Bermuda onion, cut in ⅛-inch slices
½ cup green pepper, diced in ¼-inch pieces
1 canned pimiento, cut in ¼-inch pieces
¾ cup pitted green olives, cut in ⅛-inch slices
3 cups shredded iceberg lettuce
1 cup French dressing
¾ cup crumbled blue cheese

Soak the cauliflower in slightly salted cold water for about
2 hours. Drain, then break up the cauliflower into bite-
sized pieces. If there are any thick stems, dice them into
¼-inch pieces.

Place the cauliflower pieces, diced hot dogs, garlic, onion
slices, green pepper and pimiento in a large salad bowl.
Add the sliced olives and the shredded lettuce and toss all
very lightly.

Mix the French dressing and the blue cheese thoroughly.
Drizzle the dressing over the salad greens. Chill in the refrigerator for 30 minutes before serving. Serves 6 generously.

MIXED UP HOT DOG SALAD #2

8 hot dogs
6 slices Italian salami, ⅛ inch thick
1 medium-sized head lettuce
6 strips of bacon, cut in ¼-inch cubes
¼ cup cider vinegar
1 teaspoon sugar
1 cup hot boiled potatoes, peeled and diced in ½-inch
   cubes

Dice the hot dogs and the salami into ¼-inch cubes. Break
the lettuce up into bite-sized pieces. Mix the lettuce, hot
dog cubes and salami cubes together by tossing lightly.

Place the bacon in a skillet and saute until it is crisp and
brown. Using a slotted spoon, remove the bacon pieces
from the fat and add them to the salad greens.

Add the vinegar and sugar to the bacon fat and simmer
over very low heat for 3 minutes.

Pour the hot vinegar and bacon dripping mixture over the salad ingredients. Add the hot diced potatoes and toss all lightly. Serve at once. Serves 6.

Variations:

Substitute Thuringer sausage for the Italian salami.
Add ½ cup commercial croutons to the salad at the last minute for added flavor and crunchiness.

KIDNEY BEAN SALAD WITH HOT DOGS

1 1-pound can kidney beans
2 cups celery, finely chopped
½ cup chopped sweet pickle relish
1 tablespoon grated onion
2 hard-boiled eggs, coarsely chopped
2 tablespoons fresh lemon juice
½ teaspoon salt
1½ teaspoons prepared yellow mustard
8 hot dogs, diced in ½-inch cubes
6 lettuce cups

Drain the kidney beans and rinse under cold running water. Drain again and set aside.

Mix the celery, pickle relish, grated onion, chopped eggs, lemon juice, salt, mustard and diced hot dogs together. Add the drained kidney beans. Mix well and place in the refrigerator for at least 1 hour before serving.

Place a portion of the salad in each of the lettuce cups and serve. Serves 6.

Variations:

Substitute a 1-pound can of yellow butter beans for the kidney beans.
Substitute 2 tablespoons vinegar for the lemon juice.
Mix the chopped egg whites into the salad; reserve the chopped yolks for a garnish over each portion.
If you like a thicker salad, do not rinse the kidney beans, but just drain them slightly.

HOT DOG AND BEAN SALAD #1

6 hot dogs, diced in ¼-inch cubes
1 #2 can French-cut green beans, drained
1 #2 can French-cut yellow wax beans, drained
1 #2 can chick peas, drained and rinsed with cold water
1 5-ounce can water chestnuts, drained and thinly sliced
2 red Italian onions or 1 large Bermuda onion; peeled,
  sliced ¼ inch thick and separated into rings
½ cup cider vinegar
½ cup granulated sugar
1 teaspoon Accent
¼ cup olive oil
3 tablespoons soy sauce
1 teaspoon celery seed
½ teaspoon paprika

Place the hot dog pieces, the green beans, the wax beans, chick peas, water chestnuts and onion rings in a large bowl and toss gently so that all the ingredients are evenly mixed.

In your blender or in a fruit jar, place the vinegar, sugar, Accent, olive oil, soy sauce, celery seed and paprika. Blend or shake for a few minutes so that all the ingredients are thoroughly mixed. Pour over the salad ingredients. Chill in the refrigerator at least 2 hours, turning the salad ingredients over several times so that all the flavors unite. Serves 8.

HOT DOG AND BEAN SALAD #2

6 hot dogs, diced in ¼-inch cubes
2 1-pound cans pork and beans
2 cups pascal celery, diagonally sliced
¼ cup diced green pepper
½ teaspoon salt
¼ teaspoon seasoned pepper (available in spice section of
  most supermarkets)
4 tablespoons lemon juice
6 to 8 large lettuce leaves
3 medium-sized red Italian onions, peeled, sliced ¼ inch
  thick and separated into rings

Mix the diced hot dogs with the pork and beans. Add the pascal celery and the green pepper. Add the salt, seasoned pepper and the lemon juice. Mix all together lightly so the beans do not become crushed.

Arrange the lettuce leaves around the outer edge of a large salad bowl, then arrange the rings of onion on top of the lettuce. Pour the bean salad mixture into the middle. Chill in the refrigerator for at least an hour. Serves 8.

POTATO SALAD AND HOT DOG STICKS

12 hot dogs
12 2-inch diameter salad potatoes, cooked, peeled and sliced (about 6 cups)
½ cup pascal celery, diced in ¼-inch cubes
6 green onions, sliced paper thin (use a little of the green too)
½ teaspoon salt
½ teaspoon celery salt
¼ cup radishes, thinly sliced
1 16-ounce carton dairy sour cream
¼ cup French dressing
1 drop Tabasco
3 hard-boiled eggs, peeled and sliced
1 tablespoon parsley, finely chopped

Place the hot dogs in a saucepan with cold water to cover. Place over moderate heat until the water barely reaches the boiling point. Remove from the heat and let stand for 5 minutes. Drain and slice each hot dog into quarters lengthwise and then cut in half crosswise, ending up with 8 "sticks" per hot dog. If you cut them while they are hot they will curl backwards, making a more decorative dish. Place the cut-up hot dogs in the refrigerator to chill.

Mix the sliced potatoes, celery, green onions, salt, celery salt and radishes together lightly. Mix the sour cream, French dressing and Tabasco together thoroughly. Pour this over the potato mixture and again mix lightly so that all of the potato slices are covered with the dressing. Chill in the refrigerator at least 2 hours.

Arrange the chilled hot dog sticks around the outside of a platter. Place the chilled potato salad in the middle and garnish with slices of egg. Sprinkle the parsley over all. Serves 6.

199

HOT GERMAN POTATO SALAD AND HOT DOGS

3 cups cooked, peeled salad potatoes, sliced ¼ inch thick
12 hot dogs
6 slices lean bacon
¼ cup juice from sweet and sour pickles
¼ cup vinegar
4 tablespoons granulated sugar
¼ teaspoon powdered mustard
½ teaspoon salt
¼ teaspoon pepper
3 tablespoons flour
½ cup water
½ onion, diced in ¼-inch cubes
½ cup celery, diced in ¼-inch cubes

Cut the hot dogs up into ¼-inch slices and mix lightly with the potato slices. Set aside.

Dice the bacon into ¼-inch pieces and place in a large oven-proof skillet. Saute the bacon until it is crisp and golden. Lower the heat and add the pickle juice, vinegar, sugar, powdered mustard, salt and pepper. Simmer for 2 minutes.

Mix the flour with the half cup of water until it is smooth and add to the bacon mixture. Stir well and continue to simmer for a few minutes longer until the mixture has thickened and become somewhat transparent. Add the potatoes and hot dogs, onion and celery. Turn the entire mixture over several times so that the dressing is evenly distributed. Place in a 300° F. oven for 15 minutes or until warmed through. Serve at once. Serves 6.

WILTED LETTUCE MADE WITH HOT DOGS

1 pound leaf lettuce (this is usually sold in fan-like bunches,
   but have it weighed so that you have approximately 1
   pound)
1 cup celery, diagonally sliced ⅛ inch thick
½ cup onion, finely chopped
1 cup white radishes, thinly sliced (white is preferred,
   but you can use red)
3 tablespoons butter
2 tablespoons granulated sugar
¼ cup cider vinegar
¼ cup water
1 tablespoon cornstarch
6 strips bacon, cut in ½-inch pieces
4 hot dogs, cut in ½-inch cubes
4 medium-sized potatoes, peeled and boiled until tender
4 hard-boiled eggs, peeled and sliced
4 additional hot dogs, cut in half lengthwise

Wash the lettuce and dry it well. Using a shears, snip
the lettuce up into 1-inch strips. Toss together lightly with
the onion, celery, and radishes.

Melt the butter in a saucepan. Stir in the vinegar and
sugar. Mix the water with the cornstarch and add to the
vinegar mixture. Cook over low heat until it is thickened
and transparent.

Saute the bacon until it is crisp and golden; pour off
half of the fat and discard. Add the hot dog cubes and saute
until slightly browned. Add the vinegar mixture to the hot
dog-bacon mixture; cook over low heat for a few seconds.

Drain the potatoes and break them up with a fork. They
should not be mashed, but left in uneven lumps. Add the
potato pieces to the lettuce, and then pour the hot vinegar-
bacon-hot dog mixture over the lettuce and potatoes. Mix
well; turn the entire salad over in the bowl several times
so that the flavors are well blended.

Place mixture in a salad bowl. Decorate the top with the
slices of egg. Place the hot dog halves around the outside
edge. Serves 6.

JELLIED HOT DOG LOAF

12 hot dogs
1 tablespoon unflavored gelatin
¼ cup cold water
1 cup boiling water
¼ cup fresh lemon juice
½ cup sweet-sour pickles, very finely sliced
½ cup pimiento-stuffed olives, very finely sliced
1 tablespoon onion, finely grated
1 teaspoon prepared Dusseldorf-style mustard
½ cup mayonnaise

Chop six of the hot dogs until they are the consistency of coarse corn meal. Set aside.

Soften the gelatin in the cold water for 5 minutes. Add the hot water and stir until all of the gelatin is completely dissolved. Add the lemon juice. Place in the coldest part of the refrigerator for 1 hour or until thickened.

Beat the thickened gelatin with an electric or rotary beater until it is light and fluffy. Fold in the chopped hot dogs, pickles, olives, grated onion, mustard and mayonnaise.

Place three of the whole hot dogs in the bottom of a loaf pan which has been rinsed in ice cold water. Pour one half of the gelatin mixture over them. Place the remaining three hot dogs over the gelatin. Pour the remainder of the gelatin mixture over them. Place in the coldest part of the refrigerator for at least 4 hours.

Unmold on a thick bed of shredded lettuce. Slice in generous slices and serve with additional mayonnaise which has been slightly flavored with horseradish. Serves 6.

IN THE PINK POTATO AND HOT DOG SALAD

6 medium potatoes, cooked, peeled and chilled; diced in
   ½-inch cubes
6 hot dogs, cut in ½-inch cubes
2 eggs
½ cup sugar
1 teaspoon powdered mustard
1 teaspoon flour
1 teaspoon cornstarch
¾ cup cider vinegar
1 tablespoon butter
1 teaspoon salt
1 cup canned, diced beets, drained

Mix the cubed potatoes and the cubed hot dogs together lightly. Set aside.

Beat the eggs until they are light and frothy. Make a mixture of the sugar, mustard, flour and cornstarch. Add this mixture gradually to the beaten eggs and continue to beat until smooth. Continue beating, and add the vinegar a little at a time. Beat for 1 minute longer. Place the mixture in the top of a double boiler over slowly boiling water and cook until thickened. Add the butter and salt. Mix well and remove from the heat. Allow the dressing to cool to room temperature.

Pour the dressing over the potatoes and the hot dogs; mix lightly. Add the diced beets and mix again lightly. Chill in the refrigerator for 2 hours before serving. Serves 6 generously.

Chapter XV

HOT DOG CASSEROLES

IF YOU HAVE casserole fans in your family, try making them with hot dogs. Due to their total meat content and delicate flavor, hot dogs in casseroles are wonderful.

Hot dog casseroles can be frozen with great success. Make two casseroles at the same time. Serve one and freeze the other for a future meal. This will save you precious time and money.

If you have hit the doldrums when it comes to making casseroles, try some of the delicious recipes in this chapter. If you have casserole recipes that contain meat, try substituting hot dogs the next time you make them, and you will be pleasantly surprised.

Protein packed hot dogs enhance the flavors of casseroles like nothing else!

HOT DOG CHILI PIE

8 hot dogs, diced in ½-inch cubes
1 cup taco-type corn chips, coarsely crushed
1 cup garlic-flavored potato chips, coarsely crushed
1 #300 can barbecue-style beans (1¾ cups)
1 10¼-ounce can chili con carne with kidney beans
⅓ cup warm water
¾ cup onion, diced in ¼-inch cubes
¾ cup mild Cheddar cheese, diced in ¼-inch cubes

Mix the hot dogs, corn chips and potato chips by tossing together lightly. Add the barbecue beans, the chili con carne, the warm water and the diced onion. Again, mix all the ingredients lightly.

Place in a 1½-quart buttered casserole. Press the mixture down lightly. Place in a 350° F. oven for 15 minutes.

Sprinkle the cubed cheese over the top and return to the oven for an additional 8 minutes or until the cheese has melted. Serve at once. Serves 6.

HOT DOG AND CHEESE BAKE

4 slices enriched white bread, lightly buttered
8 hot dogs
1 8-ounce package Velveeta cheese spread
2 eggs, slightly beaten
3 cups milk
½ teaspoon salt
¼ teaspoon pepper

Stack the buttered bread and then cut up into 1-inch squares. Cut the hot dogs into ¼-inch thick circles.

Place ¼ of the buttered bread squares and ¼ of the hot dog circles in the bottom of a buttered casserole. Slice the cheese and place ¼ of the slices over the hot dogs and the bread. Repeat, ending with a layer of cheese and hot dogs as the top.

Add the beaten eggs to the milk. Add the salt and pepper and mix well. Pour this mixture over the bread, cheese and hot dogs. Bake, uncovered, in a 350° F. oven for 1 hour. Serve piping hot. Serves 6.

HOT DOGS AND POTATOES IN ONE DISH

5 cups raw potatoes, sliced ¼ inch thick
10 hot dogs, sliced in ¼-inch circles
2 tablespoons melted butter
¾ cup onion, diced in ¼-inch cubes
½ teaspoon salt
½ teaspoon pepper
2 cups warm milk
1 cup shredded mild Cheddar cheese
8 slices of bacon, fried crisp and crumbled

Place a layer of half of the sliced potatoes and half of the hot dog circles over the bottom of a 2-quart casserole. Drizzle with half the butter and sprinkle on half the onions. Season with half the salt and pepper. Repeat again, using the remainder of the ingredients.

Pour the warm milk over the top of the casserole and bake in a 350° F. oven for 1 hour or until you can pierce the potatoes easily with a fork. Just before serving, sprinkle the cheese and crumbled bacon over the top and place under the broiler for 3 minutes or until the cheese has melted. Serves 6.

HOT DOG AND BEAN BAKE #1

1 1-pound can vegetarian baked beans, undrained
1 1-pound can butter beans, undrained
1 1-pound can kidney beans, undrained
1 tablespoon prepared yellow mustard
1 teaspoon Worcestershire sauce
½ cup onion, finely chopped
8 hot dogs, cut in 1-inch pieces
½ cup dark brown sugar
⅛ teaspoon ground cloves

Mix the three bean varieties together just as they come from the can. Add the mustard, Worcestershire sauce and onion. Mix very well, taking care not to mash the beans. Add the hot dog pieces and turn the mixture over several times so that they are evenly distributed throughout.

Place in a buttered casserole. Mix the brown sugar and cloves together until completely blended and then sprinkle this over the top of the beans.

Bake, uncovered, in a 350° F. oven for 35 minutes. Serve at once, piping hot. Serves 6 to 8.

HOT DOG AND BEAN BAKE #2

2 1-pound cans pork and beans
1 cup diced onion
¼ cup diced green pepper
1 teaspoon powdered mustard
1 tablespoon Worcestershire Sauce
6 hot dogs
6 slices bacon

Drain the beans and discard the pieces of pork. If left in, this makes the dish much too greasy. Add the onion, green pepper, mustard and Worcestershire sauce. Mix well, taking care not to mash the beans.

Place the beans in a shallow baking dish. Wrap each hot dog in one of the slices of bacon, fastening the bacon at each end with a toothpick. Place the bacon-wrapped hot dogs over the surface of the beans. Bake in a 350° F. oven for 35 minutes or until the bacon begins to get crisp. Place under the broiler for 5 minutes to thoroughly crisp the bacon before serving. Serves 6.

HOT DOG AND BEAN BAKE #3

8 hot dogs, sliced ⅛ inch thick
2 1-pound jars New England-style baked beans
¾ cup heavy whipping cream
1 3-inch diameter Bermuda onion, peeled and sliced ¼ inch
  thick
½ cup diced bacon

Distribute the hot dog slices over the bottom of a shallow baking dish. Remove any pork pieces from the beans and discard, for this will make the dish too greasy.

Gently fold the whipping cream into the baked beans, taking care not to mash the beans. Pour this mixture over the wiener slices. Break the onion slices up into rings and place them over the beans. Sprinkle the diced bacon over the top of the onions and beans.

Place in a 350° F. oven for 1 hour or until the bacon pieces have become crisp and the top of the beans have developed a crust. Serve piping hot. Serves 6 to 8.

HOT DOG AND BEAN BAKE #4

2 10-ounce packages French-style frozen green beans,
  thawed
8 hot dogs
8 10-inch slices bacon
1½ cups tomato sauce
1½ cups grated American cheese

Spread the thawed green beans over the bottom of a shallow baking dish. Wrap each hot dog in a slice of bacon; fasten with a toothpick. Place the hot dogs wrapped in bacon over the top of the green beans.

Pour the tomato sauce over the hot dogs and green beans. Sprinkle the American cheese over the top. Place in a 350° F. oven for 25 minutes or until the cheese is melted and bubbly. Serve at once, piping hot. Serves 4.

HOT DOG AND BEAN BAKE #5

1 #2 can yellow butter beans, drained
1 #2 can green baby lima beans, drained
1 #2 can cut green beans, drained
1 #2 can red kidney beans, drained
8 hot dogs, quartered
1 pound sliced American cheese with pimiento pieces

Place the butter beans, baby limas, green beans and kidney beans in a large bowl. Mix all well, taking care not to mash the beans.

In a buttered casserole, place half of the bean mix over the bottom. Smooth out, and place the hot dogs in a layer over the top. Cover the hot dogs with half of the slices of cheese.

Place the remainder of the beans over the hot dogs and cheese. Again smooth them out, and cover with the remaining pieces of cheese.

Place in a 350° F. oven for 35 minutes or until the cheese on top is melted and bubbly. Serve piping hot. Serves 8.

ORIENTAL HOT DOG CASSEROLE

1 #2 can French-style green beans, drained
1 1-pound can Chinese vegetables, drained
1 5-ounce can water chestnuts, drained and sliced ⅛ inch thick
½ cup chopped onion
6 hot dogs, cut in ¼-inch circles
1 10-ounce can cream of mushroom soup
1 cup shredded mild American cheese

Mix the green beans, Chinese vegetables, chestnuts, chopped onion and hot dogs together lightly. Add the cream of mushroom soup and mix again. Place in a buttered casserole. Press the mixture down with the back of a spoon and then sprinkle the cheese over the top.

Bake in a 350° F. oven for 1 hour or until the cheese is slightly browned and bubbly. Serve piping hot. Serves 6.

DOG AND YAM CASSEROLE

6 hot dogs
½ cup crunchy-style peanut butter
½ cup chopped Virginia-style peanuts
1 1½-pound can yams packed in syrup, drained
½ cup currant jelly
2 tablespoons water

Split the hot dogs lengthwise and spread the insides with the peanut butter. Arrange them over the bottom of a buttered baking dish. Sprinkle the chopped peanuts over the wieners.

Cut the yams in half; arrange the halves over the top of the hot dogs.

Mix the currant jelly and water together and pour a portion of the mixture over each of the yam halves. Place in a 375° F. oven for 25 minutes. Serves 6.

LAZY BONES CASSEROLE WITH HOT DOGS

6 medium-sized potatoes, scrubbed but not peeled
4 medium-sized onions, peeled
10 hot dogs
1 #300 can kidney beans, drained
3 strips of very lean bacon, diced in ¼-inch cubes
1 can condensed tomato soup
1 beef bouillon cube dissolved in ½ cup boiling water

Slice the unpeeled potatoes into uniform ¼-inch slices. Slice the onions into ¼-inch slices. Slice the hot dogs into ¼-inch circles.

In a lightly buttered 1½-quart casserole, place a layer of half of the sliced potatoes, a layer of half of the onions. Cover the surface with the hot dog slices. Layer the kidney beans over the hot dogs. Sprinkle half of the bacon cubes over the kidney beans and hot dogs. Repeat the layers, using up the remainder of the potatoes, kidney beans, hot dogs and bacon.

Mix the tomato soup with the boiling bouillon. Pour over the ingredients in the casserole. Cover and bake at 375° F. for 1 hour. Remove the cover and bake for an additional 30 minutes. Serve at once, piping hot. Serves 6.

RED AND GOLD HOT DOG CASSEROLE

12 hot dogs
¼ cup butter or margarine
¼ cup chopped onion
1 4-ounce can mushroom stems and pieces, drained
2 medium-sized boiled potatoes, diced in ½-inch cubes
1 3-inch dill pickle, sliced paper thin
½ cup pimiento-stuffed green olives, thinly sliced
½ teaspoon salt
¼ teaspoon pepper
½ teaspoon Accent
1 16-ounce carton dairy sour cream or sour half-and-half
2 hard-boiled eggs, diced in ¼-inch cubes
¾ cup grated American cheese
¼ cup chopped pimiento
3 medium-sized tomatoes, peeled and quartered

Cut the hot dogs up into ¼-inch circles and set aside. Melt the butter in a large skillet; add the chopped onion and saute until the onion is limp and transparent. Add the mushroom stems and pieces and continue to cook until they are slightly browned. Add the diced hot dogs and continue to cook until they begin to brown on the edges. Remove from heat.

Stir in the diced potatoes, the dill pickle slices, the olives, salt, pepper and Accent. Add the sour cream and turn the mixture over several times to mix well. Place in a 2-quart buttered casserole. Press the mixture down slightly and smooth the top. Sprinkle the diced eggs over all. Sprinkle with the grated cheese and the chopped pimiento. Place the 12 wedges of the tomato around the outer edge. Bake in a 350° F. oven for 30 minutes or until the cheese is melted and bubbly. Serves 6.

FRANK AND POTATO CASSEROLE

8 wieners, cut in thirds
6 medium-sized potatoes, peeled and quartered
2 tablespoons Heinz 57 Sauce
½ cup half-and-half cream
¼ cup melted butter
1 teaspoon baking powder
½ cup grated Cheddar cheese

Boil the potatoes in a small amount of salted water until they are tender enough to pierce with a fork. Drain and mash the potatoes well. Using a wire whisk or an electric mixer, beat in the Heinz 57 sauce and the cream. Add the melted butter and the baking powder and continue beating until the potatoes are very light and fluffy.

Place half of the wiener pieces over the bottom of a suitable buttered baking dish. Top the wiener pieces with the mashed potato mixture. Place the remainder of the wieners over the top of the mashed potatoes. Press them down into the potatoes. Sprinkle the grated Cheddar cheese over the top.

Bake in a 450° F. oven for 15 minutes or until the cheese has melted and become bubbly. Serve piping hot. Serves 6.

HOT DOG AND KRAUT CASSEROLE

2 1-pound cans sauerkraut
12 hot dogs
2 tablespoons caraway seed
6 whole peppercorns
12 juniper berries (optional but nice)
1 8-ounce can tomato sauce
1 cup dairy sour cream
1 tablespoon brown sugar

Rinse the sauerkraut under cold running water. Allow to drain well.

In the bottom of a 3-quart buttered casserole with a tightly fitting cover, place four of the hot dogs. Sprinkle a 1-inch layer of sauerkraut over the hot dogs. Sprinkle ⅓ of the caraway seed, 2 peppercorns and 4 juniper berries over the sauerkraut. Place four more hot dogs over the sauerkraut and follow with another layer of sauerkraut and spices. Repeat, ending with a layer of sauerkraut and spices.

Mix the tomato sauce, dairy sour cream and brown sugar together and pour over the casserole ingredients. Cover tightly and bake in a 350° F. oven for 45 minutes. Serve piping hot. Serves 6.

HOT DOG TAMALE PIE

2 tablespoons bacon fat
1 tablespoon chili powder
1 tablespoon flour
1 teaspoon onion salt
½ teaspoon garlic powder
½ cup water
10 hot dogs, diced in ¼-inch cubes
1 12-ounce can niblet corn, drained
½ cup sliced, pitted ripe olives
2 cups taco-type corn chips, coarsely crushed
½ cup grated American cheese

Melt the bacon fat in a saucepan; mix the flour and chili powder together and then stir into the melted fat. Add the onion salt and garlic powder. Cook over moderate heat until the mixture begins to bubble slightly. Add the water and continue to cook, stirring constantly, over moderate heat until thickened. Remove from heat and stir in the diced hot dogs, niblet corn and ripe olives. Mix all very well.

In the bottom of a buttered casserole, place ¾ cup of the crushed corn chips. Follow this with a layer of the hot dog mixture. Sprinkle with more corn chips and another layer of the hot dog mixture. Continue, alternating the layers, ending up with a layer of corn chips. Sprinkle the grated cheese over the top. Place in a 350° F. oven for 15 minutes or until the cheese has melted. Serve at once, piping hot. Serves 6.

WIENER RICE CASSEROLE

8 wieners, sliced ⅛ inch thick
1 cup instant rice, cooked according to package directions, or 2 cups fluffy cooked rice
2 cups milk
1½ cups cubed mild Cheddar cheese
2 eggs, beaten until lemon yellow
½ teaspoon salt
¼ teaspoon pepper
1 cup pimiento-stuffed olives, sliced ⅛ inch thick
¼ cup melted butter
½ cup fine breadcrumbs

Place the milk in the top of a double boiler over rapidly boiling water. Add the Cheddar cheese and continue to cook until the cheese has melted, stirring frequently to smoothly blend the mixture. Remove from heat and stir 3 tablespoons of the cheese sauce into the beaten eggs; then add the eggs to the cheese sauce and mix well. Add the cooked rice, salt and pepper. Mix very well.

In a suitable buttered baking dish, spread ¼ of the rice mixture over the bottom. Place ¼ of the wiener slices and ¼ of the olive slices over the rice. Add another layer of rice and another layer of wiener pieces and olive pieces. Continue, alternating layers, ending up with the rice mixture last.

Stir the bread crumbs into the melted butter; mix well. Sprinkle the buttered crumbs over the top of the layered rice mixture. Place in a 350° F. oven for 20 minutes or until the top is a golden brown. Serve at once, piping hot. Serves 6.

BAKED HOT DOG DELIGHT

2 #2 cans macaroni and cheese
1 1-ounce bag garlic-flavored potato chips
8 hot dogs, cut in ⅛-inch circles
1 tablespoon chopped green pepper
1 teaspoon Worcestershire sauce
1 tablespoon parsley, finely chopped
¼ cup butter
1 cup soft bread crumbs

Mix the macaroni and cheese and the hot dog circles together. Add the potato chips, green pepper, Worcestershire sauce and chopped parsley. Mix again and place in a suitable buttered casserole.

Melt the butter in a skillet and stir in the bread crumbs. Mix well so that all of the crumbs are evenly buttered. Spread the buttered crumbs over the surface of the casserole.

Place in a 350° F. oven for 25 minutes or until the crumbs are a rich golden brown. Serve at once, piping hot. Serves 6.

HOT DOG, CHEESE, OLIVE AND RICE BAKE

2 cups milk
1½ cups grated Cheddar cheese
2 eggs, slightly beaten
2 cups fluffy cooked rice
½ teaspoon salt
¼ teaspoon pepper
¼ cup parsley, finely chopped
1 cup pimiento-stuffed green olives, sliced ⅛ inch thick
12 hot dogs, halved lengthwise
½ cup buttered bread crumbs

Heat the milk in the top of a double boiler to just below the scalding point. Gradually add the grated cheese, stirring after each addition. Continue to cook until all of the cheese has melted. Stir three tablespoons of the hot mixture into the beaten eggs, and then add the beaten eggs to the cheese sauce. Mix well and continue to cook for a few minutes longer until thickened. Add the salt, pepper and parsley. Add the cooked rice, mix well and remove from heat.

Place 8 pieces of the sliced hot dogs, cut side down, over the bottom of a buttered 9x5x3-inch loaf pan or oblong baking dish. Place ⅓ of the olives over the hot dogs. Pour ⅓ of the cheese and rice mixture over the hot dogs and olives. Follow this with another layer of 8 hot dog pieces, olives and ⅓ of the rice and cheese mix. Repeat with the remainder of the hot dogs and olives, ending with the rice and cheese mixture as the last layer. Sprinkle the top with the buttered bread crumbs.

Bake in a 325° F. oven for 30 minutes or until the crumbs are a golden brown and the loaf is firm. Allow to cool for 5 minutes and then loosen the sides of the loaf with a sharp knife and turn out on a heated platter. Slice in 1½-inch thick slices. Garnish with additional sprigs of parsley for color. Serves 6.

POTATO SALAD CASSEROLE

4 cups cooked potatoes, peeled and diced in ½-inch cubes
2 tablespoons butter
½ cup onion, finely chopped
½ cup green pepper, finely chopped
½ cup water
¼ cup vinegar
1 tablespoon granulated sugar
2 teaspoons flour
½ teaspoon salt
¼ teaspoon pepper
2 tablespoons pimiento, finely diced
½ teaspoon celery seed
6 hot dogs, cut in half crosswise
6 10-inch strips lean bacon, cut in half crosswise
2 tablespoons parsley, finely chopped

Place the diced potatoes in a 2-quart buttered casserole.

Melt the butter in a small skillet and add the chopped onion and the green pepper. Saute over very low heat until the onion is transparent.

Place the water, vinegar, sugar, flour, salt, pepper, pimiento and celery seed in a bowl and mix well. Add to the onion and green pepper; continue to cook over low heat until the mixture has thickened and become somewhat transparent. Pour over the diced potatoes in the casserole.

Wrap each half of a hot dog in one of the half strips of bacon and fasten in place with a toothpick. Place the hot dog halves like the spokes of a wheel over the potato mixture. Place in a 375° F. oven for 20 minutes or until the bacon has become crisp and golden. Turn the hot dogs over once during the baking time to crisp the bacon evenly on both sides. Serves 6.

SURPRISE CASSEROLE

¼ pound dried chipped beef
1 cup boiling water
¼ cup butter or margarine
¼ cup chopped green pepper
1 cup chopped celery
¼ cup all-purpose flour
¼ teaspoon pepper
2 cups milk
1 12-ounce can vacuum-packed corn, drained
6 hot dogs, diced in ¼-inch cubes
1 cup lightly buttered bread crumbs

Using a kitchen shears, snip the beef up into ⅛-inch strips. Pour the boiling water over the strips of beef and allow to stand for 5 minutes.

Melt the butter in a 1½-quart saucepan. Drain the chipped beef well and discard the water. Add the drained beef to the melted butter. Add the green pepper and the celery. Saute over low heat until the celery is soft. Stir in the flour; add the pepper. Continue to cook over low heat until the mixture begins to bubble. Slowly add the milk, stirring constantly. Continue to cook over low heat until thickened. Remove from heat.

Mix the corn and hot dog cubes together. Place half the corn and hot dogs over the bottom of a buttered 1½-quart casserole; sprinkle with half the bread crumbs; follow this with half the chipped beef sauce mixture. Repeat with the remainder of the hot dogs and corn and the sauce mixture. Sprinkle the remaining ½ cup of crumbs over the top. Place in a 350° F. oven for 35 minutes or until the crumbs are a rich golden brown. Serves 6.

HOT DOG LAYERED CASSEROLE

1 12-ounce can niblet corn with pimiento
1 cup instant rice, as it comes from the package
½ teaspoon salt
¼ teaspoon pepper
2 8-ounce cans tomato sauce
¾ cup water
10 hot dogs, finely chopped
¾ cup onion, coarsely chopped
½ cup green pepper, diced in ¼-inch cubes
4 10-inch strips very lean bacon

Mix the niblet corn and the instant rice together. Sprinkle with the salt and pepper and place in the bottom of a buttered 1½-inch quart casserole which has a tightly fitting cover. Mix one of the cans of the tomato sauce with the water and pour this over the rice and corn.

Distribute the chopped hot dogs over the rice, corn and tomato sauce. Sprinkle the chopped onion over the hot dogs; sprinkle the green pepper over the onion. Pour the remaining can of tomato sauce over the top of the casserole. Do not disturb the layered arrangement. Lay the bacon strips over the top.

Bake, covered, in a 350° F. oven for 45 minutes. Then remove cover and reduce heat to 300° F. Bake for an additional 30 minutes or until the bacon strips are crisp and golden. Serve at once, piping hot. Serves 6.

Variation:

Add 1 4-ounce can of drained mushroom stems and pieces to the corn and rice mixture for a delightful flavor variation.

HOT DOG CASSEROLE WITH SOUR CREAM

8 hot dogs
4 tablespoons butter
3 tablespoons all-purpose flour
4 tablespoons milk
¼ teaspoon salt
¼ teaspoon pepper
¼ teaspoon paprika
1½ cups dairy sour cream
¾ cup mushroom stems and pieces, coarsely chopped
1 tablespoon onion, finely minced
½ cup buttered bread crumbs

Cut the hot dogs up into ¼-inch circles. Place the butter in a skillet over moderate heat and saute the hot dog circles until they just begin to turn a rich brown.

Place the flour and milk in the top of a double boiler and mix until smooth and blended. Add the salt, pepper, paprika and sour cream. Mix until well blended. Place over barely bubbling hot water and cook, stirring constantly, until the cream has thickened. Keep the heat very low or you will curdle the sour cream. Remove from heat and add the mushroom pieces and the minced onion. Mix well.

Place the sauteed hot dog circles and any butter you have left in the pan in the bottom of a suitable casserole. Pour the sour cream sauce over the hot dog pieces. Sprinkle the buttered bread crumbs over the top. Place in a 300° F. oven for 25 minutes or until the crumbs are a rich golden brown. Serve piping hot. Serves 6.

BEAN CURRY WITH FRANKS

3 packages frozen baby lima beans
2 beef bouillon cubes, dissolved in 1 cup boiling water
1 cup grated Cheddar cheese
1 cup diced onion
¼ cup melted butter
1½ cups seedless raisins
½ teaspoon salt
¼ teaspoon pepper
1 teaspoon curry powder
¼ teaspoon nutmeg
8 wieners, cut in thirds
6 lemon wedges

Place the lima beans in a large mixing bowl; break up any large frozen parts of the beans so that they can be evenly mixed with the other ingredients. Add the bouillon, Cheddar cheese and onion. Mix all well.

Add the melted butter, the raisins, salt, pepper, curry powder and nutmeg and again mix well.

Place half of the hot dogs over the bottom of a buttered casserole. Follow this with half of the bean mixture. Place the remainder of the hot dogs over the bean mixture. Top with the remainder of the bean mixture.

Place in a 350° F. oven for 25 minutes or until the raisins are puffy and the beans are tender. Invert the top of the casserole once during the baking period to prevent drying out. Serve at once, piping hot. Serve each portion with a wedge of lemon. Serves 6.

Chapter XVI

HOT DOG MAIN DISHES

MEAT HAS ALWAYS been the most costly item of a meal. Perhaps that's why restaurants always price their meals by the type of meat cut they are serving.

Steaks, chops and roasts are costly no matter what the tide of the economic times is. Hot dogs, made of pure, lean meat contain the same proteins as steaks, chops and roasts. Isn't it good economy to substitute the economical, tasty hot dog for these more expensive cuts?

If you want good, nourishing meals for your family, plan them around hot dog main dishes. Hot dogs offer you triple savings.

First of all, they take less cooking time than any other meat on the market because they have been completely cooked before you buy them.

Secondly, hot dogs are loaded with pure economy when you compare their price to the other cuts of meat on your butcher's counter.

Thirdly, there is not a speck of waste to a hot dog. You are getting all meat—no bones, no thick fat, no inedible gristle. You are purchasing pure, waste-free meat for your precious food dollar. Hot dogs are great—especially when they form the main dish of your family's meal.

HOT DOG LOAF #1

8 ounces medium egg noodles, cooked until tender according to package directions
3 eggs, slightly beaten
½ cup milk
½ teaspoon salt
½ teaspoon Accent
1½ cups grated mild American cheese
¼ cup parsley, finely chopped
8 hot dogs

Mix the cooked noodles, eggs, milk, salt, Accent, grated cheese and parsley together well.

In a greased loaf pan, place one third of the mixture evenly over the bottom. Place 4 of the hot dogs the long way over the noodles. Place another third of the noodles over the hot dogs. Place the remaining 4 hot dogs lengthwise on top of this addition of noodles. The hot dogs should be placed so that when you slice the loaf, you will have circles of hot dog interspersed with noodles in each slice. Top with the remaining third of the noodles. Press the mixture down in the pan well so that there are no air pockets.

Bake in a 350° F. oven for 1 hour. Remove from the oven and allow to cool for 8 to 10 minutes, to set before slicing. Loosen from the loaf tin with a sharp knife and invert on platter. Slice in 2-inch thick slices with a very sharp knife. Serves 6.

HOT DOG LOAF #2

12 hot dogs
1 cup grated sharp Cheddar cheese
1 egg, beaten until lemon yellow
1 cup milk
1 teaspoon Worcestershire sauce
¾ cup fine cracker crumbs
1 teaspoon baking powder
2 tablespoons minced parsley
1 10-ounce package peas frozen in cream sauce

Chop the hot dogs until they are the consistency of coarse corn meal. Mix the chopped hot dogs and grated Cheddar together thoroughly. Add the beaten egg to the milk along with the Worcestershire sauce; mix well and then add to the hot dogs and cheese. Mix the finely crushed cracker crumbs and baking powder together; add to the hot dog mixture along with the parsley and stir well.

Place in a lightly buttered loaf pan. Bake in a 350° F. oven for 1 hour. Turn out on a heated platter.

Cook the peas as directed on the package. Cut the hot dog loaf into generous slices and pour the creamed peas over the top. Serves 6.

HOT DOG LOAF #3

10 hot dogs
1 cup canned tomatoes
1 cup canned peas, drained
1 cup canned diced carrots, drained
½ cup chopped cashew nuts
½ teaspoon salt
⅛ teaspoon pepper
½ teaspoon Accent
¼ cup minced onion
1 cup soft, white enriched bread crumbs
½ cup half-and-half cream
3 eggs, beaten until lemon yellow
1 tablespoon melted butter

Chop the hot dogs until they are the consistency of coarse corn meal. Mix the chopped hot dogs, tomatoes, peas, carrots, cashews, salt, Accent, pepper, onion and bread crumbs thoroughly.

Mix the cream and beaten eggs together and add to the mixture. Stir in the melted butter. Mix thoroughly and place in a lightly buttered loaf tin. Bake in a 350° F. oven for 1 hour or until the center is firm. Serve in 1½-inch slices. Serves 6 generously.

HOT DOG LOAF #4

12 hot dogs, very finely chopped
1½ pounds ground veal (double ground if possible)
1½ cups enriched white bread crumbs
1 teaspoon salt
¼ teaspoon pepper
½ cup onion, finely chopped
¼ cup parsley, finely chopped
1 canned pimiento, finely chopped (optional)
3 eggs, beaten until lemon yellow
1 cup milk
4 slices lean bacon

Mix the ground veal and the chopped hot dogs together. Add the bread crumbs, salt, pepper, onion, parsley, pimiento, beaten eggs and milk. Mix all very thoroughly and then knead much as you would bread. Form into an oblong loaf and place in a lightly greased baking pan. Lay the four strips of bacon over the top diagonally.

Bake in a 350° F. oven for 1½ hours. After removing the loaf from the oven, let it rest for 5 minutes before slicing. Serves 6 generously.

Note: This hot dog loaf is delicious when served cold. It is a good partner to potato salad, and it also makes delicious cold sandwiches.

TETRAZZINI HOT DOGS

½ cup butter or margarine
1 8-ounce can mushroom stems and pieces, drained
¼ cup flour
2 tablespoons instant chicken bouillon granules
2 cups boiling water
1 cup half-and-half cream
1 teaspoon Heinz 57 Sauce
½ teaspoon salt
¼ teaspoon pepper
12 hot dogs, sliced in ¼-inch circles
1 12-ounce package medium egg noodles, cooked according to package directions
¾ cup grated Parmesan cheese
½ teaspoon paprika

Melt the butter in a large skillet. Add the mushroom stems and pieces and saute until slightly browned. Push the mushrooms to one side and stir in the flour. Cook until bubbly. Mix the chicken bouillon granules in the boiling water and add to the flour, butter and mushrooms. Add the cream and the Heinz 57 sauce; cook over very low heat, stirring constantly, until the mixture has thickened and coats the spoon. Add the sliced hot dogs; mix until the hot dog pieces are coated with the thickened sauce. Set aside.

Place the cooked and drained noodles in a buttered baking dish and pour the sauce and the hot dogs over the top. Sprinkle the top of the dish with the grated cheese, then with the paprika. Bake in a 350° F. oven for 20 minutes or until the cheese turns a golden brown. Serves 6 generously.

SPAGHETTI HOT DOG DINNER

6 slices bacon, diced in ½-inch pieces
8 hot dogs, diced in ¼-inch cubes
¾ cup onion, diced in ¼-inch cubes
¼ cup green pepper, diced in ¼-inch cubes
1 #2 can tomatoes
1 pound Velveeta cheese
½ teaspoon salt
⅛ teaspoon pepper
1 4-ounce can mushroom stems and pieces, drained
8 ounces vermicelli spaghetti, cooked until tender according to package directions

Place the diced bacon in a large skillet and saute until it is a golden brown. Do not drain the bacon, for the drippings form part of the flavor of this dish. Add the cubed hot dogs to the bacon and saute until the edges begin to turn brown.

Add the onion, green pepper and tomatoes to the bacon and hot dogs. Bring to a boil and cook over moderate heat for 8 minutes or until the onion begins to become limp and transparent. Reduce the heat to simmer and add the Velveeta cheese, salt, pepper and mushroom stems and pieces.

Continue to cook over very low heat, stirring constantly, until the cheese has completely melted and is smoothly blended. Place the hot, cooked spaghetti in a deep serving dish and pour the cheese and hot dog mixture over the top. Serve at once. Serves 6 generously.

HOT DOGS AND BAKED BEANS DINNER

2 #303 cans baked beans in tomato sauce
½ teaspoon garlic salt
¼ teaspoon salt
⅛ teaspoon pepper
1 cup dairy sour cream
8 hot dogs, sliced in ½-inch circles
½ cup chopped parsley
¼ cup chopped onion

Drain away most of the juice from the canned beans. Place the beans in a 2-quart buttered baking dish along with the garlic salt, salt, pepper and ½ cup of the sour cream. Stir in the hot dog pieces, parsley and chopped onion.

Bake, uncovered, in a 375° F. oven for 20 minutes or until the beans are bubbling in the center. Serve with a dab of the remaining sour cream on each portion. Serves 6.

HOT DOGS WITH CRUNCHY NOODLES

1 12-ounce package enriched broad egg noodles
1 teaspoon salt
1 tablespoon cooking oil
6 hot dogs, cut in ⅛-inch slices
½ cup butter
1 tablespoon dehydrated parsley flakes

Set aside approximately 1 cup of the dry egg noodles just as they come from the package.

Bring 3 quarts of water to a rolling boil; add the salt and the remainder of the noodles. Cook over moderate heat until the noodles are tender and can be cut when pressed against the side of the kettle with a spoon or fork. Add the cooking oil to the cooked noodles, mixing well. (The addition of the oil to the cooking noodles prevents them from sticking together after they are drained.) Drain the noodles through a collander. Return the hot noodles to the pan in which they were cooked. Add the hot dogs and mix well with a light hand. Cover and set aside.

Place the cup of egg noodles between two dish towels and crush fairly well with a rolling pin. Melt the butter in a skillet and add the crushed (uncooked) egg noodles. Saute the egg noodle pieces until they turn a rich brown. Stir constantly to avoid burning. Remove the skillet from the heat immediately.

Mix the cooked noodles and hot dog slices with the browned noodle pieces and their butter. Add the dried parsley flakes and mix again lightly. Serve at once. Serves 6.

Note: This is a very popular dish with youngsters, because they enjoy the crunchiness of the "toasted" noodle pieces.

HOT DOG AND BEEF LOAF

1½ pounds ground chuck
½ pound hot dogs, either ground or chopped very finely
½ cup soft white enriched bread crumbs
2 eggs, beaten until lemon yellow
1 cup milk
1 teaspoon salt
1 teaspoon celery seed
¼ teaspoon pepper
1 teaspoon prepared yellow mustard
½ cup onion, finely grated

Mix the ground chuck and the ground hot dogs together thoroughly. Add the bread crumbs, eggs, milk, salt, celery seed, pepper, mustard and onion. Mix again until all is smoothly blended. Place the mixture in a lightly buttered 10x5x3-inch loaf pan. Press the mixture down to expel any air pockets.

Place in a 350° F. oven for 1 hour. Slice 1½ inches thick. Serves 6.

Note: This loaf is excellent if served cold for sandwiches. When using for sandwiches, chill thoroughly and slice ¼ inch thick. This loaf will make 18 sandwiches.

BAKED HOT DOG DINNER

12 hot dogs, cut crosswise into thirds
4 cups cooked, hot instant mashed potatoes, prepared according to package directions
2 tablespoons minced green onion
¼ cup chopped pimiento-stuffed green olives
2 tablespoons parsley, finely chopped
⅛ teaspoon pepper
¼ teaspoon paprika

Place the cut-up hot dogs in a lightly buttered shallow baking dish. Mix the hot mashed potatoes with the onion, green olives, parsley and pepper. Spread this mixture over the hot dogs. Arrange in decorative peaks.

Sprinkle the paprika over the mashed potatoes and bake in a 350° F. oven for 30 minutes or until the top has turned a golden brown. Serve piping hot. Serves 6.

HOT DOG JAMBALAYA

¼ cup bacon, diced in ¼-inch pieces
½ cup onion, diced in ¼-inch cubes
½ cup green pepper, diced in ¼-inch cubes
1 4-ounce can mushroom stems and pieces, drained
1 8-ounce can tomato sauce
1 cup instant rice, uncooked
12 hot dogs, cut up in ½-inch cubes
1 beef bouillon cube dissolved in 1 cup boiling water
½ teaspoon Worcestershire sauce
2 tablespoons parsley, finely chopped

Place the diced bacon in a 2-quart saucepan and saute until it begins to brown. Add the onion, green pepper and mushrooms, and saute until the onion begins to get limp and transparent.

Remove from heat and add the tomato sauce, instant rice, hot dog cubes, bouillon water and Worcestershire sauce. Mix all well and pour into a lightly buttered 1½-quart casserole.

Cover and place in a 350° F. oven for 40 minutes. Sprinkle the chopped parsley over the top and serve at once. Serves 6.

SKILLET HOT DOG DINNER

2 #300 cans of chili con carne (with kidney beans)
1 #2 can chick peas, drained
2 12-ounce cans vacuum packed corn niblets with pimiento, drained
10 hot dogs
1 cup grated American cheese

In a large skillet with a tightly fitting cover, combine the chili con carne, chick peas and the corn niblets. Mix all very well, cover and place over low heat for 10 minutes, stirring occasionally to prevent scorching.

Cut the hot dogs into 1-inch lengths and add to the chili mixture. Mix all gently, taking care not to mash the beans and chick peas. Press the mixture down and smooth it over with a rubber spatula.

Sprinkle the grated cheese over the top. Continue to cook, covered, for 5 minutes longer or until the cheese has melted and become soft. Serve piping hot. Serves 6.

SKILLET OF HOT DOGS, PINEAPPLE AND BEANS

8 hot dogs, cut into thirds
½ cup onion, coarsely chopped
¼ cup butter
2 1-pound cans pork and beans
1 #211 can (13½ ounces) pineapple chunks, drained
1 tablespoon Worcestershire sauce
1 teaspoon powdered mustard
¼ cup parsley, finely chopped

Place the hot dog pieces, onion and butter in a large heavy saucepan. Saute over low heat until the onion is glazed and transparent and the hot dogs begin to brown slightly.

Remove the pork pieces from the pork and beans and discard, as this added pork will make the dish too greasy. Add the beans to the onions and hot dogs; add the pineapple chunks and Worcestershire sauce. Sprinkle the powdered mustard over the surface. Mix all well, using a light touch so that the beans do not get mashed. Continue to cook over low heat for an additional 20 minutes or until all is heated through.

Remove from the heat and stir in the chopped parsley. Serve at once. Serves 6 generously.

HAWAIIAN BARBECUE WITH HOT DOGS

1 8-ounce can tomato sauce
¼ cup brown sugar, tightly packed
¼ cup cider vinegar
1 tablespoon minced onion
1 tablespoon celery seed
1 teaspoon powdered mustard
1 teaspoon chili powder
1 tablespoon Worcestershire sauce
12 hot dogs
1 14-ounce can pineapple spears, drained
1 #303 can Kadota figs, drained

In a 1-quart saucepan, mix the tomato sauce, brown sugar, cider vinegar, onion, celery seed, mustard, chili powder and Worcestershire sauce thoroughly. Place over moderate heat and bring to a rolling boil for 5 minutes. Stir frequently to prevent scorching.

Alternate the hot dogs with the pineapple spears in a lightly buttered shallow baking pan. Arrange the Kadota figs around the hot dogs and the pineapple spears. Pour the hot barbecue sauce over all.

Place in a 325° F. oven for 35 minutes. Turn the hot dogs and figs over several times during the baking period to distribute the flavors of the sauce. Serve piping hot with hot fluffy rice. Serves 6.

HOT DOGS WITH CHIVE POTATOES

12 to 15 small pink salad potatoes (approximately 2
    pounds)
10 hot dogs, cut crosswise in 1-inch pieces
½ cup butter
3 tablespoons chives, finely chopped
2 tablespoons lemon juice
1 teaspoon grated lemon peel
¼ teaspoon salt
½ teaspoon Accent
⅛ teaspoon black pepper

Wash and scrub the potatoes well. Place in salted water to cover and boil until they are tender enough to pierce with a fork. Remove from the heat, drain and peel.

Add the hot dog pieces to the peeled hot potatoes and set aside.

Melt the butter in a large skillet; add the chopped chives, lemon juice and lemon peel. Stir well and then add the salt, Accent and black pepper. Place the hot dogs and the potatoes in the butter sauce and turn over lightly until all are coated with sauce.

Cook over very low heat for 10 minutes, turning gently from time to time. Serve at once, piping hot. Serves 6 generously.

Variations:

Substitute ¼ cup thinly-sliced scallions for the chives. Be sure to include a portion of the green.

If you cannot obtain small salad potatoes, use the larger variety and cut them into quarters after they are cooked and peeled.

229

HOT DOGS AND HASH-BROWNED POTATOES

8 hot dogs sliced in ¼-inch circles
6 medium-sized potatoes, scrubbed well but not peeled
4 tablespoons olive oil
4 tablespoons butter
2 cloves garlic, sliced 1/16 inch thick
½ teaspoon salt
¼ teaspoon pepper
3 scallions, cut into ⅛-inch slices (use a portion of the green too)
3 tablespoons parsley, finely chopped
1 tablespoon caraway seed

Boil the potatoes in their jackets until they are tender enough to pierce with a fork. Do not overcook or let them get too soft. Drain and peel. Slice the hot, peeled potatoes about ¼ inch thick; place in a mixing bowl, cover and set aside.

Place the olive oil, butter and garlic in an oven-proof skillet over moderate heat. Saute the garlic until it begins to turn brown. Using a slotted spoon, remove the garlic from the butter and olive oil. Add the potatoes to skillet and mix lightly with the olive oil and butter.

Add the sliced hot dogs, salt, pepper, scallion pieces, parsley and caraway seed. Mix all very well. Press down firmly in the skillet; smooth the top with a rubber spoon. Place the skillet over moderate heat until the bottom of the potatoes are a golden brown. Do not stir, but using a spatula, lift up a small portion to see if they are sufficiently browned.

Place the skillet about 6 inches away from the broiler heat and brown the top side. Loosen the potatoes and hot dogs with a spatula and turn out on to a heated platter. Serve at once, piping hot. Serves 6.

HOT DOG SPANISH RICE

6 slices lean bacon
8 hot dogs
¾ cup onion, coarsely chopped
¾ cup instant rice just as it comes from the package
1 cup boiling water
1 8-ounce can tomatoes (1 cup)
½ teaspoon salt
¼ teaspoon pepper

Cut the bacon into ¼-inch cubes and saute over low heat until slightly transparent but not crisp. Pour off any excess grease. Dice the hot dogs into ¼-inch cubes and add to the bacon along with the chopped onion. Continue to saute over low heat until the onion is limp and transparent. Remove from heat.

Mix the instant rice and the hot water; allow to stand for 5 minutes; then add the rice and water to the hot dog and onion mixture. Stir in the tomatoes, salt and pepper. Pour into a deep buttered baking dish. Cover and bake in a 350° F. oven for 20 minutes or until the rice has absorbed all of the liquid. Serve at once. Serves 6.

HOT DOG AUTUMN DISH

1 #2 can sweet potatoes, drained
4 medium-sized tart apples
12 hot dogs
½ cup dark brown sugar, tightly packed
¼ teaspoon cinnamon
¼ teaspoon grated lemon rind
1 teaspoon lemon juice
¼ cup melted butter
½ cup soft bread crumbs

Slice the sweet potatoes ½ inch thick. Peel, core and quarter the apples and then chop them coarsely. Cut the hot dogs crosswise diagonally into 1-inch pieces.

Place a layer of sweet potato slices over the bottom of a buttered 10x5x2-inch baking dish with a cover. Follow this with a layer of chopped apples and half of the diagonally-cut hot dogs.

Mix the brown sugar, cinnamon, lemon rind and lemon juice together. Sprinkle half of this mixture over the ingredients in the baking dish. Follow with the remainder of the sweet potato slices, apples and hot dogs. Again sprinkle with the remainder of the brown sugar mixture.

Mix the melted butter and the bread crumbs together and sprinkle this over the top of the other ingredients. Cover and place in a 350° F. oven for 1 hour. Remove the cover and bake for 5 minutes longer. Serves 6.

HOT DOG AND HAM LOAF

10 hot dogs, very finely chopped
¾ pound ground lean ham
1 cup dry bread crumbs
¼ cup onion, finely chopped
¼ cup celery, finely chopped
¼ teaspoon freshly ground pepper
1 egg, beaten until lemon yellow
¾ cup milk

Sauce:

⅓ cup grated horseradish, pressed dry
¼ cup mayonnaise
½ cup heavy whipping cream

Mix the chopped hot dogs, ground ham, bread crumbs, onion, celery and ground pepper together. Mix the egg and milk together and add to the hot dog mixture. Stir and mix all well.

Pour into a lightly buttered 9x5x3-inch loaf pan and bake in a 350° F. oven for 1 hour.

Whip the cream until it is stiff and stands in peaks. Fold in the mayonnaise and the horseradish.

Serve the hot ham loaf in 1½-inch slices topped with a portion of the sauce. Serves 6.

HOT DOGS AND ONION RINGS

8 hot dogs
1 8-ounce can tomato sauce
1 teaspoon powdered mustard
¼ teaspoon ground cloves
⅛ teaspoon sweet basil
1 teaspoon granulated sugar
1 tablespoon raw rice
1 10-ounce package frozen French fried onion rings

Quarter the hot dogs and place in a 1-quart saucepan along with the tomato sauce, mustard, cloves, basil, sugar and rice. Mix all well.

Cook over low heat, covered, for 20 minutes or until the rice grains are tender and the sauce has thickened to the consistency of catsup. Stir gently from time to time during this cooking period.

Place the French fried onion rings on an oven-proof serving platter. Place in a 375° F. oven for 10 minutes or until the rings are heated through and crisp.

Pour the hot dogs and their sauce over the heated onion rings and serve at once, piping hot. Serves 6.

HOT DOG NOODLE RING WITH SAUERKRAUT

1 #2½ can sauerkraut
1 cup tart baking apples, peeled and sliced
½ cup Rhine wine
½ teaspoon Accent
2 tablespoons dark brown sugar
¼ teaspoon pepper
6 juniper berries
1 16-ounce package medium-wide egg noodles, cooked until tender according to package directions; drained and slightly cooled
8 hot dogs, cut in ⅛-inch circles
¼ cup melted butter
¼ teaspoon pepper
½ teaspoon salt
¼ cup parsley, finely chopped
3 eggs, beaten until lemon yellow

Place the sauerkraut in a saucepan with a tightly fitting cover. Add the apple, Rhine wine, Accent, brown sugar, pepper and juniper berries. Mix well and bring to a rolling boil; turn heat down to low and simmer for 30 minutes, stirring occasionally.

In a large mixing bowl, mix the cooked noodles, hot dog slices, melted butter, salt, pepper and parsley. Fold in the beaten eggs. Place the mixture in a well-buttered 8½-cup ring mold. Press down so that there are no air pockets. Place in a 375° F. oven for 20 minutes or until the ring is firm in the center.

Remove the noodle ring by loosening the edges with a sharp knife; then invert on a platter. Spoon the hot sauerkraut mixture into the middle. Serve at once, piping hot. Makes 4 generous servings.

HOT DOGS, CHEESE AND POTATOES

12 hot dogs, diced in ¼-inch cubes
2 cups mild American cheese, diced in ¼-inch cubes
1 3-ounce can pimientos, drained and diced in ¼-inch
   cubes
3 cups cooked potatoes, diced in ½-inch cubes
¼ cup melted butter or margarine
¼ cup all-purpose flour
2 cups milk
½ teaspoon salt
¼ teaspoon pepper
2 tablespoons parsley, finely chopped

Place the diced hot dogs, cheese cubes, diced pimientos and diced potatoes in a large mixing bowl. Toss all together until uniformly mixed.

Melt the butter in the bottom of a 2-quart saucepan; stir in the flour and cook over low heat until bubbly. Add the milk. Stirring constantly, cook over low heat until the mixture has thickened. Add the salt, pepper and parsley to the sauce. Mix well.

Add the hot dog-potato mixture to the sauce and continue to cook over very low heat for 8 minutes or until warmed through, stirring frequently. Serve at once, piping hot. Serves 6.

Note: Do not be concerned if the cheese cubes do not melt thoroughly during the cooking time, for this is part of the deliciousness of this dish.

HOT DOGS AND AU GRATIN POTATOES

12 hot dogs
4 tablespoons butter
¼ cup green pepper, finely chopped
¼ cup canned pimiento, finely chopped
¼ cup onion, finely chopped
½ teaspoon salt
¼ teaspoon pepper
¼ teaspoon paprika
2 cups milk
2 cups grated American cheese
3 cups cooked potatoes, diced in ½-inch cubes

Cut the hot dogs in ¼-inch circles. Set aside. Melt the butter in a 1½-quart saucepan. Add the green pepper, pimiento, onion, salt, pepper, paprika and saute until the onion is limp and slightly transparent. Gradually add the milk, stirring constantly. Continue to cook over low heat. Add the grated cheese a little at a time; continue to cook until the cheese is melted. Remove from the heat.

Add the diced potatoes and mix well, taking care not to mash up the potato pieces. Place half of the sliced hot dogs in the bottom of a buttered casserole. Follow this with half of the potato mixture. Place the remainder of the hot dogs over the potatoes and again follow with the remainder of the potato mixture.

Place in a 350° F. oven for 30 minutes. Serve at once, piping hot. Serves 6.

HOT DOG-GHETTI DINNER

8 small onions, about 1 inch in diameter
1½ cups water
1 8-ounce can tomato sauce
1 #303 can tomatoes (2 cups)
1 cup spaghetti bends (small curved pieces of spaghetti)
1 package garlic-flavored salad dressing mix
½ cup sweet pickle relish, drained
8 hot dogs, cut in thirds

Peel the onions and place them in a saucepan with the water. Boil over moderate heat until the onions can be pierced with a fork. Drain, reserving the water in which they were boiled.

Place the reserved onion water in a 1½-quart saucepan along with the tomato sauce and tomatoes. Bring to a rolling boil, then add the spaghetti. Turn the heat back to simmer and cook for 25 minutes or until the spaghetti is tender, stirring occasionally.

Add the salad dressing mix, the pickle relish, whole onions and the hot dog pieces. Continue to cook over low heat for 10 minutes longer, stirring occasionally. Serve piping hot. Serves 6.

GONE TO THE DOGS HASH

2 tablespoons butter or margarine
¼ cup onion, thinly sliced
10 hot dogs, diced in ¼-inch cubes
1 tablespoon grated horseradish
1 tablespoon cider vinegar
1 teaspoon caraway seed
1½ cups cabbage, finely shredded (or leftover cole slaw
    which has been drained and pressed dry)
2 cups cooked potatoes, diced in ½-inch cubes

Melt the butter in a large skillet. Add the sliced onion and cook over low heat until the onion is limp and transparent. Add the hot dog cubes, horseradish, vinegar and caraway seed. Continue to cook over low heat for 8 minutes. Stir from time to time to mix the flavors.

Add the shredded cabbage, spreading over the top of the hot dogs; add the diced potatoes, spreading them over the top of the cabbage. Cover and continue to cook over very low heat for 5 minutes. Then completely turn the mixture over so that the potatoes are on the bottom of the pan. Continue to cook over very low heat for 5 additional minutes. Serve piping hot. Serves 6.

CREOLE HOT DOGS

3 tablespoons butter or margarine
¾ cup onion, coarsely chopped
½ cup celery, diagonally sliced ¼ inch thick
1 #2 can Italian tomatoes
1 8-ounce can tomato sauce
1 teaspoon chili powder
1 teaspoon brown sugar
½ teaspoon Accent
½ teaspoon salt
½ cup green pepper strips, 1x¼ inch thick
8 hot dogs, cut into fourths crosswise
4 cups cooked hot fluffy rice
2 tablespoons dehydrated parsley

Melt the butter in a large skillet; add the chopped onion and saute until the onion is limp and transparent. Add the celery. Continue to saute until the celery becomes transparent around the edges.

Add the tomatoes and the tomato sauce. Stir well; add the chili powder, brown sugar, Accent and salt. Continue to cook over low heat until it reaches a bubbling boil.

Add the green pepper strips and the pieces of hot dog. Turn the heat back to simmer and cook for 8 minutes longer or until the hot dog pieces are warmed through.

Stir the dehydrated parsley into the hot cooked rice. Spread the rice on a heated platter and pour the hot dog mixture over the rice. Serve at once, piping hot. Serves 6.

HOT POT KRAUT AND HOT DOGS

8 hot dogs, sliced in ¼-inch circles
1 #2½ can sauerkraut, undrained
1 cup water
1 #1 can small white onions, undrained
1 10-ounce package frozen carrots and peas
½ cup celery, diced in ¼-inch cubes
½ teaspoon caraway seed
½ teaspoon celery seed
¼ cup parsley, finely chopped
1 cup canned tomatoes
1 10-ounce package French-style frozen green beans
1 10-ounce can cream of celery soup
1 10-ounce can frozen potato soup

Place the hot dog slices, sauerkraut, water, onions and peas and carrots in a 2-quart saucepan over low heat. Add the celery, caraway seed, celery seed and parsley. Cook over low heat for 20 minutes. Do not cover; otherwise you will lose the bright colors of the vegetables. Turn the mixture over several times during cooking so that all is heated through and done evenly.

Add the tomatoes and the frozen green beans and continue to cook for 5 minutes longer or until the beans just begin to get tender. Stir in the celery soup and add the potato soup. Cook for an additional 8 minutes or until the potato soup is melted. Stir the mixture lightly so that the vegetables do not get crushed. Serve piping hot with saltine crackers or with crisp pieces of French bread. Serves 6.

HOT DOG AND NOODLE BAKE

1 6-ounce package medium egg noodles, cooked according
   to package directions
¼ cup butter or margarine
¼ cup chopped onion
¼ cup all-purpose flour
½ teaspoon powdered mustard
½ teaspoon salt
⅛ teaspoon pepper
1¼ cups milk
1 16-ounce package creamed cottage cheese
½ cup mushroom stems and pieces, drained
½ cup toasted sliced almonds
8 hot dogs, diced in ¼-inch cubes
1 cup grated American cheese

Drain and rinse the cooked noodles in cold water. Set
aside to drain thoroughly. Melt the butter in a 2-quart
saucepan and add the chopped onion. Cook the onion over
moderate heat until it is transparent and limp. Mix the mustard, flour, salt and pepper together. Push the onions to one
side of the saucepan and add the flour mixture to the
melted butter. Stir well and cook over very low heat until
it begins to bubble. Stir in the milk and continue to cook
and stir over low heat until the mixture is smooth and
thickened.

Stir in the drained noodles, the cottage cheese, the mushroom stems and pieces, the sliced almonds and the hot dog
cubes. Mix all well with a light touch. Pour into a buttered
2½-quart baking dish.

Smooth the top of the mixture with the back of a spoon
and then sprinkle the grated American cheese over the top.
Bake in a 350° F. oven for 30 minutes or until the cheese
is bubbly and lightly golden. Let stand for 5 minutes before
serving for firmer portions. Serves 6.

HOT DOG 'N LIVER SAUSAGE LOAF

12 hot dogs
½ pound smoked liver sausage (at room temperature)
1½ cups soft enriched white bread crumbs
1 egg, beaten until lemon yellow
¾ cup half-and-half cream
½ teaspoon salt
½ teaspoon Accent
⅛ teaspoon pepper
4 strips bacon

Sauce (optional but good):

1 8-ounce can tomato sauce
½ cup celery, finely chopped
¼ cup green pepper, finely chopped
1 teaspoon brown sugar
1 drop Tabasco
1 teaspoon prepared yellow mustard
⅛ teaspoon ground cloves

Chop the hot dogs until they are the consistency of coarse corn meal. Peel and mash up the liver sausage; add to the chopped hot dogs along with the bread crumbs, beaten egg, cream, salt, Accent and pepper. Mix all thoroughly and pack into a lightly buttered loaf pan. Cut the bacon in half crosswise and place diagonally over the top.

Bake in a 350° F. oven for 45 minutes or until the bacon and the top of the loaf are a crisp golden brown. Slice in generous slices. Can be served hot or cold.

To make the sauce, combine all of the ingredients and simmer over low heat for 30 minutes or until thickened. Serve separately, allowing each person to spoon the sauce over the slice of loaf.

Serves 6.

DUCHESS POTATOES AND HOT DOGS

6 medium-sized potatoes, halved
¼ cup butter or margarine
½ cup hot half-and-half cream
½ teaspoon salt
½ teaspoon Accent
⅛ teaspoon pepper
2 egg yolks, beaten until lemon yellow
6 hot dogs
¼ cup melted butter (additional)
1 teaspoon paprika

Wash, peel and cook potato halves in water to cover for about 25 minutes or until tender enough to pierce with a fork. Drain and again place over the hot burner for 2 or 3 seconds to thoroughly dry them. Mash the potatoes thoroughly.

Using a whisk or electric mixer whip the butter into the potatoes. Gradually add the hot half-and-half cream and continue beating. Add the salt, Accent and pepper. Mix well. Beat two tablespoons of the hot potato mixture into the egg yolks and then beat the egg yolks into the mixture.

Slice the hot dogs lengthwise about half way through leaving a "hinge" at one side. Lay the hot dogs, cut side down, about 2 inches apart on a lightly buttered cooky sheet.

Using a pastry bag and the star-shaped tip, force the mashed potatoes over and around the hot dogs. For added color, leave each end of the hot dog peeking out from under the potatoes. Drizzle the melted butter over the mounds of potato. Sprinkle with paprika.

Place in a hot, 450° F. oven for 8 minutes or until golden brown. Remove from the cooky sheet with a spatula on to each plate. Serves 6.

Note: Leftover mashed potatoes can also be used for this dish. Place the leftover potatoes in a double boiler over barely boiling water until heated through. Whip again until fluffy and then add the egg yolks.

Packaged instant mashed potatoes can also be used in this recipe if you desire.

HOT DOGS IN PIQUANT MUSTARD SAUCE

12 hot dogs
1 cup granulated sugar
½ cup prepared horseradish mustard, Dusseldorf style
¼ cup vinegar
2 beef bouillon cubes dissolved in ½ cup water
2 egg yolks, beaten until lemon yellow
¼ cup butter
1 teaspoon flour

Cut the hot dogs in half lengthwise and arrange in the bottom of a lightly buttered shallow baking dish with a tightly fitting cover.

Mix the sugar, horseradish mustard, vinegar and bouillon in the top of a double boiler. Add the beaten eggs, butter and flour. Cook over rapidly boiling water, stirring constantly, until the mixture has thickened and coats the spoon.

Pour the mixture over the hot dogs in the baking dish. Cover and place in a 350° F. oven for 15 minutes or until the hot dogs are warmed through. Serve at once. Serves 6, allowing 4 hot dog halves per person.

HOT DOG AND ROASTED RICE CASSEROLE

8 hot dogs, sliced in ½-inch circles
1 cup raw long grain rice
1 foil package onion soup mix (1¼-ounce size)
2 cups boiling water or clear soup stock
1 tablespoon butter
1 tablespoon dehydrated parsley

Spread the rice over the bottom of an ungreased large shallow baking pan. Place in a 400° F. oven for 8 minutes or until the rice has toasted to a golden brown color. Shake the pan from time to time so that the rice is evenly browned. Remove from the oven and set aside.

In a 2-quart casserole with a tightly fitting cover, place the onion soup mix and the boiling water or soup stock. Stir to dissolve. Add the butter, parsley and the golden toasted rice. Add the hot dog slices. Mix all well, cover and bake at 350° F. for 30 minutes or until all of the liquid has been absorbed and the rice is light and fluffy. Serve at once, piping hot. Serves 6.

HOT DOG PICNIC LOAF

1 8-ounce package elbow macaroni, cooked according to package directions
1 teaspoon grated lemon rind
2 tablespoons lemon juice
1 teaspoon salt
¼ teaspoon pepper
2 teaspoons prepared yellow mustard

Sauce:

¼ cup all-purpose flour
2 cups milk
2 cups shredded Cheddar cheese
½ cup diced green pepper
¼ cup scallions, finely sliced (include some of the green please)
¼ cup canned pimiento, finely diced
¼ cup green olives, finely chopped
8 hot dogs
6 large lettuce leaves
3 tomatoes, quartered

Drain the macaroni and place in a 2-quart mixing bowl. Add the grated lemon, lemon juice, salt, pepper and mustard. Mix lightly. Set aside while you make the sauce.

Mix the flour and milk together in a saucepan. Place over low heat and cook, stirring constantly, until the mixture begins to coat the spoon. Add the cheese and continue to cook over low heat until the cheese is melted and the mixture just begins to bubble. Add the green pepper, scallion pieces, pimiento and olives. Mix well; add to the macaroni mixture and stir well.

Pour about two cups of the mixture into the bottom of a buttered 1½-quart loaf pan. Place four of the hot dogs lengthwise on the surface of the macaroni. Follow this with another cup of the macaroni mixture and four more hot dogs staggered in position from the first four hot dogs. Place the remainder of the macaroni mixture over the top. Press down with a spoon to force out any air pockets. Place in the refrigerator for at least six hours or overnight.

Place the lettuce leaves around the edge of a platter

and unmold the loaf on top of the lettuce leaves. Place six wedges of tomato on each side of the loaf. Serves 6 generously.

Variations:

Instead of leaving the hot dogs whole, chop them coarsely and mix them with the cheese sauce before combining with the macaroni.

Substitute ½ cup pitted ripe olives for the green olives; chop them coarsely; eliminate the pimiento.

SHOESTRING HOT DOG DISH

12 hot dogs
¼ cup chopped onion
¼ cup butter or margarine
1 tablespoon brown sugar
1 teaspoon prepared yellow mustard
⅛ teaspoon pepper
2 beef bouillon cubes dissolved in ½ cup boiling water
¼ cup cider vinegar
1 tablespoon Worcestershire sauce
1 drop Tabasco
½ cup tomato sauce

Slice the hot dogs into quarters the long way; then cut the quarters in half crosswise. Each hot dog should yield 8 pieces. Set aside.

Melt the butter in the bottom of a 1-quart kettle with a tightly fitting cover. Add the onions to the melted butter and saute until they are limp and slightly transparent. Add the sugar, mustard, pepper, bouillon water, vinegar, Worcestershire sauce, Tabasco and tomato sauce. Mix all well and bring to a boil.

Add the hot dogs to the boiling sauce and mix lightly so that all the hot dog pieces are coated. Turn the heat back to simmer, cover and cook for 20 minutes, turning the hot dogs occasionally so that the flavors are evenly blended. Serve piping hot. Serves 6.

Note: This dish is excellent with hot fluffy rice.

Chapter XVII

HOT DOG SANDWICHES SUPREME

THAT SUCCULENT MORSEL, a hot dog in a soft bun with mustard and relish, is not to be looked down upon. However, there are many other ways to make a hot dog sandwich.

Since the hot dog is thoroughly cooked when purchased, it lends itself to chopping, grinding and slicing. Due to the hot dog's delicate flavor, it bends over backwards to get along with other good ingredients. Using hot dogs in sandwiches is a natural.

When you mention a hot dog sandwich, most people conjure up a vision of that wiener in a bun; that's only natural because this is how they were introduced to the U. S. A.

Down with mere wieners in a bun! Revolutionize your sandwich-making by introducing your family to some of the delicious combinations in this chapter.

HOT DOG CANOES

12 slices soft enriched white bread, crusts removed
½ cup melted butter
6 slices process American cheese 3x3x⅛ inch thick
2 tablespoons Dusseldorf-style mustard
12 hot dogs

Brush one side of each slice of bread with the melted butter. Cut the slices of cheese into 4 equal strips and place a strip on the unbuttered side of the bread. Brush the bread and cheese with the mustard. Place a hot dog on top of the cheese and bring up two opposite corners of the bread to meet on top of the hot dog. Fasten the bread in place with a toothpick.

Place on a cooky sheet in a 350° F. oven for 8 to 10 minutes or until the bread has toasted to a crisp brown on the outside. Serve at once, piping hot. Serves 6, allowing two hot dog canoes per person.

HOT DOG SANDWICH

8 hot dogs, halved lengthwise
4 tablespoons Kitchen Bouquet
½ cup melted butter
1 clove garlic, minced
8 slices enriched white bread
1 cup grated American Cheese

Brush the hot dogs on their cut side with the Kitchen Bouquet and set aside.

Place the minced garlic in the melted butter over very low heat for about 5 minutes to allow the flavors to unite. Brush each piece of bread with some of the garlic butter.

Place the pieces of buttered bread on a cooky sheet. Sprinkle each piece with a portion of the grated cheese. Place two halves of the flavored hot dogs, cut side up, on top of the cheese.

Place in a 400° F. oven for 8 minutes or until the cheese has melted and the hot dogs are just beginning to get brown. Serve at once. Serves 8, allowing 1 open sandwich per person.

HOT DOG OPEN FACE SANDWICHES

8 hot dogs
1 3-ounce package cream cheese, at room temperature
1 teaspoon horseradish-flavored mustard
2 tablespoons half-and-half cream or milk
1 tablespoon parsley, finely chopped
8 hamburger buns
1 teaspoon paprika

Chop the hot dogs until they are the consistency of hamburger. Mix the chopped hot dogs, cream cheese, mustard, cream and parsley together well.

Split the hamburger buns in half, and spread each half with the mixture. Sprinkle each with a portion of the paprika.

Place on a cooky sheet, spread side up, and broil about 6 inches from the heat for 8 minutes or until the sandwiches begin to brown. Serve at once. Serves 8.

245

DOG-BEANWICHES

1 10-ounce can bean soup with bacon
6 hot dogs, diced in ¼-inch cubes
3 slices American cheese with pimiento, 3x3x⅛ inch thick
4 scallions, sliced 1/16 inch thick (include a little of the green)
½ cup drained ripe olives, thinly sliced
6 hamburger buns, halved
¼ cup melted butter

Place the bean soup in a mixing bowl just as it comes from the can. Add the cubed hot dogs. Cut the cheese up into ¼-inch cubes and add to the beans and the hot dogs. Add the sliced scallions and the sliced ripe olives. Scoop out the soft center of the top of each hamburger bun, leaving about a ½-inch wall. Crumble up the soft bread center and add it to the bean mixture. Stir until all is well blended.

Brush the bottom and the scooped out half of each bun with the melted butter; place, open sides up, under the broiler for a few seconds or until they have just turned a crisp golden brown.

Fill the top half cavity of each bun with the hot dog-bean filling. Place on the bottom half of the bun and wrap tightly in a square of aluminum foil. Place the foil-wrapped buns on a cooky sheet and bake at 350° F. for 10 minutes. Serves 6, allowing 1 sandwich per person.

DOWN EAST BAKED BEAN AND HOT DOG RAREBIT

1 cup baked beans; these can be leftovers or drained pork and beans
8 hot dogs, diced in ¼-inch cubes
1 cup milk
1 tablespoon butter
1 cup grated mild American cheese
1 egg, slightly beaten
¼ teaspoon salt
¼ teaspoon prepared yellow mustard
¼ teaspoon Worcestershire sauce
3 4-inch diameter English muffins, cut in half and toasted or 6 thick slices enriched white bread, toasted

246

Mash the baked beans until they are fairly smooth. Mix with the diced hot dogs and set aside.

Heat the milk in the top of the double boiler to just below the scalding point; add the butter and gradually stir in the grated cheese. Continue to cook and stir until smooth. Take 2 tablespoons of the cheese mixture and stir it into the beaten egg; then add the beaten egg to the cheese mixture. Stir well. Add the salt, mustard and Worcestershire sauce. Add the mashed beans and the hot dogs. Mix all well, and continue to cook for 5 minutes longer or until all is warmed through.

Serve in generous portions over the toasted English muffin halves or over toasted bread. Serves 6.

HOT DOG RIB LINERS

10 hot dogs
2 cups chopped, roasted, lean pork
⅔ cup grated sharp American cheese
¼ cup grated onion
⅓ cup mayonnaise
12 hamburger buns, halved

Chop the hot dogs until they are the consistency of coarse corn meal. Add the chopped roast pork, cheese and grated onion. Add the mayonnaise and mix all thoroughly.

Scoop out a portion of the dough from the top half of the hamburger buns, leaving about ½-inch wall. Fill this cavity with a portion of the hot dog mixture. Cover with the bottom half. Wrap each bun in aluminum foil.

Place the foil-wrapped sandwiches in a 375° F. oven for 15 minutes. Serve piping hot. Serves 6, allowing 2 sandwiches per person.

Variations:

Substitute ¼ cup French dressing for the mayonnaise for a different flavor.

Use a mixture of chopped roast pork and chopped roast veal instead of all pork.

Place a thin slice of tomato on top of the sandwich filling before wrapping in foil and placing in the oven.

Add ¼ cup chopped tart apple to the filling for a different flavor.

247

TACO HOT DOGS

12 hot dogs
¾ cup taco-type corn chips
2 cups grated American cheese
2 tablespoons grated onion
1 teaspoon Worcestershire sauce
½ cup mashed avocado pear
1 cup lettuce, finely shredded
12 hot dog buns

Cut the hot dogs open the long way, leaving a "hinge" at one side. Set aside. Crush the corn chips until they are very fine. Add ½ cup of the grated cheese. Reserve the rest. Add the grated onion, Worcestershire sauce and the avocado pear. Mix all very well. Stuff the center of each hot dog with the mixture.

Cut the hot dog buns open also leaving a "hinge" at one side. Place them, open side up, on a cooky sheet. Sprinkle each bun with a bit of the shredded lettuce. Place a filled hot dog on top of the lettuce in each bun and sprinkle a portion of the grated cheese over all.

Broil about 8 inches away from the heat until the cheese just begins to melt. Serve at once. Serves 6, allowing two per person.

HOT DOG POPS

12 hot dogs
1½ cups sifted flour
2 teaspoons baking powder
¼ teaspoon salt
1 cup milk
1 egg, beaten until lemon yellow
1 tablespoon melted butter
12 wooden skewers such as the butcher uses for mock chicken legs
Deep vegetable oil for frying

Sift the flour, baking powder and salt together twice. Mix the milk and egg together and stir into the flour until you have a smooth batter. Add the melted butter gradually and mix well.

Dry the hot dogs with paper toweling so that they contain absolutely no moisture. Stick a skewer into one end of the hot dog so that it reaches about halfway up into the inside. Using the skewer as a handle, dip each hot dog into the batter, allowing the batter to come up about ½ inch on to the skewer. Drop the batter covered hot dogs into 350° F. vegetable oil and fry until the batter turns a golden brown.

Remove the hot dogs to paper toweling and allow to drain slightly. Serve piping hot. Serves 6, allowing 2 hot dogs per person.

Note: These batter covered hot dogs can be made in advance and reheated in the oven on a pan with a rack. These hot dogs are very popular for children's parties. If very tiny tots are involved, omit using skewers in the hot dogs, for they can prove dangerous. The hot dogs can be dipped and fried without the sticks.

GLAZED HOT DOGS

12 hot dogs
1 cup apple butter
1 teaspoon grated lemon rind
1 teaspoon grated orange rind
12 hot dog buns
½ cup melted butter
½ cup chopped walnut meats

Place the hot dogs side by side in a shallow baking dish.

Mix the apple butter thoroughly with the lemon and orange rind. Pour the apple butter over and around the hot dogs. Place in a 325° F. oven for 25 minutes or until the apple butter is bubbly. Turn the hot dogs over once during this baking time.

Split the hot dog buns open just half way through. Place the buns, open side up, on a broiler rack. Brush the interior of each bun with melted butter; sprinkle the interior of the buns with a portion of the nut meats. Broil about 6 inches away from the heat for 5 minutes or until lightly toasted. Serve the glazed hot dogs in the toasted buns. Spoon a little of the apple butter left in the pan over each hot dog. Serves 6, allowing two per person.

SUPER SUPER HOT DOGS

½ pound ground chuck
¼ cup onion, finely chopped
2 tablespoons green pepper, finely chopped
1 clove garlic, finely crushed
½ teaspoon salt
¼ teaspoon seasoned pepper (obtainable in spice section of
   supermarkets)
½ teaspoon chili powder
½ teaspoon powdered mustard
2 tablespoons brown sugar
juice of ½ lemon
1 cup tomato sauce
8 hot dogs
8 hot dog buns

Place the ground chuck in a skillet over low heat. Saute until the meat loses its reddish color and begins to brown slightly. Add the onion and continue to saute until the edges of the onion begin to get transparent. Add the green pepper, garlic, salt, seasoned pepper, chili powder, mustard, brown sugar, lemon juice and tomato sauce. Cook over low heat for 25 minutes, stirring frequently.

Place three tablespoons of the beef-barbecue mixture in each hot dog bun; place the hot dog on top of the barbecue sauce; wrap each hot dog sandwich in aluminum foil, sealing tightly. Place the hot dog sandwiches on a cooky sheet in a 375° F. oven for 20 minutes. Serve at once, piping hot. Serves 8, allowing one hot dog per person.

HOT DOG CHEESE RAREBIT

4 English muffins, halved and lightly toasted
8 hot dogs
¼ cup soft butter
1 cup grated Cheddar cheese
¼ teaspoon salt
⅛ teaspoon pepper
¼ teaspoon paprika
2 tablespoons brandy
¾ cup mushroom stems and pieces, finely chopped
1 egg

Cut the hot dogs in half lengthwise and place the 2 halves, cut side down, on each toasted muffin half.

Mix the soft butter and cheese together until you have a soft spreadable mixture. Add the salt, pepper, paprika, brandy and the chopped mushrooms. Mix well, and then add the egg and beat until all is well blended.

Spread a portion of the mixture over and around the hot dog halves. Place the muffin halves on a cooky sheet in a 350° F. oven for 20 minutes or until the tops are bubbly and slightly browned.

Serve at once. Serves 4, allowing 2 muffin halves per person.

Variations:

Use ¾-inch thick slices of enriched white bread in place of each muffin half.
Use halves of hard rolls in place of the muffins.
Substitute American cheese for the Cheddar cheese.
Substitute Swiss cheese for the Cheddar cheese.

HOT DOG SURPRISE

10 hot dogs
5 hard-boiled eggs, chilled and peeled
½ cup sweet pickle relish, pressed dry
1 cup grated sharp Cheddar cheese
½ cup onion, finely chopped
½ cup peanuts, finely chopped
¼ cup mayonnaise
1 tablespoon prepared mustard
12 hot dog buns, halved

Chop the hot dogs and the hard-boiled eggs together until they are the same consistency as the pickle relish. Add the pickle relish, the grated cheese, chopped onion, chopped peanuts, mayonnaise and prepared mustard. Mix all thoroughly.

Scoop out about half the dough from the top half of the hot dog buns, leaving a ½-inch wall. Fill this cavity with the hot dog mixture. Cover with the bottom half. Wrap each filled bun in a square of aluminum foil. Place the foil-wrapped buns on a cooky sheet in a 300° F. oven for 20 minutes. Serve piping hot. Serves 6, allowing 2 sandwiches per person.

SWISS 'N WIENER SANDWICHES

4 hot dogs
4 hard-boiled eggs, cooled and peeled
½ cup cabbage, very finely chopped
¾ cup Swiss Cheese, diced in ¼-inch cubes
3 tablespoons ripe olives, finely chopped
2 tablespoons parsley, finely chopped
½ cup dairy sour cream
¼ cup mayonnaise
16 slices rye bread, lightly buttered

Chop the hot dogs and the hard-boiled eggs until they are about the size of small peas. Add the finely-chopped cabbage, the diced Swiss cheese, the ripe olives and the parsley.

Mix the sour cream and the mayonnaise together and add to the hot dog mixture. Mix all very well.

Spread the mixture on 8 of the slices of buttered rye bread; top with the remaining 8 slices. Cut each sandwich diagonally into thirds. Garnish with ripe or green olives. Makes 8 generous sandwiches.

Variations:

Substitute mild American cheese for the Swiss cheese.
Substitute mild Cheddar cheese for the Swiss cheese.
Use whole wheat bread in place of the rye bread.
Add 1 tablespoon of finely grated onion for more zip.
Add 2 tablespoons of chili sauce and reduce the mayonnaise to 3 tablespoons.

SURPRISE SANDWICHES

4 hard-boiled eggs, peeled and coarsely chopped
1 cup American cheese, diced in ¼-inch cubes
½ cup mayonnaise
2 tablespoons green pepper, finely chopped
2 tablespoons onion, finely chopped
2 tablespoons parsley, finely chopped
2 tablespoons sweet pickles, finely chopped, or drained pickle relish
8 hot dogs, finely chopped
8 hamburger buns

Mix the chopped eggs, cheese, mayonnaise, green pepper, onion, parsley, sweet pickle and hot dogs together well. Place a heaping spoonful of the mixture in the center of each hamburger bun. Wrap tightly in aluminum foil and place on a cooky sheet.

Bake in a 350° F. oven for 30 minutes. Serve at once. Serves 8.

HOT DOG ROUND-UP SANDWICHES

8 hot dogs
8 round hard rolls, 3 inches in diameter
1 #2½ can sauerkraut
1 teaspoon celery seed
½ cup catsup
2 tablespoons capers, finely chopped
1 teaspoon caraway seed
½ cup soft butter
1 tablespoon grated horseradish
1 teaspoon prepared yellow mustard

Drain the sauerkraut and press dry. Chop with a chopping blade until quite fine. Add the celery seed, catsup, capers and caraway seed. Place in the top of double boiler over slowly boiling water for 20 minutes to unite all of the flavors.

Mix the butter, horseradish and mustard together thoroughly. Cut off the top quarter of the hard rolls. Dig out the soft dough in the center forming a cup-like indentation in the roll. Spread the interior of each roll with some of the flavored butter. Place on a cooky sheet in a 450° F. oven for 5 minutes or until a delicate golden brown.

Make 12 slashes along one side of each hot dog. Make the slashes about halfway through the hot dogs. Drop the hot dogs into boiling water. Bring up to a full boil, cover and remove from the heat. Set aside for 5 minutes.

Remove the hot dogs from the water, and form into circles, slashed side out. Place the hot dog circles inside the buttered rolls. Fill the center of each hot dog circle with some of the sauerkraut mixture. Return to the 450° F. oven for 5 minutes longer. Serve at once. Serves 8.

FRENCH-TOASTED SURPRISES

8 hot dogs
1 cup pitted ripe olives
½ cup diced green pepper
½ cup diced sweet onion
1 clove garlic
¾ cup mayonnaise
½ cup catsup
½ teaspoon Accent
½ teaspoon salt
¼ teaspoon pepper
½ teaspoon paprika
12 slices enriched white bread
2 eggs, beaten until lemon yellow
½ cup half-and-half cream
½ cup sesame seed
½ cup soft butter

Chop the hot dogs, pitted olives, green pepper, onion and garlic until they are the consistency of hamburger. Add the mayonnaise, catsup, Accent, salt, pepper and paprika. Mix all very well. Spread the mixture on six slices of the bread. Top with the remaining six slices and press together firmly.

Mix the beaten eggs and the cream together. Dip each sandwich in it, and then sprinkle lightly with the sesame seed. Saute in the butter in a large skillet over moderate heat. Saute the sandwiches as you would French toast until they are a golden brown on each side. Serve piping hot with pickle chips or sweet-and-sour pickles as a garnish. Serves 6.

HOT DOGWICHES

8 hot dogs
½ cup chopped onion
¾ cup Velveeta cheese, diced in ¼-inch cubes
½ cup fresh tomato, diced in ¼-inch cubes
½ cup mayonnaise
1 teaspoon prepared yellow mustard
1 tablespoon dehydrated parsley
8 hamburger buns, sliced in half

Chop the hot dogs fairly fine; add the chopped onion, Velveeta, diced tomato and mix all well.

Mix the mayonnaise, mustard and parsley together; add to the hot dog mixture. Mix all well.

Scoop out the soft dough in the top part of the hamburger buns. Fill this cavity with a portion of the hot dog mixture. Place on top of the bun bottom. Wrap each bun in a square of aluminum foil.

Place the foil-wrapped sandwiches on a cooky sheet in a 350° F. oven for 30 minutes. Serve at once, piping hot. Serves 8, allowing 1 sandwich per person.

HOT DOG PASTIES

8 hot dogs
1 tablespoon vegetable shortening
¼ cup raw carrots, finely chopped
2 tablespoons onion, finely chopped
1 medium-sized tomato, peeled and chopped
1 medium-sized cooked potato, coarsely chopped
¼ teaspoon pepper
2 cups biscuit mix
⅓ cup milk

Chop the hot dogs until they are the consistency of peas. Melt the shortening in a skillet and saute the carrots and onion until lightly browned. Add the chopped hot dogs and saute until they are warmed through and just lightly browned. Add the chopped tomato, potato, salt and pepper. Mix well; cook for a few seconds and then remove from heat and set aside.

Mix the biscuit mix and the milk together until smooth. Turn out on a floured board or pastry cloth and knead until you have a smooth dough. Roll out to ¼ inch thickness. Cut into 4-inch circles. Place a spoonful of the hot dog mixture on one half of the circle. Wet the outer edge of the circle with a little cold water and fold over to form a half circle over the filling. Press the dampened edge of the circle tightly so that the filling is completely sealed inside.

Place the half circles on a lightly buttered cooky sheet and bake in a 350° F. oven for 15 minutes or until a delicate golden brown. Serve at once. Serves 6.

OVERNIGHT HOT DOG SANDWICHES

Here is a dish that your family will not tire of. It takes a little time, for it has to marinate in the refrigerator overnight or at least 8 hours. However, the reward in unique flavors is well worth it.

2 cups grated mild American cheese
8 hot dogs, finely chopped
1 3-ounce package cream cheese, at room temperature
18 slices square sandwich-style enriched white bread, crusts removed
4 eggs, beaten until lemon yellow
2½ cups milk
⅛ teaspoon salt
⅛ teaspoon pepper

Sandwich topping:

1 tablespoon butter
½ cup chopped onion
1 10-ounce can cream of mushroom soup
1 cup half-and-half cream
3 hard-boiled eggs, peeled and coarsely chopped
1 tablespoon parsley, finely chopped

Mix the grated American cheese, chopped hot dogs and the cream cheese together until it is of spreading consistency.

Spread this mixture on one side of twelve of the pieces of bread. The remaining six are reserved for the top. Place six of the spread slices, spread side up, on the bottom of a suitable baking dish. Follow this by placing the remaining six slices of spread bread on top, again with the spread side up. Top with the remaining six slices of unspread bread. You will end up with a three-layer sandwich. Press down on each sandwich slightly so that the layers are firmly adhered.

Mix the eggs, milk, salt and pepper together well. Pour this over the three-layer sandwiches. Cover with aluminum foil and place in the refrigerator overnight.

The following day, remove the foil cover and place in a 325° F. oven for 45 minutes or until firm and just slightly browned.

For the topping, melt the butter in a saucepan; add the

onion and saute until it is slightly transparent. Add the mush-room soup and cream and. stir well. Continue to cook over low heat for 5 minutes or until warmed through. Add the chopped eggs and the parsley; cook for 3 minutes longer. Stir from time to time to prevent sticking.

Using a broad spatula, remove each sandwich from the baking dish to individual serving dishes. Top each baked sandwich with generous spoonfuls of the sauce. Serve pip-ing hot. Serves 6.

HOT DOG SLOPPY JOES

8 hot dogs
½ cup onion, finely chopped
2 tablespoons butter
1 cup celery, finely chopped
2 8-ounce cans tomato sauce
2 tablespoons cornstarch
½ cup chili sauce
½ teaspoon salt
¼ teaspoon pepper
8 hamburger buns

Slice the hot dogs up into ⅛-inch circles. Set aside. Place the butter in a large skillet and add the onion. Saute until the onion is transparent; add the celery and continue to cook until the largest pieces of celery are tender and soft.

Stir the cornstarch into the tomato sauce until it is com-pletely dissolved. Add to the onion and celery mixture. Stir in the chili sauce, salt, pepper and hot dog pieces.

Cook over very low heat for 25 minutes or until thick-ened. Stir frequently to prevent sticking.

Serve by placing large spoonfuls between heated ham-burger buns. Serves 8.

SAUERKRAUT AND WIENER SANDWICHES

1 #2 can sauerkraut, drained and pressed dry
1 cup raw carrot, finely grated
¼ cup chopped green pepper
¼ cup chopped sweet red pepper
1 cup mayonnaise
1 teaspoon celery seed
1 teaspoon poppy seed
8 hot dogs, cut in half lengthwise
8 slices enriched white bread

Chop the sauerkraut with a chopping knife until it is as fine as the grated carrots. Combine the sauerkraut, grated carrot, green pepper, red pepper, mayonnaise, celery seed and poppy seed; mix all thoroughly.

Spread each piece of bread with a portion of the mixture. Place the hot dog halves, skin side up, on top of the kraut mixture. Place the slices of bread on a cooky sheet, broil about 6 inches from heat for 8 minutes or until the hot dogs begin to brown slightly. Serve at once. Serves 8, allowing 1 sandwich for each person.

Note: The relish mixture can also be used in hot dog buns with separately grilled or boiled hot dogs.

HOT DOG TRIOS

4 slices rye bread
4 slices white bread
4 slices whole wheat bread
½ cup soft butter
2 slices Swiss cheese (sandwich size)
2 slices Brick cheese (sandwich size)
2 slices American cheese (sandwich size)
6 hot dogs
3 eggs, beaten until lemon yellow
1 teaspoon Worcestershire sauce
2 drops Tabasco
1½ cups milk
1½ cups grated Cheddar cheese
6 slices tomato, ½ inch thick, approximately 3 inches in diameter

Lightly butter each slice of bread on one side. Place two

slices each, buttered side up, of the three kinds of bread over the bottom of a lightly buttered baking pan. Place a slice of Swiss cheese on the rye bread, a slice of Brick cheese on the whole wheat, a slice of American on the white bread.

Cut each hot dog into 3 slices lengthwise and place on top of the cheese. Place the corresponding slice of buttered bread on top of each hot dog.

Mix the eggs, Worcestershire sauce, Tabasco and milk together and pour over and around the sandwiches. Sprinkle the grated Cheddar over the top. Place in a 350° F. oven for 20 minutes or until the cheese topping has melted and become slightly puffed up. Place a slice of tomato on top of each sandwich and return to the oven for 8 minutes longer. Serve by using a broad spatula to transfer each sandwich to the plate; spoon some of the pan sauce over each. Serves 6.

HOT DOGS SUPREME

12 hot dogs
4 tablespoons onion juice, either fresh or bottled
6 pieces American cheese, 3x3x⅛ inch thick
12 10-inch strips bacon
12 hot dog buns

Slit the hot dogs on one side, but do not cut all the way through. Leave a "hinge" at one side. Brush the inside of each hot dog with the onion juice.

Cut the cheese into ½-inch strips and place two of the strips inside each slit hot dog. Fasten a strip of bacon to one end of the hot dog with a toothpick and spiral it around the cheese-filled hot dog barber-pole style. Fasten the bacon on the other end of the hot dog with a toothpick. Brush the bacon with some of the onion juice.

Place in the broiler or on the grill about 6 inches away from the heat. Broil, turning the hot dogs with tongs, until the bacon is crisp and golden on all sides.

Place the wrapped hot dogs in a bun, remove the toothpicks and serve. Serves 6, allowing two hot dogs per person.

Chapter XVIII

HOT DOGS AND VEGETABLES

HOT DOGS and vegetables go together like ham and eggs. In this day of frozen vegetables, beautifully canned vegetables and fresh crisp produce, the average homemaker has a choice that would have made her grandmother's head whirl.

Our daily diets and our tables probably boast more good vegetables than granny's did even on Thanksgiving day. If you want to send your vegetable platter from the "no-thank-you" class to the "may-I-have-seconds?" class, try cooking them with hot dogs.

Because hot dogs are delicately spiced, they boost vegetable flavors but still firmly retain their own identity. Vitamins, minerals and protein all in one dish is what you will offer your family when you combine vegetables with hot dogs. If you have never joined a hot dog with a vegetable, start today—you will please your family if you do.

HOT DOG SUCCOTASH

8 hot dogs
1 #2 can lima beans, drained
1 #2 can creamed corn
4 tablespoons butter
½ cup half-and-half cream
½ teaspoon salt
¼ teaspoon pepper
1 tablespoon dehydrated parsley

Cut the hot dogs into 1-inch lengths. Place in the top of the double boiler. Add the drained lima beans, creamed corn, butter, cream, salt, pepper and parsley.

Mix all thoroughly, cover, and cook over slowly boiling water for 20 minutes. Serve piping hot. Serves 6.

HOT DOGS AND GREEN BEANS

2 pounds green beans
6 slices lean bacon
6 hot dogs
¼ cup onion, finely chopped
1 tablespoon vinegar

Wash and remove the stems and ends from the green beans. Cut each bean in half or in quarters diagonally, depending upon their size. Cover with cold water and cook over moderate heat until the beans are tender but not mushy. Drain and set aside in the kettle in which they were cooked.

Dice the bacon in ¼-inch cubes and place in a skillet over moderate heat. Saute the bacon until it just begins to get crisp and golden. Dice the hot dogs in ½-inch cubes and add them to the bacon. Saute until the hot dog pieces just begin to brown.

Remove from the heat and stir in the onion and the vinegar. Pour this mixture over the beans and mix well. Return to the heat for 5 minutes or until the beans are piping hot. Serves 6.

ZUCCHINI AND HOT DOG SAUTE

6 hot dogs, sliced in ⅛-inch thick circles
2 pounds small zucchini, about 1-inch in diameter
⅓ cup olive oil
2 tablespoons parsley, finely chopped
1 clove garlic, finely chopped
¼ teaspoon oregano
½ teaspoon salt
¼ teaspoon black pepper

Wash the zucchini thoroughly and remove the stem ends. Slice, without peeling, into ⅛-inch thick slices. Place the olive oil in a large skillet over moderate heat. When hot, add the zucchini and hot dog circles. Saute over moderate heat until the zucchini has browned, turning frequently.

Reduce the heat to simmer and add the parsley, garlic, oregano, salt and pepper. Stir lightly to distribute the flavors. Simmer for 5 minutes longer. Serves 6.

HOT DOGS AND CABBAGE WITH SOUR CREAM DRESSING

6 cups cabbage, coarsely shredded
8 hot dogs
1 tablespoon all-purpose flour
¼ teaspoon powdered mustard
½ teaspoon salt
⅛ teaspoon pepper
2 eggs, beaten until lemon yellow
½ cup dairy sour cream
3 tablespoons cider vinegar
2 drops Tabasco

Place the shredded cabbage in a suitable saucepan with water to cover over moderate heat. Bring to a rolling boil and cook for 5 minutes or until the thick portions of the cabbage can barely be pierced with a fork. The cabbage should remain fairly crisp.

Slice the hot dogs lengthwise into quarters and then slice them in half crosswise, ending up with 8 strips each. Drop the hot dog pieces into the boiling cabbage and turn several times so that all of the hot dog pieces become heated through. Remove from the heat and set aside.

Mix the flour, mustard, salt and pepper together in the top of a double boiler. Add the eggs, sour cream, vinegar and Tabasco and mix well. Cook over slowly boiling water until thickened. Stir constantly to keep the mixture smooth and creamy.

Drain the hot dogs and the cabbage well. Place in a heated serving dish and pour the thickened dressing over all. Serves 6.

HOT DOG AND SPINACH BAKE

10 hot dogs
2 10 ounce packages of frozen chopped spinach, cooked according to package directions and drained
1½ cups grated American cheese
1 teaspoon garlic salt
2 tablespoons dehydrated onion
¾ cup instant rice, just as it comes from the package
2 eggs, beaten until lemon yellow
2 cups milk

Cut the hot dogs into ½-inch thick circles and place over the bottom of a buttered 10x8x2-inch deep baking dish.

Place the drained, cooked, chopped spinach into a large mixing bowl. Add the cheese, garlic salt, onion and rice. Mix all well. Add the beaten eggs to the milk and mix well. Add the eggs and milk to the spinach and rice mixture. Mix thoroughly and pour over the sliced hot dogs.

Place in a 325° F. oven for 40 minutes or until the center is firm to the touch. Serve by scooping up a portion of the hot dogs at the bottom and inverting over the rice and spinach custard. Serves 6.

GREEN AND YELLOW BEAN AND HOT DOG MEDLEY

1 #2 can green beans, undrained
1 #2 can yellow wax beans, undrained
8 hot dogs
¾ teaspoon powdered mustard
1 teaspoon flour
½ teaspoon salt
⅛ teaspoon pepper
2 egg yolks, beaten until lemon yellow
1 tablespoon butter or margarine
1 cup scalded milk
2 tablespoons fresh lemon juice

Place both cans of beans and their liquid in a 1½-quart saucepan over moderate heat. Cut the hot dogs into quarters the long way and then cut them in half crosswise. After the beans have reached the boiling point, turn off the heat and add the hot dog strips. Set aside while preparing the sauce.

In a 1-quart saucepan, mix the mustard, flour, salt and pepper together. Add the beaten egg yolks and blend until smooth. Gradually add the scalded milk; add the butter and mix well. Place over very low heat and cook, stirring constantly, until the mixture has thickened. Rapidly stir in the lemon juice. Turn off the heat.

Drain the bean and hot dog mixture and place on a heated serving dish. Pour the sauce over all. Serve at once. Serves 6.

TOMATOES WITH HOT DOG STUFFING #1

6 ripe but firm tomatoes, about 3 inches in diameter
½ teaspoon salt
½ teaspoon seasoned pepper
1 10-ounce package frozen tiny peas
½ cup onion, finely diced
1 cup water
6 hot dogs, diced in ¼-inch cubes
6 tablespoons grated Parmesan cheese

Cut off a ½-inch slice from the blossom end of the tomatoes and discard. Scoop out the inside of the tomatoes, leaving a firm wall about ½ inch thick. Sprinkle the salt and seasoned pepper inside the tomatoes and set aside inverted upside down so that they drain.

Discard the seedy sections from the scooped-out tomatoes. Cut the remainder into ¼-inch cubes.

Place the frozen peas, the onion and the water in a saucepan over moderate heat. Bring to a rolling boil for about 3 minutes. Drain and discard the water.

Add the cubed tomato pieces to the peas and onions. Add the diced hot dogs and mix all well. Place a portion of the mixture in each drained tomato shell. Place in a baking dish, and then put 1 tablespoon of the Parmesan cheese on top of each filled tomato.

Bake in a 350° F. oven for 5 to 8 minutes; they should just be heated through, but not baked until mushy or shriveled. Serve at once. Serves 6.

TOMATOES WITH HOT DOG STUFFING #2

6 large ripe firm tomatoes
1 teaspoon Accent
4 tablespoons butter
1 tablespoon onion, finely chopped
6 hot dogs, finely chopped
½ cup bread crumbs
½ teaspoon salt
¼ teaspoon celery salt
¼ teaspoon pepper
2 eggs, beaten until lemon yellow
2 additional tablespoons butter

264

Cut the tops from the tomatoes and discard. Scoop out the inside pulp, leaving about ½-inch wall. Reserve the pulp until later. Invert the tomatoes on paper toweling and allow the excess juice to drain away. Let drain for ½ hour. Then turn the open side up and sprinkle the cavity with a portion of the Accent.

Melt the butter in a skillet over moderate heat. Add the onions and saute until limp and transparent. Chop the tomato pulp until it is fairly fine and add to the onion and butter; cook over low heat for 5 minutes or until the pulp is slightly thickened.

Add the hot dogs, bread crumbs, salt, celery salt and pepper. Remove from the heat and mix all well. Add the beaten eggs and mix well again.

Stuff each tomato with the mixture and place in a lightly buttered baking dish. Place a portion of the butter on top of each stuffed tomato. Bake in a 350° F. oven for 35 minutes. Serves 6.

HOT DOG TOMATO SCRAMBLE

4 slices bacon, diced in ¼-inch pieces
6 hot dogs, diced in ¼-inch pieces
3 medium-sized fresh tomatoes; firm but ripe
½ teaspoon salt
¼ teaspoon pepper
6 eggs, beaten until frothy

Saute the bacon in a suitable skillet over moderate heat until it just begins to turn a golden brown. Add the diced hot dogs and continue to saute until the hot dogs begin to get brown on the edges. Remove the bacon and hot dogs from the skillet with a slotted spoon and set them aside on absorbent toweling in a warm oven.

Peel the tomatoes, cut them up into eighths and place them in the remaining bacon fat over low heat. Sprinkle the tomatoes with the salt and pepper. Cover, and cook for 8 minutes or until the tomatoes are bubbling and slightly thickened. Stir from time to time.

Add the beaten eggs to the tomatoes and continue to cook over low heat. Stir slowly until the eggs are light and fluffy and completely cooked. Place on a heated platter. Sprinkle the top with the diced hot dog and bacon pieces. Serve at once. Serves 6.

GREEN BEANS AND HOT DOGS IN MUSTARD SAUCE

2 10-ounce packages frozen French-style green beans
10 hot dogs, cut crosswise in 1-inch pieces
1 cup half-and-half cream
2 tablespoons granulated sugar
2 tablespoons powdered mustard
1 tablespoon cornstarch
½ teaspoon salt
1 egg yolk, beaten until lemon yellow
2 tablespoons cider vinegar

Cook the frozen French-style beans according to the package directions. Do not drain, but turn off the heat and add the hot dog pieces so that they are warmed through in the hot bean water.

Place ¾ cup of cream in the top of a double boiler over slowly boiling water. Cook until the cream is scalded. In the remaining ¼ cup of cream, stir in the sugar, mustard, cornstarch and salt. Mix well and then slowly add to the scalded milk. Turn the heat to very low, and continue to cook, stirring constantly, for 8 minutes or until the mixture thickens. Stir about 2 tablespoons of the thickened sauce into the beaten yolk and then add to the sauce. Continue to cook over simmering water for an additional 3 minutes, stirring constantly. The sauce should be fairly thick. Remove from the heat and add the vinegar.

Drain the beans and hot dogs and place them on a heated platter. Pour the sauce over the hot dogs and beans and serve. Serves 6.

HOT DOG STUFFED ONIONS

6 large onions, about 3 inches in diameter
6 hot dogs
1 cup soft white enriched breadcrumbs
1 teaspoon ground sage
⅛ teaspoon pepper
¼ cup melted butter
½ cup grated American cheese

Peel the onions and place in a 2-quart kettle with enough water to cover. Boil until just tender enough to pierce with a fork. Drain and cool. Using a teaspoon, scoop out the centers of the onion, leaving about a ½-inch wall.

Place the scooped-out onion centers and the hot dogs in a chopping bowl. Chop until they are the consistency of coarse corn meal. Add ½ cup of the bread crumbs, the sage and pepper. Fill each onion cavity with the mixture, mounding the mixture up on each onion. Place the onions in a shallow baking dish. Brush the tops with a portion of the melted butter. Cover the dish with aluminum foil and place in a 350° F. oven for 20 minutes.

At the end of this baking time, mix the remainder of the bread crumbs, melted butter and grated cheese together and sprinkle it over and around the onions. Return to the 350° F. oven for an additional 10 minutes or until the cheese and crumbs have turned a rich golden brown. Serve piping hot. Serves 6.

ENDIVE CHARLOTTE WITH HOT DOGS

1 medium-sized head endive
6 slices bacon
2 tablespoons butter
4 hot dogs
4 eggs, well beaten
¼ cup granulated sugar
½ teaspoon salt
⅛ teaspoon pepper
3 tablespoons cider vinegar

Wash the endive thoroughly, discarding any tough outside leaves. Using a kitchen shears, snip the endive up into 3-inch long pieces. Set aside.

Dice the bacon in ½-inch pieces; place in a large skillet over moderate heat. Saute the bacon until it is just barely crisp. Dice the hot dogs in ¼-inch cubes and add to the sauteed bacon along with the butter. Continue to cook until the butter has melted. Remove from the heat and allow to cool slightly.

Add the well-beaten eggs gradually to the bacon mixture. Stir constantly. Add the sugar, salt, pepper and vinegar. Mix all well. Return the mixture to very low heat and add the snipped endive. Cook over very low heat, stirring and turning over constantly, until the endive has wilted and is coated with the mixture. Serve at once. Serves 6.

BEANS AND HOT DOGS, GREEK STYLE

1 pound dried white beans, soaked overnight in water to cover
½ cup olive or peanut oil
4 cloves garlic, very finely chopped
1½ cups onion, sliced ¼ inch thick
3 tablespoons dehydrated parsley
1 bay leaf, broken into bits
¼ teaspoon marjoram
¼ teaspoon savory
¼ teaspoon thyme
1 #2½ can tomatoes
1 teaspoon Accent
½ teaspoon salt
¼ teaspoon pepper
8 hot dogs, cut in 2-inch lengths

Drain the water from the soaked beans and discard. Rinse the drained beans under cold running water for a few seconds and then drain again. Set aside.

Heat the oil in the bottom of a 2-quart kettle. Add the garlic and onions and saute until the onions are limp and transparent. Add the bay leaf, marjoram, savory, thyme and tomatoes. Cook over moderate heat, stirring frequently, until the sauce becomes as thick as catsup. Add the drained beans, Accent, salt and pepper. Mix well. Add enough water to cover the beans. Cover and cook at simmer for 1 hour and 30 minutes. Remove the cover, add the hot dog pieces, mix well, and continue to cook, uncovered, for 30 minutes longer. The sauce around the beans and the hot dogs should be thick and a rich tomato color. Serve piping hot. Serves 6.

HOT DOGS, RED CABBAGE AND CHESTNUTS

½ pound chestnuts
1 head red cabbage (about 2 pounds)
1 teaspoon salt
½ cup brown sugar
1 tablespoon caraway seed
¼ cup butter
8 hot dogs, cut in 1-inch pieces
⅓ cup cider vinegar

Using a very sharp knife, cut a slit in the side of each chestnut. Place the gashed chestnuts in a saucepan with enough water to cover. Bring to a boil and cook for 20 minutes. Remove from the heat, but do not drain. Remove two or three chestnuts from the water at a time, when they are cool enough to handle, and remove the brown outer shell and the brown membrane covering. Slice each peeled chestnut into ⅛-inch slices. Set aside.

Remove any wilted outer leaves from the cabbage and discard. Rinse under running water. Cut the head of cabbage into quarters and remove the hard center core. Cut the cabbage up into ½-inch slices.

Bring enough water to cover the cabbage to a rolling boil. Add the salt, brown sugar and caraway seed. Add the shredded cabbage. Cook for 10 minutes or until the thickest parts of the cabbage can be pierced with a fork. Remove from the heat and drain; discarding the water in which the cabbage was boiled. Set the cabbage aside.

Melt the butter in a skillet; add the hot dog pieces and saute until they just begin to brown. Add the sliced chestnuts and the cider vinegar. Mix well, and pour over the boiled cabbage. Toss lightly so that all is evenly mixed. Serve at once. Serves 6.

BARBECUED HOT DOGS AND ONIONS

8 hot dogs
1 8-ounce can tomato sauce
½ teaspoon powdered mustard
¼ teaspoon ground cloves
⅛ teaspoon sweet basil
1 teaspoon granulated sugar
1 10-ounce package frozen French fried onion rings

Cut the hot dogs diagonally into thirds and place in a 1-quart saucepan along with the tomato sauce, mustard, cloves, basil and sugar. Cook over low heat, uncovered, for 20 minutes or until the sauce has thickened to the consistency of catsup, stirring gently from time to time.

Place the French fried onion rings on an oven-proof serving platter. Place in a 375° F. oven for 8 to 10 minutes or until the rings are heated through and crisp.

Pour the hot dogs and their sauce over the heated onion rings and serve at once. Serves 6.

269

ASPARAGUS AND HOT DOGS #1

6 slices enriched white bread
¼ cup soft butter
6 hot dogs
1 #2 can asparagus spears, either green or white, undrained
4 egg whites
¼ teaspoon cream of tartar
¼ cup mayonnaise
½ teaspoon salt
½ teaspoon prepared mustard
1 tablespoon fresh lemon juice
1 teaspoon Accent

Butter one side of the bread and toast it under the broiler until a golden brown. Butter the other side and toast it until golden brown. Slice each hot dog the long way and lay the two halves diagonally across the toasted bread. Set aside.

Place the asparagus and its juice in a saucepan, taking care not to break off any of the tender tips. Bring to a rolling boil for 5 minutes and then drain. Place two of the hot asparagus spears diagonally on each side of the hot dogs. Do not worry if the spears extend over the edge of the toast.

Beat the egg whites until they are frothy and bubbly. Add the cream of tartar and continue to beat until they stand in stiff peaks. Mix the mayonnaise, salt, mustard, lemon juice and Accent together well. Fold this mixture into the stiff egg whites. Using a rubber spoon, spread this mixture over the hot dogs and asparagus. Heap it up slightly in the center. Broil about 6 inches from heat until a delicate golden brown. Serve at once. Serves 6.

ASPARAGUS AND HOT DOGS #2

1 #2 can white asparagus spears, drained
8 hot dogs
4 hard-boiled eggs, chilled and peeled
1 cup grated American cheese
2 tablespoons butter
2 tablespoons flour
1 cup milk
½ teaspoon salt
¼ teaspoon pepper
1 cup coarse cracker crumbs

270

Alternate the asparagus spears and the hot dogs in a baking dish. Slice the hard-boiled eggs and place egg slices over the asparagus and hot dogs. Sprinkle the grated cheese over the top of the eggs.

Melt the butter in a saucepan over low heat. Stir in the flour and continue to cook until it begins to bubble. Gradually add the milk. Continue to cook over low heat, stirring constantly, until the mixture is thickened and coats the spoon. Add the salt and pepper, mix, and pour over the grated cheese.

Sprinkle the coarse cracker crumbs over the top of the dish and place in a 350° F. oven for 20 minutes or until the cracker crumbs are brown. Serve immediately. Serves 6.

KIDNEY BEANS WITH HOT DOGS

2 cups dry kidney beans, soaked overnight in water to cover
4 cups water (additional)
¾ cup dark corn syrup
¼ cup cider vinegar
1 teaspoon salt
¼ teaspoon pepper
½ cup green pepper, diced in ¼-inch cubes
½ cup celery heart, cut in ⅛-inch slices
8 hot dogs, cut in 1-inch pieces

Drain the kidney beans, discarding the water in which they were soaked. Bring the four cups of water to a rolling boil in a suitable saucepan with a tightly fitting cover. Add the soaked beans to the boiling water gradually so that the water does not stop boiling. Cover tightly, and cook over moderate heat for 1 hour or until the beans are tender enough to pierce with a fork. Keep the beans covered with water during the cooking; if some of the water evaporates away, add more.

Do not drain the beans, but add the corn syrup, vinegar, salt and pepper right to the beans and the water in which they were boiled. Mix thoroughly, and cook over moderate heat, uncovered, for an additional 30 minutes or until the juice has thickened. Stir frequently and gently. Add the green pepper, celery and hot dog pieces and cook over low heat for an additional 8 minutes. Serve immediately. Serves 6.

CHICK PEAS AND HOT DOGS

1 pound dried chick peas, soaked overnight in water to
   cover
½ teaspoon salt
1 medium-sized bay leaf
¼ cup peanut oil
2 cloves garlic, finely minced
1½ cups onion, finely chopped
½ teaspoon chili powder
8 hot dogs, cut crosswise in 1-inch pieces
1 tablespoon wine vinegar
1 8-ounce can tomato sauce

Add more water to the chick peas while they are soaking
if necessary. Often, depending upon the degree of dryness,
they will expand and absorb much of the water, leaving
the top layers uncovered. After soaking, drain and discard
the water in which they were soaked. Rinse under cold
running water for several minutes. Place in a 2-quart kettle
with water to cover, add the salt and the bay leaf. Place
over moderate heat and cook for 1½ hours or until the
peas can be pierced with a fork. Drain, reserving 2 cups
of the water in which they were boiled.

Heat the peanut oil in a skillet; add the garlic and onions.
Saute them until the onion becomes slightly browned. Add
the chili powder. Mix well and then add the hot dog pieces.
Saute for 5 minutes longer or until the hot dogs begin to
turn slightly brown. Mix the wine vinegar and tomato sauce
and add to the onion-hot dog mixture. Stir well and remove from the heat.

Place the drained chick peas in a suitable casserole; add
the reserved 2 cups of water and the hot dog mixture.
Stir well and cover; place in a 350° F. oven for 40 minutes.
Uncover and bake for 15 minutes longer. Serve piping
hot. Serves 6.

HOT DOGS AND PINTO BEANS

1 pound dried pinto beans, soaked overnight in water to cover
6 strips lean bacon, cut in ¼-inch pieces
¾ cup onion, coarsely chopped
1 clove garlic, finely chopped
½ cup warm water (additional)
1 teaspoon salt
¼ teaspoon pepper
½ teaspoon powdered mustard
1 teaspoon pulverized sage
2 teaspoons brown sugar
8 hot dogs, cut in 1-inch pieces

Drain the beans and discard the water in which they were soaked. Rinse the beans under cold running water for several seconds, and then drain again. Place the beans in a 2-quart kettle and cover with cold water. Place over moderate heat and bring to a boil; turn the heat back to low and continue to cook the beans at low while you prepare the other ingredients.

Place the bacon in a skillet over moderate heat and saute until the bacon is crisp and golden. Using a slotted spoon, remove the pieces of bacon and add them to the boiling beans.

In the remaining bacon fat, saute the onions and garlic until they are limp and transparent and just beginning to brown. Drain off the excess fat and discard. Add the sauteed onions and garlic to the boiling beans.

To the ½ cup of warm water, add the salt, pepper, mustard, sage and brown sugar. Mix well and add to the boiling beans. Stir the beans so that all of the flavors are distributed, cover, and continue to cook at low heat for 1 hour and 45 minutes, stirring occasionally.

At the end of this cooking period, add the hot dog pieces and continue to cook, without covering, for an additional 15 minutes. Serve piping hot. Serves 6.

SAUERKRAUT AND WIENERS

2 #2 cans sauerkraut
6 slices very lean bacon, cut in 1-inch pieces
1 cup sliced onion
1 12-ounce bottle ale
8 wieners, cut diagonally into thirds
2 tablespoons butter
¾ cup domestic red wine, such as Burgundy
1 clove garlic, finely minced

Saute the bacon in the bottom of a heavy saucepan with a tightly fitting cover until it is a delicate golden brown. Pour off the excess grease.

Rinse the sauerkraut under cold running water and then drain thoroughly and press dry. Place the rinsed sauerkraut on top of the crisped bacon. Distribute the sliced onion over the top of the sauerkraut. Add the bottle of ale and cook over moderate heat, tightly covered, for 45 minutes.

While the sauerkraut is cooking, melt the butter in a skillet and saute the wieners until they begin to brown slightly. Add the wine and the minced garlic. Turn the heat down to simmer and continue to cook over low heat until the wine has almost completely evaporated. Turn the hot dogs frequently during this cooking period.

Using a slotted spoon, remove the cooked sauerkraut and bacon pieces from their juice and mound on a platter. Place the pieces of hot dog around the outside edge. Serve piping hot. Serves 6.

HOT DOGS WITH BEANS AND CORN

8 hot dogs, cut in thirds
½ cup butter
1 cup diced celery
½ cup diced onion
½ teaspoon salt
¼ teaspoon pepper
¼ teaspoon cinnamon
⅛ teaspoon ground cumin seed (optional)
2 10-ounce cans cream of celery soup
1 10-ounce package frozen French-style green beans, thawed
1 10-ounce package frozen corn niblets, thawed

274

Melt the butter in a 2-quart saucepan; add the celery and onions. Saute over low heat until the celery is transparent on the edges and tender. Add the hot dogs and continue to saute until they are lightly browned. Add the salt, pepper, cinnamon and cumin. Mix well, and then add the celery soup. Continue to cook over low heat until the soup begins to bubble.

Add the green beans and the niblet corn and cook over low heat for 8 minutes longer or until the beans are tender. Turn the mixture over from time to time, taking care not to mash the vegetables. Serve piping hot. This dish is excellent with plain boiled potatoes or with broad egg noodles. Serves 6.

HOT DOG AND BEAN LOAF

2 cups dry lima beans, soaked overnight in water to cover
12 hot dogs
1 cup soft enriched bread crumbs
¼ cup peanut butter
¼ teaspoon pepper
1 teaspoon poultry seasoning
¼ cup onion, finely grated
1 tablespoon bacon or ham fat
2 eggs, slightly beaten
1 cup milk

Drain the lima beans after soaking. Cover with fresh cold water and cook. over moderate heat until the beans are tender enough to pierce with a fork. Drain through a collander and allow them to cool. Chop the lima beans until they are the consistency of large peas.

Dice the hot dogs into ¼-inch cubes and add to the chopped beans. Add the bread crumbs, peanut butter, pepper, poultry seasoning, grated onion and bacon fat. Mix all very well; then gradually add the beaten egg and the milk. Mix well again. Place in a lightly greased 9x5x3-inch loaf pan. Place in a 350° F. oven for 40 minutes.

Allow the loaf to cool for 5 minutes; then loosen with a sharp knife and turn out on to a heated platter. Cut into 1½-inch slices. Serve with chili sauce or catsup.

CHINESE CABBAGE AND HOT DOGS

1 large head Chinese cabbage (about 2½ pounds)
8 hot dogs, sliced in ½-inch circles
2 teaspoons powdered mustard
¼ teaspoon salt
¼ cup soy sauce
2 teaspoons cider vinegar

Wash the Chinese cabbage under cold running water. Cut away any tough outside leaves and any tough root portion. Slice the cabbage across the grain in ¾-inch slices. Place the slices in a suitable kettle with water to cover. Bring to a rolling boil over moderate heat. Cook for 1 minute or just enough to wilt slightly. Drain thoroughly in a collander.

Place the cabbage in a large mixing bowl along with the hot dog slices. Mix the mustard, salt, soy sauce and vinegar thoroughly. Pour this mixture over the cabbage and the hot dogs. Turn several times so that the cabbage is evenly coated. Chill in the refrigerator for 2 hours before serving. Serves 6.

BRUSSEL SPROUTS AND HOT DOGS

2 10-ounce packages frozen Brussel sprouts
1 envelope dehydrated onion soup mix
2 cups hot water
8 hot dogs
1 tablespoon dehydrated parsley

Place the Brussel sprouts in a suitable saucepan. Mix the onion soup and the hot water together and pour over the Brussel sprouts. Place over moderate heat and cook for 8 minutes or until the sprouts are tender but not mushy.

Cut the hot dogs up into 1-inch lengths and add to the Brussel sprouts. Turn the heat to very low and cook for 5 minutes. Turn off the heat and allow the hot dogs and the sprouts to stand in the hot liquid for an additional 5 minutes. Do not cover.

Drain off the liquid and discard. Sprinkle the dehydrated parsley over the sprouts and hot dogs. Mix lightly and serve immediately. Serves 6.

HOT DOG ZUCCHINI COMBO

6 fairly large zucchini, about 5 inches long and 1½ inches in diameter
1 tablespoon salt
3 strips lean bacon, cut in ¼-inch cubes
6 hot dogs, finely chopped
½ cup onion, finely chopped
½ cup fine cracker crumbs
1 8-ounce can tomato sauce
⅛ teaspoon crushed sweet basil
½ teaspoon celery seed
1 tablespoon parsley, finely minced
⅛ teaspoon pepper
½ cup grated Cheddar cheese
½ cup grated Parmesan cheese

Wash the zucchini well, but do not peel. Place the squash in a large kettle with water to cover. Add the salt and cook over moderate heat, uncovered, for 15 minutes or until tender enough to pierce with a fork. Drain and allow to cool slightly.

Using a very sharp knife, cut the squash lengthwise; scoop out the seedy inside portion and place in a large mixing bowl.

Saute the bacon in a skillet until it just begins to turn brown. Add the chopped hot dogs and continue to cook until they begin to brown. Drain away any excess grease. Add the bacon and the hot dogs to the squash centers. Mix well. Add the onion, cracker crumbs and tomato sauce. Add the sweet basil, celery seed, parsley and pepper. Mix all thoroughly. Fill each half of the squash with the mixture and place in a lightly buttered baking dish.

Mix the Cheddar and the Parmesan cheese together and sprinkle this over each of the stuffed squash. Place in a 325° F. oven for 25 minutes or until the cheese has become bubbly and slightly browned. Serve at once, piping hot. Serves 6, allowing 2 halves per person.

CABBAGE ROLLS WITH HOT DOGS

1 3-to-4-pound head cabbage, with nice outside green leaves
3 cups boiling water
2 bay leaves
1 teaspoon garlic salt
¼ cup butter
1 cup chopped onion
12 hot dogs, chopped until the consistency of hamburger
⅔ cup instant rice, just as it comes from the package
½ cup dairy sour cream
½ teaspoon salt
½ teaspoon Accent
¼ teaspoon seasoned pepper
⅛ teaspoon nutmeg
1 #1 can tomato sauce (2 cups)

Remove 12 large outer leaves from the head of cabbage and wash them well. Place the leaves in a saucepan with a tightly fitting cover along with the 3 cups of boiling water. Bring to a rolling boil; then turn the heat back to simmer, cover and continue to cook for 5 minutes or until the cabbage leaves are soft and tender. Drain and set aside.

Cut the remainder of the cabbage into 4 wedges; remove the center core and discard. Using a very sharp knife, shred the remainder of the cabbage into 1/16-inch thick slices. Place this shredded cabbage over the bottom of a buttered 2-quart casserole with a tightly fitting cover. Add the bay leaves and sprinkle with the garlic salt. Set aside until you finish the stuffed rolls.

Melt the butter in a skillet and add the onion; saute until the onion begins to get transparent. Add the chopped hot dogs and saute until they just begin to get brown. Remove from the heat and add the rice, sour cream, salt, Accent, seasoned pepper and nutmeg. Mix all very well.

Place about ¼ cup of the hot dog mixture on the stem end of the softened cabbage leaf. Roll towards the outer edge, tucking in the sides as you go along. Fasten tightly with a toothpick.

Place the stuffed cabbage rolls on top of the shredded cabbage in the casserole. Pour the tomato sauce over the rolls and the shredded cabbage. Cover tightly and place in a 325° F. oven for 45 minutes. Turn the cabbage rolls over, and continue to bake for an additional 15 minutes.

Serve at once, piping hot. Serves 6, allowing two cabbage rolls per person.

SWEET AND SOUR LIMA BEANS WITH HOT DOGS

3 cups dried lima beans
1 clove garlic, finely chopped
½ teaspoon salt
¼ teaspoon pepper
½ cup onion, finely chopped
¼ cup parsley, finely chopped
⅓ cup cider vinegar
3 tablespoons granulated sugar
8 hot dogs, cut in thirds

Soak the lima beans overnight in water to cover. Then drain and cover with water again. Bring to a rolling boil and skim off any froth which may gather. Cover and continue to cook over low heat for 1 hour or until the beans are tender enough to pierce with a fork. Drain, reserving 1 cup of the liquid. Keep the beans covered so they remain warm.

Place the cup of bean liquid in a suitable saucepan; add the garlic, salt, pepper and chopped onion. Bring to a boil and continue to cook for 5 minutes. Add the parsley, vinegar, sugar and the cut-up hot dogs. Cook for an additional 3 minutes or until the hot dogs are heated through. Mix with the cooked beans and serve at once, piping hot. Serves 6.

Chapter XIX

HOT DOGS IN DOUGH

BECAUSE OF the subtle spices and naturally good flavor of hot dogs, they lend themselves well to being combined with doughs and baking.

On today's grocery shelves there are so many convenience doughs for breads and biscuits that the young homemaker hardly needs knowledge beyond having a degree in carton-opening. Convenience foods are wonderful and, for the most part, foolproof. However, if you want some delightful thrills and flavors, try combining your own basic ingredients for biscuits and breads. After you have accomplished this minor feat, try adding hot dogs!

In this chapter you will find deliciously garbed hot dogs both in doughs which are made from scratch and from convenient packages.

Combining meat and bread doughs is about as old as the art of cooking itself. One finds meat and dough combined in the recipes of those countries where meat is at a premium both supply and price-wise. You will find that when hot dogs are united with dough, they turn into wonderful budget stretchers and even greater flavor abettors.

HOT DOGS IN POTATO BISCUITS

3 cups hot mashed potatoes
3 eggs, separated
3 tablespoons melted butter
3 tablespoons grated Cheddar cheese
2 tablespoons parsley, finely chopped
½ teaspoon salt
¼ teaspoon pepper
3 tablespoons flour
¼ cup dairy sour cream
6 hot dogs, cut in half crosswise

Beat the egg yolks until they are lemon yellow. Add three tablespoons of the hot potato mixture to the yolks; mix well and then add the remainder of the yolks to the potatoes. Beat well; add the melted butter, cheese, parsley, salt, pepper and flour. Add the sour cream and beat the mixture for 1 minute.

Beat the egg whites until they are stiff and stand in peaks. Fold the egg whites into the potato mixture. Mound the potato mixture into 12 muffin tins which have been lightly buttered. Insert one hot-dog half, cut side down, into the center of each muffin and then mound up the muffin mixture around the hot dogs.

Place in a 350° F. oven for 20 minutes or until the surface of the muffins turn a rich golden brown. Serve at once, piping hot. Serves 6, allowing two potato biscuits per person.

HOT DOGS IN HERB BISCUITS

2 cups all-purpose flour
3 teaspoons baking powder
1 teaspoon salt
1 teaspoon poppy seed
½ teaspoon thyme
½ cup butter or margarine
¾ cup ice cold milk
6 hot dogs

Sift the flour, baking powder and salt together twice. Place in a mixing bowl along with the poppy seed and thyme. Add the butter and cut with a pastry blender until the consistency of corn meal. Stir in the ice cold milk and mix until you have a soft dough.

Place the dough on a floured board or pastry cloth and pat until about ½ inch thick. Using a floured doughnut cutter, cut into 12 doughnut-like circles.

Cut the hot dogs in half and place half a hot dog over the center of each circle. Bring up each side of the circle and pinch together, leaving the hot dog sticking out at each end. Place on a lightly buttered cooky tin and bake at 375° F. for 10 minutes or until the dough is a golden brown. Serves 6, allowing 2 per person.

HOT DOG, CHEESE AND ONION SURPRISE PIE

8 hot dogs
1 tablespoon butter
¾ cup chopped onion
1 egg, beaten until lemon yellow
½ cup water
1½ cups prepared biscuit mix
½ cup grated mild Cheddar Cheese
2 tablespoons poppy seeds
2 tablespoons melted butter (additional)

Melt the tablespoon of butter in a skillet and then add the chopped onions. Saute the onions until they are transparent and limp. Set aside to cool.

Mix the egg, water and biscuit mix until you have a soft dough, free of lumps. Add the cooled sauteed onion and the grated cheese. Mix well; divide the dough into two equal parts. Place one portion of the dough over the bottom of a buttered 8x2-inch deep round glass baking dish. Arrange the hot dogs over the dough from the center to the outer edge like the petals of a flower. Place the remaining dough on top of the hot dogs. Press it into place so that you can faintly see the outline of each hot dog. Using a sharp knife, score the dough between the hot dogs just as you would cut a pie.

Sprinkle the poppy seeds over the top of the dough and drizzle the two tablespoons of butter over the top. Place in a 400° F. oven for 25 minutes or until the top crust is a rich golden brown. Cut into portions along your previously scored markings and serve with additional chips of butter. Serves 6 to 8.

SURPRISE BISCUITS

10 hot dogs
1 teaspoon powdered mustard
¼ cup chopped sweet pickles
1 egg, slightly beaten
¼ cup chili sauce
1 tube refrigerated baking powder biscuits

Chop the hot dogs until they are the consistency of coarse corn meal. Add the mustard, sweet pickle, egg and chili sauce. Mix together thoroughly.

Flatten each half of the refrigerated baking powder biscuits until they are about 1 inch larger than they come in the can. Mound up a portion of the hot dog mixture in the middle of half the flattened biscuits. Moisten the outer edge with a little water. Press the top half of each biscuit in place over the filling; seal the outer edges well.

Place each filled biscuit in a buttered muffin tin or on a buttered cooky sheet. Bake at 400° F. for 15 minutes or until the biscuits are puffed up and a golden brown.

These hot dog filled biscuits are delightful served with a tossed green salad. Makes 12 biscuits.

HOT DOG ONION PIE

3 slices bacon, diced in ½-inch pieces
4 hot dogs, cut in ⅛-inch circles
2 cups sweet onion, such as Bermuda, cut into ½-inch cubes
3 eggs, beaten until lemon yellow
½ teaspoon salt
¼ teaspoon pepper
¾ cup half-and-half cream
1 9-inch unbaked deep pie crust
3 tablespoons grated Swiss cheese

Saute the bacon pieces until they are golden and crisp. Using a slotted spoon, remove the crisp bacon pieces from the grease and sprinkle them over the bottom of the 9-inch pie crust. Add the hot dog slices and the onion pieces to the hot bacon grease and saute until the onion is limp and transparent. Remove from the heat and set aside to cool to room temperature.

Mix the beaten eggs, cream, salt and pepper together. Stir this into the hot dog-onion mixture. Pour into the unbaked pie shell. Sprinkle the grated Swiss cheese over the top. Place in a 325° F. oven for 35 minutes or until the center is firm and a table knife comes out clean when inserted. Serve at once, piping hot. Serves 6.

HOT DOG BISCUIT PIE

1½ cups all-purpose flour
3 teaspoons baking powder
½ teaspoon salt
1 teaspoon paprika
¼ teaspoon pepper
1 teaspoon celery salt
5 tablespoons vegetable shortening
¾ cup cold milk
3 tablespoons butter
¼ cup onion, sliced ⅛ inch thick
1 10-ounce can tomato soup
8 hot dogs, finely chopped

Mix the flour, baking powder, salt, pepper, paprika and celery salt together well. Using a pastry blender or two table knives, cut in the shortening until it is the consistency of coarse corn meal. Add the cold milk and mix into a soft dough. Place on a floured board, knead lightly, and pat out until about ½ inch thick. Cut into 2-inch circles. Set aside.

Melt the butter in a skillet; add the onion and saute until it is transparent and tender. Add the tomato soup and mix well. Add the chopped hot dogs and cook until the mixture bubbles. Pour into a buttered casserole or baking dish. Place the biscuit rounds on top. Bake in a 450° F. oven for 20 minutes or until the biscuits are puffed up and a golden brown. Serve at once. Serves 6.

HOT DOG CORN BREAD PIE

8 hot dogs, cut in ¼-inch circles
½ cup onion, coarsely chopped
1 tablespoon margarine
1 8-ounce can tomato sauce
1 #2 can red kidney beans, drained
½ teaspoon salt
¼ teaspoon pepper
½ teaspoon chili powder (increase to 1 teaspoon if you like chili flavor)
½ teaspoon Accent

Corn Bread Topping:

1½ cups all-purpose flour
1 teaspoon salt
4 teaspoons baking powder
1 teaspoon granulated sugar
1 cup yellow corn meal
1½ cups milk
⅓ cup melted butter
3 eggs, beaten until lemon yellow

Place the hot dog pieces, onion and margarine in a large skillet; saute over low heat until the onion is transparent and the hot dogs begin to brown slightly. Add the tomato sauce, kidney beans, salt, pepper, chili powder and Accent. Mix all well and pour into a 2-quart, buttered casserole.

Sift the flour, salt, baking powder, sugar and corn meal together twice. Place in a suitable mixing bowl. Mix the milk, melted butter and the beaten eggs together, then pour into the dry ingredients. Beat with a wire whisk until smooth and free of lumps. Spoon over the top of the hot dog mixture. Bake in a 375° F. oven for 25 minutes. Serves 6.

HOT DOG CORN FRITTERS

6 eggs, separated
1 12-ounce can niblet corn with pimiento, drained
6 hot dogs, diced in ¼-inch pieces
½ cup all-purpose flour
½ teaspoon salt
1 tablespoon cooking sherry (optional but good)

Beat the egg yolks until they are light and fluffy; add the corn, the diced hot dogs, flour, salt and sherry. Mix very well.

Beat the egg whites until they stand in peaks. Fold the egg whites into the hot dog mixture, taking care not to lose the air.

Fry on a hot, lightly greased griddle as you would pancakes, using about ¼ cup of the mixture per cake. Serve at once, piping hot. Serves 6, generously.

HOT DOG PIE #1

2 cups all-purpose flour
½ teaspoon salt
⅔ cup margarine or vegetable shortening
5 brimming tablespoons ice water
1 10-ounce package frozen cauliflower, thawed to room temperature
1 10-ounce package frozen green beans, thawed to room temperature
6 hot dogs, diced in ½-inch cubes
½ cup onion, thinly sliced
1 10-ounce can Cheddar cheese soup

Sift the flour and salt together; add the margarine and cut with a pastry blender until it is crumbly and about the size of peas. Add the ice water, one tablespoon at a time, and work into a soft dough.

Place the ball of dough on a floured board and divide into thirds. Take ⅔ of the dough and roll out until you have a circle which will fit the bottom and sides of a 1½-quart casserole. Place the dough in the casserole and pinch the edges into flutes so that the juices of the casserole will not run out during baking.

Place the remaining ⅓ of the dough on the floured board and roll out into a circle which will fit the top of the casserole. Cut into six wedges just as you would cut a pie. Place the 6 wedges on a cooky sheet. Place the lined casserole and the wedges in a 400° F. oven for 10 minutes or until a very pale golden brown.

Cut any large pieces of cauliflower in half; place in a large mixing bowl along with the beans, hot dog cubes, onion and the cheese soup just as it comes from the can. Mix all together well.

Leaving your baked pastry shell right in the casserole in which it was baked, pour in the vegetable and hot dog mixture. Press the ingredients down slightly so that the top is not too mounded. Place the 6 baked wedges over the top of the casserole. Bake in a 325° F. oven for 25 minutes or until the cauliflower can be pierced with a fork. Serve piping hot. Serves 4 to 6.

HOT DOG PIE #2

2 cups sifted all-purpose flour
1 teaspoon salt
⅔ cup shortening
4 brimming tablespoons ice water
1 10-ounce package frozen cauliflower, cooked according to package directions
1 10-ounce package frozen carrots and peas in cream sauce, cooked according to package directions
½ cup onion, finely chopped
1 10-ounce can Cheddar cheese soup
½ cup milk
8 hot dogs, cut in ½-inch cubes

Sift the flour and salt together twice. Place in a mixing bowl along with the shortening. Cut with a pastry blender until it is the consistency of corn meal. Add the water a little at a time, and work into a soft dough. Divide the dough in half; roll out one half to fit the bottom and sides of a 1½-quart casserole. Roll out the remainder to fit the top of the casserole. Set aside while you prepare the rest of the ingredients.

Place the cauliflower and carrots and peas in a saucepan over very low heat. Add the chopped onion, the Cheddar cheese soup and milk. Cook until all is smoothly blended. Stir lightly from time to time. Add the hot dogs and mix lightly.

Pour the mixture into the waiting bottom crust in the casserole. Cut the top crust into 6 equal wedges and lay them on top of the hot dog and vegetable mixture. Flute and seal the edges of the pastry where they meet on the outer rim.

Place in a 350° F. oven for 20 minutes or until the crust is golden brown. Serves 6.

HOT DOG DUMPLINGS

8 medium-sized potatoes
2 egg yolks, beaten until lemon yellow
1 teaspoon salt
¼ teaspoon pepper
6 strips lean bacon
6 hot dogs
½ cup chopped onion
1 tablespoon parsley, finely chopped
3 cups sifted, all-purpose flour
3 quarts water
1 tablespoon salt

Peel and quarter the potatoes. Place in a saucepan with water to cover. Cook over moderate heat for about 20 minutes or until they can be pierced with a fork. Drain and mash until light and fluffy. Allow to cool to room temperature, then add the egg yolks, salt and pepper. Whip again until the mixture is light and fluffy. Set aside.

Dice the bacon into ¼-inch pieces and place in a skillet over moderate heat. Dice the hot dogs and add to the bacon. Add the chopped onion and saute until the onion is soft and transparent. Pour off any excess grease. Remove from the heat and stir in the parsley. Set aside.

Add one half of the flour to the potato mixture; stir until mixed and smooth. Add the remaining flour and knead into a dough just as you would bread. Place on a floured board or pastry cloth and continue to knead until slightly elastic. Flatten out the dough until it is uniformly ½ inch thick. Using a 2-inch diameter biscuit cutter, cut the dough into circles. Place 1 tablespoon of the hot dog mixture on one circle and cover with another circle. Press the edges together firmly to seal and then shape into a ball.

Bring the three quarts of water to a rolling boil in a 4-quart saucepan with a tightly fitting cover. Add 1 tablespoon salt. Add the dumplings one at a time to the boiling water; cover tightly and cook for 15 minutes without removing the cover. Remove the dumplings with a slotted spoon; drain well. Place on a warm platter and serve at once. Serves 6.

Note: These dumplings may be served plain or they may be served with melted butter drizzled over them. They make a good companion to sauerkraut and also make an excellent

288

main dish when sprinkled with ¾ cup buttered bread crumbs and placed under the broiler long enough to brown the crumbs. The dumplings can also be served in a clear soup or broth. Do not cook the dumplings in the soup, but cook them separately as directed and then add them to the hot soup at the last minute.

If you have any leftover hot dog dumplings, they are delicious if sauteed until golden brown in butter.

SWISS PIE WITH HOT DOGS

1 unbaked 10-inch pie shell
5 strips lean bacon
6 hot dogs, diced in ¼-inch cubes
1 cup shredded Swiss cheese
4 eggs, beaten until lemon yellow
2 cups half-and-half cream
½ teaspoon salt
¼ teaspoon pepper
¼ teaspoon sugar
2 drops Tabasco
⅛ teaspoon nutmeg, freshly grated

Place the unbaked crust in a 400° F. oven for 8 minutes or until it just begins to turn a pale brown. Remove from the oven and set aside. Turn oven to 450° F. to preheat while making the rest of the pie.

Place the bacon in a skillet and saute until it is crisp and brown. Remove the bacon to paper toweling to drain. Saute the hot dog cubes in the bacon drippings until they get brown around the edges; remove to paper toweling to drain. Discard the remainder of the bacon drippings.

Crumble the crisp bacon into bits and spread over the bottom of the pie crust. Sprinkle the hot dog pieces over the bacon. Sprinkle the shredded Swiss cheese over the bacon and the hot dogs.

Mix the eggs, cream, salt, pepper, sugar, Tabasco and nutmeg together well. Pour over the ingredients in the pie shell. Place in a 450° F. oven and immediately reduce the heat to 400° F. Bake at 400° F. for 10 minutes and then reduce the heat to 325° F. and bake for 30 minutes or until the center of the pie is firm and the top is a rich brown. Cut in wedges and serve. Serves 6.

PEEKING DOGS

1 cup milk
1 envelope dry, granulated yeast
¼ cup lukewarm water
¼ cup sugar
¼ cup shortening
1 teaspoon salt
4 cups sifted flour
2 eggs, beaten until lemon yellow
12 hot dogs
3 tablespoons butter
2 tablespoons poppy seed

Scald the milk in the top of a double boiler over rapidly boiling water. Remove from the heat and allow to cool. Dissolve the yeast in the ¼ cup of lukewarm water. Set aside.

Place the sugar, shortening and salt in a large mixing bowl; mix slightly and then pour the scalded milk over all. Stir until the shortening has melted. When cooled to lukewarm, add 1 cup of the sifted flour gradually. Beat until smooth. Add the softened yeast. Mix well. Gradually add half of the remaining flour and beat until smooth. Add the two well beaten eggs and mix again. Beat in enough of the remaining flour to make a soft dough. Place the dough on a well-floured board and allow it to stand in a warm place, away from drafts, for 10 minutes.

Knead the dough until it is elastic. Form the dough into a ball, and place in a greased mixing bowl. Turn the dough over so that the top is greased and shiny from being in the greased bowl. Cover, and set in a warm place for about ½ hour or until double in size. Knead again, and let rise once more until doubled in size. Knead again, and place on a lightly floured board.

Roll the dough out into a rectangle about ½ inch thick. Cut into strips ½ x ½ x 6 inches long.

Starting at one end of a hot dog, wrap the dough around the hot dog barber pole fashion. Wrap each hot dog to within ½ inch of the other end, allowing one end of the hot dog to peek out. Pinch the end piece to the rest of the dough to seal in place. Place the dough-wrapped hot dogs on a lightly buttered baking sheet. Brush with melted butter and sprinkle with poppy seed. Cover and allow the dough to rise again for 25 minutes longer.

Place in a 425° F. oven for 15 minutes or until the crust around the hot dog is a golden brown. These peeking dogs can be served either hot or cold. Makes 1 dozen.

HOT DOG PIZZA PIE

8 hot dogs, diced in ¼-inch cubes
1 cup onion, coarsely chopped, or, if you prefer, very thinly sliced
1 clove garlic, finely chopped
1 #1 can tomato sauce (2 cups)
1 teaspoon salt
¼ teaspoon seasoned pepper
1 teaspoon fennel seed
1 teaspoon oregano
1 package (1 ounce) dry yeast dissolved in ¾ cup lukewarm water
2½ cups prepared biscuit mix
½ cup all-purpose flour
1 pound Mozzarella cheese, sliced ⅛ inch thick
½ cup grated Parmesan cheese

Mix the chopped hot dogs, onion, garlic, tomato sauce, salt, pepper, fennel seed and oregano together. Place over moderate heat and bring to a rolling boil; turn the heat down and simmer for 5 minutes longer, stirring occasionally to prevent sticking. Remove from heat and set aside.

Mix the yeast dissolved in the ¾ cup lukewarm water with the prepared biscuit mix. Beat vigorously until smooth and free of lumps. Sprinkle a portion of the flour on a board or pastry cloth and knead the dough until it is smooth and glossy. Divide the dough into two parts. On a floured surface, roll each piece of dough into a 12- to 14-inch circle. Place the circle of dough on a cooky sheet and pinch and flute the edge so that the cheese and sauce cannot run out during baking.

Spread half of the hot dog and tomato mixture on each of the dough circles. Place the Mozzarella slices over the top of the sauce. Sprinkle the tops with the Parmesan cheese.

Bake in a 450° F. oven for 12 minutes or until the cheese is bubbly and the edges of the crust are a golden brown. Serve at once. Serves 6.

291

HOT DOG ROLL-UPS

2 cups all-purpose flour
4 teaspoons baking powder
½ teaspoon salt
4 tablespoons butter or margarine
¾ cup cold milk
8 hot dogs, very finely chopped
4 tablespoons butter (additional)
1 tablespoon prepared yellow mustard

Cheese Sauce:

2 tablespoons butter
2 tablespoons all-purpose flour
1 cup milk
1 cup grated mild Cheddar cheese

Sift the flour, baking powder and salt together twice. Using a pastry blender or two knives, cut the butter into the flour until it is the consistency of coarse corn meal. Add the milk, a little at a time, and stir until all is thoroughly mixed. Place on a floured board or pastry cloth and knead into a smooth dough.

Melt the additional butter in a saucepan over low heat, add the hot dogs and the mustard; mix well. Spread the hot dog mixture over the surface of the dough. Roll up as you would a jelly roll. Cut up into 1½-inch thick slices. Flatten each slice slightly. Place on a cooky sheet and bake in a 400° F. oven for 20 minutes or until the tops are a golden brown.

For the sauce, melt the butter in a saucepan, stir in the flour and continue to cook until it begins to bubble. Slowly add the milk and, stirring constantly, continue to cook over low heat until the mixture has thickened and coats the spoon. Add the grated cheese and continue to cook over low heat until all of the cheese has melted and the mixture is smooth and creamy.

Serve each roll-up with a topping of the cheese sauce. Serves 6, allowing one roll-up per person.

Variations:

Add ½ cup finely-chopped ripe olives to the hot dog mixture for a different flavor.

Add ½ cup very finely-chopped onions to the hot dog mixture.

Add ¼ cup drained pickle relish to the hot dog mixture.

Substitute ½ cup Parmesan cheese for half of the Cheddar cheese.

HOT DOGS IN A BLANKET

1 tablespoon granulated dry yeast
½ cup lukewarm water
¾ cup milk, scalded and then cooled to lukewarm
1 teaspoon salt
2 teaspoons sugar
2 cups all-purpose flour
6 hot dogs, cut in half crosswise
2 slices American cheese 3x3x⅛ inch thick

Dissolve the dry yeast in the half cup of lukewarm water. Add the salt and sugar to the cooled, scalded milk. Mix well, and then stir in the dissolved yeast. Sift the flour into the milk mixture a little at a time; mix well after each addition. Cover and set aside, away from all drafts, until doubled in bulk.

Slit each hot dog in half lengthwise; do not cut all the way through, but leave a "hinge" at the back. Cut the cheese into ½x1½-inch pieces. Place 2 pieces of cheese in each hot-dog slit.

When the dough has doubled in bulk, take a piece about as big as an egg and roll out to about the same thickness as pie dough. Shape into a wedge and place the cheese-filled hot dog at the broad end. Roll the hot dog up in the dough, folding in the sides as you go along. Place in rows in a coffee-cake tin and bake in a 375° F. oven for 35 minutes or until puffed up and golden brown. Serve either hot or cold. Makes 6.

Chapter XX

GOURMET HOT DOGS

GOURMET COOKING usually brings to mind fabulous dishes like Polynesian chicken or a prime roast 7 ribs long.

When you mention hot dogs and the word gourmet in a single breath, people are inclined to look at you askance. Stare them down and hold your ground, for hot dogs can be made into some real gourmet dishes.

The flavor and spices in hot dogs lend themselves well to the festive touch and become loyal, agreeable companions to wine, brandy or fruits and vegetables often found on the gourmet's list.

HOT DOGS IN FRUITED BRANDY SAUCE

1 10-ounce can condensed bouillon
1 9-ounce can crushed pineapple
⅓ cup white raisins
2 tablespoons cornstarch
¼ cup water
½ cup grape brandy
12 hot dogs

Place the bouillon, crushed pineapple, juice and all, and white raisins in a saucepan over moderate heat. Mix the cornstarch with the water. When the bouillon begins to bubble, add the cornstarch and cook until thickened and transparent, stirring constantly. Remove from heat and stir in the brandy.

Place the hot dogs in a lightly buttered shallow baking dish. Pour the sauce over the hot dogs. Place in a 375° F. oven for 8 minutes or until heated through. Serve at once, piping hot. Serves 6, allowing 2 hot dogs per person.

FESTIVE HOT DOG SOUFFLE

15 hot dogs
¼ cup melted butter
1 clove garlic, sliced paper thin
¼ cup all-purpose flour
½ cup milk
1 #303 can cream-style corn
½ teaspoon salt
¼ teaspoon pepper
1 teaspoon Worcestershire sauce
2 cups grated mild Cheddar cheese
6 eggs, separated

Cut off a small portion of one end of each of the hot dogs so that they can be stood on end around the outside perimeter of a buttered 2-quart casserole. Set the hot dogs aside while you mix the soufflé.

Place the melted butter in a saucepan with the sliced garlic and cook over moderate heat until the garlic begins to brown. Using a slotted spoon, remove the pieces of garlic and discard. Add the flour to the melted butter and stir until it is smooth; slowly add the milk and, stirring constantly, continue to cook over low heat until smoothly blended and thickened. Add the corn, salt, pepper and Worcestershire sauce. Add the grated cheese and continue to cook over low heat, stirring constantly, until the cheese has melted. Remove from the heat and set aside to cool.

Beat the egg yolks until they are lemon colored. Add three tablespoons of the cheese mixture to the eggs and then add the eggs to the cheese mixture. Beat the egg whites until they stand in peaks. Gently fold the whites into the cheese mixture.

Pour the mixture into a 2-quart buttered casserole and stand each hot dog on the cut end around the outside perimeter of the casserole. Bake in a 350° F. oven for 45 minutes or until the center is firm. Serve at once, piping hot. Serves 6.

HOT DOGS IN WINE AND MUSTARD SAUCE

1 pound hot dogs
1 tablespoon cornstarch
1 tablespoon granulated sugar
1 teaspoon powdered mustard
½ teaspoon salt
½ teaspoon Accent
1 cup water
2 tablespoons butter or margarine
¼ cup cider vinegar
¼ cup Rhine wine or Sauterne
1 teaspoon grated horseradish
3 egg yolks, beaten until lemon yellow

Mix the cornstarch, sugar, mustard, salt and Accent together thoroughly. Place in the top of a double boiler along with the cup of water. Mix well, and then cook directly over the heat until slightly thickened, stirring constantly.

Now place the double boiler top over rapidly boiling water and add the butter, vinegar, Rhine wine and horseradish. Mix all thoroughly. Take 3 tablespoons of the mixture and stir into the beaten egg yolks; then add the egg yolks to the mustard mixture. Stir and mix well. Continue to cook over the boiling water until the mixture is thick and coats the spoon.

Place the hot dogs in the mustard sauce, reduce the heat under the boiling water, and cook for 15 minutes. If the hot dogs are not completely submerged in the sauce, turn them over several times during this cooking period.

Serve on warm hot dog buns with a portion of the sauce as a sandwich. These hot dogs are also delicious with potato salad. Serves 4, allowing 2 hot dogs per person.

HOT DOG OPEN FACERS

10 hot dogs, diced in ¼-inch pieces
1½ cups half-and-half cream
2 egg yolks, beaten until lemon yellow
½ teaspoon salt
¼ teaspoon pepper
2 tablespoons sherry
1 tablespoon dehydrated parsley
6 English muffins, halved and toasted

Place the cream in the top of a double boiler and heat to the scalding point. Take two tablespoons of the hot cream and stir it into the beaten egg yolks; add the beaten yolks to the cream. Cook, stirring constantly, for 3 minutes or until thickened and the mixture coats the spoon.

Add the salt, pepper, sherry and parsley. Stir well and add the diced hot dogs. Cook for an additional 3 minutes or until the hot dogs are heated through.

Place two of the English muffin halves on a serving plate and top with a generous portion of the hot-dog mixture. Serve at once, piping hot. Serves 6, allowing two muffin halves for each person.

HOT DOG SHISH KABOBS

1 pound hot dogs
2 #1 cans pineapple chunks
¼ cup soy sauce
¼ cup olive oil
¾ cup Burgundy
12 slices ranch-style bacon, approximately 10 inches long
1 #1 can pitted ripe olives, drained
24 large, pimiento-stuffed green olives
1 #2 can small boiled onions

Cut each hot dog up into 4 pieces. Place in a mixing bowl with a tightly fitting cover. Drain the pineapple chunks and reserve the juice. Place the soy sauce and olive oil in a measuring cup and then add enough of the pineapple juice to bring it up to 1 cup. Mix with the Burgundy and pour over the hot dog pieces. Cover and set aside to marinate for at least 1 hour. Turn the hot dog pieces over from time to time so that all are evenly flavored by the marinade.

Cut the bacon strips into approximate thirds and wrap a piece of bacon around each pineapple wedge. String on a skewer following with a piece of hot dog a ripe olive, a stuffed olive, a boiled onion and so on until you have used up all of the ingredients.

Brush generously with the remaining hot dog marinade. Place on a broiler rack about 4 inches from the heat or on an outside grill. Broil or grill until the bacon is crisp and golden. Baste with the marinade frequently during this time. Serve piping hot. Serves 6 generously.

HOT DOG RICH BOY SANDWICHES

8 hot dogs
8 slices Swiss cheese, ⅛ inch thick
8 slices boiled ham, 1/16 inch thick
4 miniature loaves French Bread (baked, not the bake-and-serve variety)
¼ cup melted butter
1 10-ounce package frozen broccoli spears, thawed
1 10-ounce package frozen French fried onion rings, thawed
1 cup dairy sour cream
2 egg yolks, beaten until lemon yellow
½ teaspoon salt
1 tablespoon lemon juice
⅛ teaspoon powdered mustard
1 drop Tabasco

Using a very sharp knife, make criss-cross gashes about ⅛ inch deep along the side of each hot dog. Place a slice of Swiss cheese on top of a slice of boiled ham; place the hot dog at one end of the cheese and ham and roll it up. Fasten the cheese and ham in place with a toothpick. Leave the toothpick protruding so that it can be removed before serving.

Cut the French bread loaves in half lengthwise and scoop out the soft interior, leaving a wall about ½ inch thick. Brush the insides of the bread shells with the melted butter. Place several broccoli spears at each end of the bread shell with the blossom portion facing toward the outside. Place one of the ham-cheese wrapped hot dogs on top of the broccoli stems in the center of the loaf half. Place the loaf halves on a lightly buttered cooky tin. Arrange a portion of the French fried onion rings along the sides and over the top of each hot dog. Place in a 325° F. oven for 25 minutes or until the white portion of the bread turns a golden brown.

Meanwhile, whip the sour cream until it is light and fluffy. Add the beaten eggs, salt, lemon juice, mustard and Tabasco. Whip again for a second or two so that all of the ingredients are well mixed. Place the mixture in the top of a double boiler over water which is kept just below the boiling point. Do not let the water boil, for this will curdle the sauce. Stirring constantly, cook the mixture over the warm water until it thickens and coats the spoon. Avoid overcooking, as this will cause the sauce to get lumpy. The moment it coats the spoon, remove from the heat. The sauce can be left uncovered over the hot water until you are ready to use it. Stir from time to time to prevent the surface from getting dry.

Place the baked French bread sandwiches on individual serving plates. Remove the toothpicks from the ham-cheese wrapping. Spoon a generous amount of the sauce over each sandwich. Serve at once, piping hot. Serves 8.

DRUNKEN DOGS

1 cup sour-mash bourbon
1 cup catsup
1 cup dark brown sugar
¼ cup onion, very finely chopped
1 pound hot dogs or 1 pound small Vienna-style wieners

Note: Sour-mash bourbon is an absolute "must" for this recipe; if you use an ordinary bourbon, you will not gain the same delicious flavor.

Place the sour-mash bourbon, catsup and brown sugar in a large skillet with a tightly fitting cover. Place over very low heat and cook, stirring constantly, until the sugar has melted. Add the onion and mix well.

If you are using the regular-sized hot dogs, cut them up into five pieces. Distribute the hot dogs in the sauce. Spoon some of the sauce over the hot dogs so that they are well coated. Cover and continue to cook over very low heat for 45 minutes. Keep heat just below the simmering point. Stir gently and spoon the sauce over the hot dogs frequently during this cooking time. If the liquid does diminish somewhat, add a little extra bourbon.

Serve on a hot platter or in a candle-heated serving dish with the sauce surrounding the hot dogs. Place a colorful cocktail pick in each piece of hot dog. If you wish, serve rounds of soft white bread on a separate plate for your guests. Serves 12.

HOT DOGS WITH A FRENCH TOUCH

2 10-ounce packages frozen French-style green beans,
    cooked according to package directions; do not drain
    after cooking
10 hot dogs, sliced in ½-inch circles
1 cup mayonnaise
3 hard-boiled eggs, peeled and chopped
2 tablespoons lemon juice
2 tablespoons minced onion
1 teaspoon Worcestershire sauce
½ teaspoon powdered mustard
½ teaspoon garlic salt
2 drops Tabasco

Drop the hot-dog circles into the undrained, hot cooked
French-style green beans; place over very low heat for 5
minutes.

Place the mayonnaise in the top of a double boiler over
slowly boiling water. Add the hard-boiled eggs, lemon juice,
onion, Worcestershire sauce, powdered mustard, garlic salt
and Tabasco. Mix well and cook over the slowly boiling
water for 8 minutes.

Drain the hot dogs and beans thoroughly. Place on a
heated platter and pour the hot sauce over them. Serve
at once. Serves 6.

GOURMET HOT DOG VEAL LOAF

12 hot dogs
1 pound double-ground veal
¼ pound lean salt pork, double ground with the veal
2 eggs
2 cups soft, enriched white bread crumbs
1 teaspoon salt
¼ teaspoon pepper
2 tablespoons grated onion
¼ cup lemon juice
½ teaspoon paprika
2 10-inch slices lean bacon

Chop the hot dogs until they are the consistency of coarse
corn meal. Add the chopped hot dogs to the ground veal
and ground salt pork. Mix and knead until all is well
blended. Set aside.

300

In a mixing bowl, beat the eggs until they are lemon yellow; add the bread crumbs, salt, pepper, grated onion and the lemon juice. Mix all very well. Add the veal-hot dog mixture and again mix and knead until all is thoroughly blended.

Form into an oblong loaf and place in a lightly buttered oblong baking dish. Sprinkle the top of the loaf with the paprika. Cut the bacon slices in half and place the four pieces of bacon diagonally over the top of the loaf. Bake in a 400° F. oven for 30 minutes. Then reduce the heat to 300° F. and bake for 1½ hours. Remove from the oven and allow to cool for 5 minutes before slicing. Slice in generous 1½-inch slices. Serves 6.

Note: This loaf is also delicious served cold and makes excellent sandwiches.

HOT DOGS SUPREME WITH BEANS

8 hot dogs, diced in ½-inch cubes
2 tablespoons brandy
½ cup French dressing
2 10-ounce packages frozen whole green beans, cooked according to package directions and then chilled
¼ cup red Italian onion, thinly sliced and separated into rings
1 cup celery, sliced 1/16 inch thick
6 lettuce cups

Place the hot dogs in a bowl with a tightly fitting cover. Mix the brandy and French dressing and pour over the hot dogs. Toss lightly so that all is evenly coated. Cover and place in the refrigerator for 1 hour.

Mix the chilled, cooked green beans, onion rings and celery. Add the chilled hot dogs and their dressing. Toss all lightly. Serve portions in the lettuce cups. Serves 6.

Variations:

Use 2 #2 cans green beans, drained, in place of the frozen beans.
Substitute a bed of snipped water cress for the lettuce cups.

EGGPLANT AND HOT DOG MOUNDS

1 large 4-inch diameter eggplant
1 teaspoon Accent
1 teaspoon salt
6 slices lean bacon, diced in ¼-inch cubes
6 hot dogs, finely chopped
1 tablespoon onion, finely minced
½ cup butter
2 tablespoons dehydrated parsley

Wash and peel the eggplant. Slice into ¾-inch slices. Mix the Accent and salt together and sprinkle a portion on each side of the slices. Set aside and allow the excess water to drain from the eggplant.

Place the bacon in a large skillet and saute until it is a golden brown. Add the chopped hot dogs and onion. Saute until the hot dogs are slightly browned. Remove from the grease with a slotted spoon and set aside. Add several spoonfuls of the butter to the bacon grease and permit it to melt over low heat.

Meanwhile, drain the eggplant and pat each slice dry with paper toweling. Place the slices in the melted butter and saute over low heat until each slice is golden brown and tender. Add more butter as you need it for browning. Place the browned slices of eggplant in an oven-proof baking dish.

Mound a portion of the hot dog and bacon mixture in the center of each slice of eggplant. Sprinkle with a bit of parsley. Place in a 350° F. oven for 10 minutes. Serve piping hot. Serves 6 generously.

HOT DOGS AND BAKED EGGS WITH SHERRY SAUCE

½ cup melted butter
¾ cup canned mushrooms, sliced ⅛ inch thick
6 eggs
½ teaspoon salt
¼ teaspoon pepper
6 hot dogs
1 12-ounce bottle ale
½ teaspoon marjoram
½ teaspoon savory
¼ cup cooking sherry
¾ cup chili sauce
a sprinkle of cayenne
2 tablespoons minced parsley

Place 1 tablespoon of the melted butter in the bottom of each of 6 custard cups. Swirl the butter around so that it coats the sides of the cups. Divide the mushrooms into 6 portions and place in the bottom of each custard cup. Carefully break each egg into the custard cup on top of the mushrooms. Sprinkle each egg with a bit of the salt and pepper. Place the custard cups in a shallow pan of water in a 350° F. oven for 15 minutes or until the yolk is coated over and the egg is fairly firm.

Meanwhile, mix the ale, marjoram and savory. Place over moderate heat and bring to a boil. Add the hot dogs, and allow them to stand in the hot beer for 10 minutes.

Mix the sherry, chili sauce and cayenne together and place over moderate heat until the mixture begins to bubble. Turn the heat back to simmer and cook for 5 minutes, stirring occasionally.

Remove the hot dogs from the ale and slice each hot dog into ⅛-inch slices. Place one sliced hot dog on top of the firm baked eggs. Top each hot dog with two tablespoons of the sauce and a sprinkle of parsley. Serve piping hot. Serves 6.

HOT DOGS IN SOUR CREAM SAUCE

12 hot dogs
¼ cup butter
¼ cup flour
½ cup catsup
½ teaspoon salt
¼ teaspoon pepper
2 tablespoons parsley, finely chopped
1 cup dairy sour cream

Cut the hot dogs up into thirds crosswise. Set aside. Melt the butter in a 1-quart saucepan. Stir in the flour and cook over low heat until smooth and bubbly. Add the catsup and mix again until smooth. Add the cut-up hot-dog pieces, salt, pepper and parsley. Mix well. Cook over very low heat for 8 minutes or until the hot dogs are heated through.

Add the dairy sour cream and stir lightly until thoroughly mixed. Place over very low heat for 2 minutes or until the cream is heated through. Do not overcook or bring to a boil, for the sour cream will curdle. Serve piping hot. Serves 6.

Chapter XXI

HOT DOGS AND THE OUTDOOR

GRILL

COOKING over an outdoor grill has become as much a way of food preparation as cooking on a conventional stove. Summer brings spirals of flavor-laden smoke from almost every back yard or patio. There are as many styles of grills as there are models of automobiles. Whether you boast a resplendent chrome and enamel rig on wheels or just an old bucket with holes punched in it and a piece of screening, you can turn out delicious food with that all-important charcoal flavor.

Hot dogs and grilling have always been highly compatible. The two have been going together since the days of the "wiener roast," when each person roasted his own hot dog on a long sharp stick over a circle of stones filled with a glowing fire.

This chapter not only contains recipes for the outdoor grill, but some that can be prepared right in your own oven when outdoor cooking is impossible.

DILLY DOGS

8 hot dogs
18 2-inch diameter salad potatoes
½ cup melted butter
½ cup fresh dill, very finely chopped

Boil the potatoes in their jackets until they are just barely tender. Chill under cold running water and then peel.

Cut the hot dogs into thirds. Brush the hot dogs and the potatoes on all sides with the melted butter. Using four pieces of hot dogs and three potatoes per skewer, string them alternately; start and end with a piece of hot dog. Sprinkle them on all sides with the finely-chopped dill.

Place over the grill about 6 inches from the coals for about 5 minutes. Turn to grill evenly. Serve at once, piping hot. Serves 6.

OREGANO HOT DOG GRILL

12 hot dogs
2 cloves garlic, finely minced
½ teaspoon salt
¾ cup olive oil
½ cup dry red wine
¼ teaspoon pepper
1 tablespoon oregano, finely crushed

Partially split the hot dogs in half lengthwise. Do not cut all the way through, but leave a "hinge" at the back.

Mix the garlic, salt, olive oil, wine, pepper and oregano together. Pour into the bottom of a shallow pan large enough to accomodate the hot dogs laying flat with the open side down.

Place the hot dogs, cut side down in the marinade and place in the refrigerator for 3 hours or overnight if possible.

Place the hot dogs on a grill about 6 inches away from heat with the opening closed. If necessary, fasten the hot dogs back together with a toothpick. Baste with the remainder of the marinade during the cooking. Serve at once, piping hot. Serves 6, allowing 2 hot dogs per person.

SAUCEPAN GRILL

This recipe is included under grilled hot dogs because it is an excellent way to prepare them when the charcoal just won't start or when the grill is crowded with other good things to eat.

12 hot dogs
1 cup chopped onion
3 tablespoons butter
1 cup chopped celery (include some leaves)
2 8-ounce cans tomato sauce
⅛ teaspoon pulverized sweet basil
½ teaspoon salt
½ teaspoon Accent
¼ teaspoon pepper
½ cup warm water

Place the onion and the butter in a saucepan which is large enough to hold the hot dogs without too much crowding. Cook the onions over moderate heat until they are limp and transparent. Add the celery and tomato sauce and mix well. Continue to cook over moderate heat; add the sweet basil, salt, Accent, pepper and water. Mix well and bring to a bubbling boil.

Place the hot dogs in the bubbling sauce and turn the heat back to simmer. Simmer the hot dogs, turning occasionally, for 30 minutes.

Serve on buns with a little of the sauce spread on the inside of each bun. Serves 6, allowing 2 per person.

DOGS GRILLED SUPREMELY

12 hot dogs
12 slices enriched white bread, lightly buttered
1 8-ounce can tomato sauce
2 cups grated mild Cheddar cheese
2 tablespoons grated onion
½ cup peanut oil
½ cup pimiento-stuffed olives, finely chopped
¼ teaspoon salt
¼ teaspoon pepper
1 drop Tabasco

Slice the hot dogs in half lengthwise, and then cut them in half crosswise. Arrange the four pieces of hot dog on each piece of buttered bread.

Place the tomato sauce in a bowl along with the cheese, onion, oil, olives, salt, pepper and Tabasco. Mix all very well. Put a large spoonful of the mixture over the slices of hot dog. Flatten the mixture so that it covers the hot dogs but does not go over the sides of the bread. Place the slices of bread on a cooky sheet about 6 inches away from the broiler heat. Broil until the topping is melted and bubbly. Serve at once; serves 6, allowing two sandwiches per person.

HOT DOG BARBECUE

12 hot dogs
1 cup catsup
1 cup water
¼ cup brown sugar, tightly packed
¼ cup cider vinegar
¼ cup Worcestershire sauce
1 tablespoon celery seed
1 teaspoon chili powder
½ teaspoon salt
⅛ teaspoon pepper
2 drops Tabasco
12 hot dog buns
½ cup melted butter
½ teaspoon garlic powder

Gash each hot dog diagonally in four places. Set aside. Mix the catsup, water, brown sugar, cider vinegar and Worcestershire sauce in a saucepan and place over moderate heat until it reaches a rapid boil. Add the celery seed, chili powder, salt, pepper and Tabasco. Mix well and continue to cook over low heat for 15 minutes.

Brush each hot dog with the sauce and place on a grill about 6 to 8 inches away from the hot coals. Turn and brush the hot dogs with the sauce until they are a rich brown.

Mix the butter and the garlic powder together. Brush the inside of the hot dog buns with the mixture and lightly toast them over the grill. Place the barbecued hot dog in the garlic flavored bun. Add a drizzle of the basting sauce and serve. Serves 6, allowing 2 hot dogs per person.

HOT DOG AND KRAUT GRILL

1 cup sauerkraut, drained and rinsed
½ cup tart apple, peeled, cored and sliced
¼ teaspoon caraway seed
1 teaspoon brown sugar
12 hot dogs
12 strips bacon
12 hot dog buns

Place the rinsed sauerkraut and the apple pieces in a chopping bowl. Add the caraway seed; chop until the consistency of coarse corn meal. Place in a saucepan over moderate heat and add the brown sugar. Stirring frequently, cook for 8 minutes.

Split each hot dog just halfway through lengthwise, leaving a "hinge" at the back. Fill the opening with a portion of the sauerkraut mixture. Starting at one end, wrap the bacon barber pole fashion, around the hot dog. Fasten the bacon in place with toothpicks.

Place the filled and wrapped hot dogs on the grill about 6-inches away from the heat. Grill, turning from time to time, until the bacon is crisp and golden. Place each in a warm hot dog bun and serve. Serves 6, allowing 2 per person.

HOT DOG BARBECUE IN THE OVEN

12 hot dogs, cut in half lengthwise
4 tablespoons bacon or ham fat
½ cup onion, diced in ¼-inch cubes
2 cloves garlic, finely chopped
½ cup warm water
¼ cup fresh lemon juice
1 teaspoon paprika
1 teaspoon prepared mustard
¼ teaspoon seasoned pepper
½ teaspoon salt
½ teaspoon Accent
½ teaspoon grated horseradish
1 tablespoon Worcestershire sauce
¾ cup catsup

Arrange the halves of the hot dogs, cut side down, over the bottom of a shallow baking dish.

Place the bacon fat in a saucepan over moderate heat; add the diced onion and saute until the onion is limp and transparent. Add the garlic and saute for a few minutes longer. Add the warm water, lemon juice, paprika and mustard. Bring to a boil and cook for 1 minute. Remove from the heat and then add the salt, pepper, Accent, horseradish and Worcestershire sauce. Stir in the catsup. Mix all very well and then pour over the hot dogs.

Cover the pan with aluminum foil and place in a 325° F. oven for 20 minutes. Serve piping hot. Serves 6.

HOT DOG AND SPICED CRAB APPLE GRILL

8 hot dogs
1 16-ounce jar spiced crab apples (you'll need at least 12 apples)
2 tablespoons fresh lemon juice
¼ cup honey
1 teaspoon prepared mustard
1 teaspoon grated lemon rind
1 tablespoon brandy

Cut the hot dogs into thirds. Drain the juice from the crab apples and save. Cut each crab apple in half lengthwise through the core. Alternately place six pieces of hot dog and six apple halves on a skewer.

Place on a grill about 8 inches away from the heat. Grill for 10 minutes.

Mix the crab apple juice, lemon juice, honey, mustard, lemon rind and brandy together. Brush each skewer generously with the mixture and return to the grill until the glaze begins to turn brown on the hot dogs. Serve at once. Serves 6.

HOT DOGS IN BARBECUE SAUCE #1

(A delicious way to oven-grill hot dogs)

8 hot dogs
2 tablespoons peanut oil
1 cup onion, coarsely chopped
1 clove garlic, finely chopped
¼ cup green pepper, finely chopped
2 tablespoons minced parsley
¼ cup lemon juice
½ cup water
1 teaspoon paprika
1 teaspoon prepared yellow mustard
¼ teaspoon seasoned pepper
2 tablespoons brown sugar
1 tablespoon Worcestershire sauce
1 teaspoon horseradish
½ cup chili sauce

Halve the hot dogs lengthwise. Arrange them in two rows

over the bottom of a suitable buttered baking dish, cut side down.

Place the peanut oil in a large skillet; add the onion and saute until the onion is slightly brown. Add the garlic, green pepper and parsley. Continue to cook over low heat. Combine the lemon juice, water and paprika and add to the sauteed onions.

Mix the mustard, pepper, brown sugar, Worcestershire sauce, horseradish and chili sauce well. Add to the ingredients in the skillet and simmer for 8 minutes longer. Stir frequently to prevent sticking. Pour this mixture over the hot dogs.

Cover the baking dish with aluminum foil and place in a 325° F. oven for 25 minutes. Serve piping hot. Serves 6.

HOT DOGS IN BARBECUE SAUCE #2

¾ cup onion, coarsely chopped
¾ cup green pepper, coarsely chopped
2 cups tomato juice
1 cup cider vinegar
½ cup catsup
3 tablespoons Worcestershire sauce
1 stick butter
½ teaspoon salt
½ teaspoon sugar
12 hot dogs

In a 1½-quart saucepan, place the onion, green pepper and tomato juice. Bring to a rolling boil and add the vinegar, catsup, Worcestershire sauce and butter. Continue to cook over moderate heat until the butter has melted. Add the salt and sugar. Mix well. Turn the heat to simmer, cover and continue to cook at simmer for 30 minutes or until thickened.

Place the hot dogs in the sauce and cook for 8 to 10 minutes or until heated through. Serve each hot dog with a portion of the sauce over and around it. Serves 6, allowing two per person. This sauce is also excellent when serving hot dogs on buns.

GRILLED FRANKS ON A SKEWER

8 hot dogs
18 small boiled or canned potatoes
18 small canned onions
¾ cup chili sauce
2 drops Tabasco
2 tablespoons Worcestershire sauce
½ teaspoon garlic salt
¼ teaspoon black pepper

Cut the hot dogs into thirds (this will give you 24 pieces). Mix the chili sauce, Tabasco, Worcestershire sauce, garlic salt and black pepper together. Place the hot dog pieces in this mixture and allow them to marinate for at least 2 hours. Turn the pieces over so that the flavors are evenly distributed during the marinating time.

Alternate four pieces of the marinated hot dog with one each of a potato and onion on skewers, ending up with a piece of hot dog on the end. This will fill 6 skewers.

Place the skewers on the grill about 6 inches away from the heat. Brush the hot dogs, potatoes and onions from time to time with the remaining marinade. Grill until the potatoes just begin to brown. Serve at once, piping hot. Serves 6.

Chapter XXII

HOT DOGS WITH A FOREIGN FLAIR

THOUGH THE WIENER or hot dog had its beginnings in Europe, it did not take long for it to make its way to America where it enjoyed great popularity.

Thanks to the fact that America is made up of people from all over the globe, we have on our tables and in our super markets a world-wide variety of foods. Home makers have been incorporating the hot dog into dishes handed down from the homelands of their forebears.

Today our marvelous marketing of foodstuffs permits the shopper to buy tortilla, chick peas, bamboo shoots and many other delicious ethnic foods right in the same super market where she buys all-American pork and beans. Thanks to this marvelous availability and the deliciousness of hot dogs, many delightful dishes have been invented which have a foreign flair.

TOSTADA HOT DOGS

12 flat, ready-to-serve tortilla shells (sometimes labeled Taco or Tostada shells)
1 tablespoon olive oil
8 hot dogs, coarsely chopped
1 15½–ounce can refried Mexican beans
¾ cup diced fresh tomato, in ¼–inch cubes
1½ cups finely shredded lettuce
1 cup grated mild Cheddar cheese

Place the olive oil in a skillet over moderate heat. Add the chopped hot dogs and saute gently until slightly browned on the edges. Add the refried beans and mix thoroughly.

Spread each of the flat tortilla shells with a portion of the hot dog mixture. Place the spread shells on cooky sheets in a 375° F. oven for 10 minutes.

Sprinkle each of the heated bean-topped tortilla with a few pieces of tomato; top this with a portion of the shredded lettuce. Sprinkle a portion of the grated cheese over the lettuce.

Place the tortilla, still on the cooky sheets, under the broiler about 4 inches from the heat. When the cheese just begins to

313

melt, remove from the oven and serve at once. Serves 6, allowing two per person.

MEXICAN HOT DOG CASSEROLE

8 hot dogs
1 10¼–ounce can jalapeno bean dip
8 un-cooked tortilla (obtainable in the frozen food section)
1 16–ounce can chili con carne
1 cup grated mild cheddar cheese

Split the hot dogs lengthwise, leaving a hinge at the back. Spread the inside of each hot dog with a generous portion of the jalapeno bean dip. Set aside.

Place the raw tortilla, one at a time, in a small amount of oil in a skillet over moderate heat. As soon as the tortilla begins to brown slightly on the edges and soften, remove from the skillet and roll it around the bean stuffed hot dog. Place the tortilla wrapped hot dogs in the bottom of a greased oblong casserole dish.

Pour the can of chili con carne over all. Sprinkle the top with cheese.

Bake in a moderate, 350° F. oven for 20 minutes or until the cheese has melted. Serves 4, allowing two tortilla wrapped hot dogs per person.

HOT DOGS AND SALAD ITALIENNE

8 hot dogs
1¼ cups bottled Italian Dressing
2 tablespoons finely sliced green onion
2 tablespoons finely chopped green pepper
1 tablespoon finely chopped pimento stuffed olives
5 cups cooked and sliced salad potatoes
¼ cup crumbled crisp bacon
¼ cup thinly sliced red radishes
1 teaspoon chopped chives

Place the hotdogs and ½ cup of the bottled Italian dressing in a saucepan over low heat. Cover and cook over low heat for 10 minutes. Turn the hot dogs from time to time so that they are evenly flavored with the dressing.

Place the remaining ¾ cup of Italian dressing in a 2 quart saucepan over moderate heat. Add the onions, green pepper and chopped olives. Cook, stirring frequently, until the onion and pepper are tender. Add the cooked sliced potatoes, bacon

314

and radishes. Toss all together lightly.

Place the potato salad in a suitable serving dish. Remove the hot dogs from the heat and dressing. Arrange them around the salad. Drizzle any remaining dressing from the hot dogs over the top of the salad. Sprinkle with the chives and serve. Serves 4 to 6.

ITALIAN HOT DOG NOODLE CASSEROLE

3 cups medium wide green egg noodles (*tagliatelle verde*)
1 11¼–ounce can split pea soup with ham
1 cup hot water
1½ cups grated American cheese
8 hot dogs cut into ¼–inch circles
¼ cup sliced pimento stuffed olives
¼ cup finely chopped onion
⅛ teaspoon freshly ground pepper

Cook the green noodles according to the package directions; drain and set aside.

Place the pea soup and the hot water in a sauce pan over moderate heat; stir and cook until smooth and steaming hot. Add 1 cup of the grated American cheese. Reserve the remainder of the cheese until later. Continue to cook and stir over moderate heat until the cheese has melted. Add the hot dog circles, olives, onion and freshly ground pepper. Mix well and remove from the heat.

Place one half of the cooked green noodles in the bottom of a 2–quart greased casserole. Pour half of the hot dog mixture over them. Cover this with the remainder of the noodles. Pour the remainder of the soup mixture over the noodles. Sprinkle the top with the remaining half cup of cheese.

Bake in a 350° F. oven for 25 minutes or until the cheese has melted and become bubbly. Serve piping hot. Serves 6.

ITALIAN HOT DOG EGGS

½ cup ranch style bacon diced into ¼–inch squares
½ cup finely chopped onion
6 hot dogs cut up into ⅛–inch circles
½ cup green pepper diced into ¼–inch squares
8 pimento stuffed olives sliced
1 teaspoon capers, drained well
8 eggs beaten until lemon yellow
¼ teaspoon salt
⅛ teaspoon freshly ground pepper
¼ teaspoon pulverized oregano
⅛ teaspoon freshly grated nutmeg
¼ cup half and half cream

Saute the cubed bacon in a large skillet until crisp and golden brown. Pour off all but 1 tablespoon of the bacon grease. Add the onion to the bacon and cook over moderate heat until the onion is limp and transparent.

Add the hot dogs, green pepper, olives and capers. Continue to cook over moderate heat until the green pepper is glazed and transparent on the edges.

Add the salt, pepper, oregano, nutmeg and cream to the beaten eggs. Pour the egg mixture into the ingredients in the skillet. Stir to mix and continue to cook over moderate heat until the eggs are set. Serves 4.

FRENCH FRIED POTATO AND HOT DOG CASSEROLE

8 hot dogs
1 17–ounce can of tiny peas and little white onions
1 ½–pound package frozen French fried potatoes, slightly thawed
1 10¾–ounce can cheddar cheese soup
1 teaspoon prepared yellow mustard
½ cup milk
½ cup grated Swiss cheese

Slice the hot dogs into ⅛–inch thick slices. Place in a large mixing bowl. Drain the peas and onions and add to the sliced hot dogs. Add the slightly thawed French fried potatoes and toss all together lightly.

Mix the cheese soup, mustard and milk together thoroughly. Add to the other ingredients and again toss to lightly mix. Pour into a buttered 2 quart casserole. Sprinkle the top with the grated cheese.

Bake in a 350° F. oven for 35 minutes or until the cheese has melted and browned slightly. Serves 4 to 6.

TURKISH HOT DOG DISH

1 eggplant about 3 inches in diameter
½ cup all purpose flour
½ teaspoon paprika
½ teaspoon salt
¼ teaspoon freshly ground pepper
¼ cup olive oil
¾ cup onion diced into ¼–inch pieces
2 large cloves garlic, minced
1 16–ounce can stewing tomatoes
¼ teaspoon sweet basil
pinch of pulverized oregano
8 hot dogs cut into ¼–inch circles
3 cups hot fluffy cooked rice

Peel the eggplant and cut up into ½–inch cubes. Mix the flour, salt, pepper and paprika together and then sprinkle this mixture over the eggplant cubes. Toss lightly so that all the cubes are evenly floured. Set aside.

Place the olive oil in a large skillet over moderate heat; add the diced onion and saute until limp and transparent. Add the minced garlic. Add the floured eggplant cubes and continue to saute until the eggplant is lightly browned. If necessary, add a bit more oil to prevent sticking.

Add the stewed tomatoes, basil and oregano. Bring to a bubbling boil and then reduce the heat to simmer. Cook at simmer for ½ hour. Add the hot dog circles and continue to cook for an additional 10 minutes. Stir gently from time to time and add a bit more water or tomato juice if the tomato sauce becomes too thick.

Place the rice in a deep serving platter and pour the hot dog mixture over all. Serve at once. Serves 4.

HAWAIIAN HOT DOGS

1 16–ounce can vegetable chop suey
1 8–ounce can pineapple tidbits
½ cup diced green pepper, cut into ¼–inch cubes
½ cup diced onion, ¼–inch cubes
¼ cup cider vinegar
2 tablespoons granulated sugar
2 tablespoons soy sauce
6 hot dogs sliced ¼ inch thick, then diced into quarters
1 3–ounce can chow mein noodles

Place the vegetable chop suey in a 1½–quart sauce pan which has a tight fitting cover; add the pineapple tidbits, juice and all. Add the green pepper and onion.

Mix the vinegar, sugar and soy sauce thoroughly and add to the chop suey mixture. Fold in the diced hot dog pieces.

Place over moderate heat until it reaches a bubbling boil, then cover and reduce heat to simmer. Cook at simmer for 8 minutes or until heated through.

Heat the chow mein noodles according to the directions on the can. Serve the hot dog chop suey over the hot noodles. Serves 4.

Variation:

This chop suey mixture is also delicious served over fluffy portions of rice. For added glamour, a sprinkling of pecans is good.

GERMAN HOT DOG AND KRAUT BAKE

1 1 pound 13 ounce can of sauerkraut
1 medium sized tart red apple
1 cup pitted dried prunes cut up into quarters
3 tablespoons grated onion
½ teaspoon caraway seeds
1 tablespoon dark brown sugar
8 hot dogs
3 cups cooked instant mashed potatoes

Drain the sauerkraut well; place in a mixing bowl; quarter and core the apple; do not peel. Slice the quarters as you would for pie. Add to the sauerkraut along with the quartered prunes, grated onion, caraway seeds and brown sugar. Mix and toss all together lightly.

Place in a deep, oblong baking dish. Arrange the hot dogs

over the surface. Cover with foil and bake in a 350° F. oven for 25 minutes.

Remove the foil from the top and spoon the mashed potatoes around the edge. Return to the 350° F. oven and bake for an additional 15 minutes or until the potatoes are just beginning to brown. Serve at once. Serves 4.

GREEK ONE DISH MEAL

8 hot dogs diced into ¼–inch cubes
1 12–ounce can luncheon meat (such as Spam) diced into ¾–inch squares
1 8–ounce package medium wide egg noodles
1 15½–ounce can chick peas, drained
1 8–ounce can red kidney beans, drained
1 large clove garlic, minced
1 cup sliced fresh mushroom stems and pieces
½ cup chopped green pepper
½ teaspoon salt
¼ teaspoon freshly ground pepper
1 8–ounce can tomato sauce
2 cups warm water
2 tablespoons butter or margarine

Place the diced hot dogs, diced luncheon meat and the egg noodles as they come from the package in a large mixing bowl. Add the chick peas, kidney beans, garlic, mushrooms, green pepper, salt and pepper. Turn and toss all together until uniformly mixed.

Place the mixture in a 2½–quart buttered casserole which has a tight fitting cover. Mix the tomato sauce and the warm water together and pour over the casserole ingredients. Dot the top with butter.

Cover and bake in a 375° F. oven for 30 minutes. At the end of this half hour, remove the cover from the casserole. Using a spatula, turn the top of the mixture over so that the noodles are all evenly cooked. Bake, without covering, for an additional 30 minutes. Stir gently from time to time to insure even cooking of the noodles. Serve piping hot. Serves 6 to 8.

ROTELLE SKILLET

1 8–ounce package Italian Rotelle (twisted, corkscrew noodles)
1 tablespoon olive oil
8 hot dogs cut into ½–inch circles
½ cup diced green pepper (¼–inch cubes)
⅔ cup diced onion (¼–inch cubes)
1 large clove garlic, minced
1 8–ounce can red kidney beans, drained
1 15–ounce can tomato sauce with herbs
½ cup tomato juice
1 tablespoon chili powder
½ teaspoon paprika
1 teaspoon salt
¼ teaspoon freshly ground pepper

Cook the Rotelle according to package directions; drain and set aside.

Place the olive oil in a large skillet over moderate heat; when heated, add the hot dog circles. Saute until slightly browned. Add the green pepper, onion and garlic; continue to saute until the green pepper is glazed and the onion is slightly transparent.

Add the kidney beans, tomato sauce, tomato juice, chili powder, paprika, salt and pepper. Mix all thoroughly and then fold in the cooked Rotelle noodles. Bring to a bubbling boil, and then reduce the heat to simmer. Cover and cook at simmer for 25 minutes. Stir from time to time. If the mixture becomes too thick and begins to stick to the bottom of the pan, add a little more tomato juice. Serves 4.

CHILI POT DOGS

1 tablespoon olive oil
¾ cup thinly sliced onion
1 large clove garlic, minced
6 hot dogs
1 10½–ounce can tomato puree
1 16–ounce can tomatoes
½ teaspoon salt
½ teaspoon granulated sugar
1 teaspoon chili powder
1 8–ounce package macaroni elbows, cooked according to package directions and then drained

Place the olive oil in a large skillet over moderate heat. When heated, add the sliced onion and garlic. Saute until the onion

320

is limp and transparent.

Slice the hot dogs the long way into quarters; then cut the quarters in half. Add the sliced hot dogs to the onions and saute gently until a delicate shade of brown.

Add the tomato puree and the tomatoes; add the salt, sugar and chili powder. Mix lightly. Bring to a bubbling boil, and then reduce heat to simmer. Cover and cook at simmer for ½ hour. Stir from time to time. If the mixture thickens and sticks to the bottom of the pan, add a little water.

Arrange the cooked macaroni elbows in a heated deep platter; pour the chili sauce over and serve. Serves 4.

INDEX

323

324

331